ECONOMIC THEORY, WELFARE AND THE STATE

John C. Weldon (1922–87)
(reproduced from a drawing by Julia Asimakopulos)

Economic Theory, Welfare and the State

Essays in Honour of John C. Weldon

Edited by

Athanasios Asimakopulos
William Dow Professor of Political Economy
McGill University

Robert D. Cairns
Associate Professor of Economics
McGill University

and

Christopher Green
Professor of Economics
McGill University

M
MACMILLAN

First published 1990

Published by
THE MACMILLAN PRESS LTD
Houndmills, Basingstoke, Hampshire RG21 2XS
and London
Companies and representatives
throughout the world

British Library Cataloguing in Publication Data
Economic theory, welfare and the state: essays in honour of
John C. Weldon.
1. Economics, History —— Sociological perspectives
I. Asimakopulos, Athanasios, *1930–* II. Cairns, Robert D.
III. Green, Christopher IV. Weldon, John C.
306.3'09
ISBN 978-1-349-10913-5 ISBN 978-1-349-10911-1 (eBook)
DOI 10.1007/978-1-349-10911-1

To the memory of John C. Weldon

Contents

Preface

Jack Weldon had superb analytical ability, and a deep and abiding interest in economic, social, and political problems. This collection of papers, written to honour his memory by a former teacher, his fellow students, colleagues and former students, gives some idea of the wide range of his professional interests.

It is these interests that provide a unifying theme to the papers in this collection. During the last twelve years of his life, Weldon concentrated on the history of economic thought, and at the time of his death he was beginning to edit for publication over 2000 pages of lecture notes he had prepared. It is thus appropriate that the papers by Boulding (from whom, incidentally, Weldon took a course in the history of economic thought) and Usher deal with this area. Rosenbluth's paper, with its useful examination of possible areas of conflict between group interests, and individual self-interest, would have been much appreciated by Weldon. The paper by Dales presents a neat blend of economic history and economic theory that sheds a critical light on the Canadian government's policy of settling the prairies with the provision of land grants. Rowley's critical analysis of rational expectations models and their use in econometrics, is one in a series of papers that Weldon followed with great interest. Rymes's paper, with its examination of the reasons why money should be treated as a public good, is a development of an approach to money advocated by Weldon. Two papers, one by Barber and the other by Schwartzman, deal with the problem of maintaining satisfactory levels of employment – a constant theme in Weldon's writings and comments on public policy. The two contributions to international trade theory by Chipman, and Kemp and Yabuuchi are examples of economic theory of high order that also provide useful insights on practical matters. Then finally, there are three papers, by Ascah and Asimakopulos, Burbidge, and Howitt, that examine aspects of public pensions, one of Weldon's major research interests.

We are very grateful to Marika Asimakopulos for undertaking the arduous task of preparing the index for this book.

ATHANASIOS ASIMAKOPULOS
ROBERT D. CAIRNS
CHRISTOPHER GREEN

Notes on the Contributors

Louis Ascah is Professor of Economics at the University of Sherbrooke, Sherbrooke, Canada.

Athanasios Asimakopulos is Dow Professor of Political Economy at McGill University, Montreal, Canada.

Clarence Lyle Barber is Professor Emeritus at University of Manitoba, Canada.

Kenneth E. Boulding is Distinguished Professor of Economics, Emeritus, Research Associate and Project Director of the Institute of Behavioural Science, University of Colorado, Boulder, USA.

John Burbidge is Professor of Economics at McMaster University, Hamilton, Canada.

Robert D. Cairns is Associate Professor of Economics at McGill University, Montreal, Canada.

John S. Chipman is Professor of Economics at University of Minnesota, Minneapolis, USA.

John H. Dales is Professor Emeritus at University of Toronto, Canada.

Christopher Green is Professor of Economics at McGill University, Montreal, Canada.

Peter Howitt is Professor of Economics at University of Western Ontario, London, Canada.

Murray C. Kemp is Professor of Economics at University of New South Wales, Kensington, Australia.

Gideon Rosenbluth is Professor Emeritus at University of British Columbia, Vancouver, Canada.

Robin Rowley is Professor of Economics at McGill University, Montreal, Canada.

Thomas K. Rymes is Professor of Economics at Carleton University, Ottawa, Canada.

David Schwartzman is Professor of Economics at New School for Social Research, New York, USA.

Dan Usher is Professor of Economics at Queen's University, Kingston, Canada.

Shigemi Yabuuchi is Professor of Economics at Aichi University, Aichi, Japan.

John C. Weldon (1922–87): An Appreciation

Jack Weldon's death in February 1987 deprived McGill's Department of Economics of its outstanding intellect. Lost to older colleagues and a new generation of department members alike are Weldon's incisive and inquiring mind, his encyclopedic knowledge, his thoughtful comments on his colleagues' written work, his dedication to the Department's eclectic traditions which he did so much to develop, and the engaging sense of humour which could melt friend and foe alike. He is missed!

John C. Weldon was born in Magpie Mine, Ontario. However, there were family roots in the Maritimes. His father came from Saint John, New Brunswick, and briefly attended McGill before moving on to the mining country of Ontario. The most prestigious medal given by the Dalhousie Law School Alumni Association is the Weldon Award, named after the Law School's first Dean (1883–1914), Richard Chapman Weldon, a great-uncle of Jack.

Early in his life, Weldon's family moved to Montreal, where he grew up in the working-class East End. He attended the academically prestigious High School of Montreal. In 1939, Weldon enrolled at McGill University to study mathematics and physics, but the Second World War intervened. In 1941, at the age of 19, Weldon signed up 'for the duration', joining the RCAF. On his return to Montreal in 1945, he re-entered McGill, but switched from the physical sciences to economics. Earl Beach, one of Weldon's early teachers and later a colleague, said that his intellectual brilliance was immediately apparent. It was the beginning of a notable and at times turbulent career, whose outstanding characteristic was the oral tradition that Jack built.

Weldon graduated in 1947 and immediately began graduate studies at McGill, supported by an Allen Oliver Fellowship. In 1948–9, he attended Columbia University on a fellowship, returning to McGill as a lecturer in the fall of 1949, and to finish his doctorate. His dissertation, completed in 1952, for McGill, examined the role of entrepreneurship in theories of income distribution. It is of interest that although Weldon's writing and teaching ranged over many different subjects, mostly theoretical, his last published paper returned to his beginnings. This paper, entitled 'The Classical Theory of Distribution', was described by a reviewer (*Economic Journal*, September 1988) as the 'jewel in the crown' of a volume, *Theories of Income Distribution*, every chapter of which contains 'a first class piece of work'.

Weldon's academic specialisation was in economic theory, and he was particularly interested in the logical foundations of theoretical analysis. These interests are partially reflected in published papers on the multi-product firm (1948), utility functions (1950), social welfare functions (1952), and public goods (1966). Much of Jack's work was what might be described as 'difficult' theory. His chief concern was the behaviour of individuals as part of a group (society) making time-specific, sometimes intergenerational, decisions. Social welfare functions, their significance, and how they could be conceptualised in an historical context as the corpus of society changed, with one set of generations trying to affect the actions of succeeding generations, was an ongoing theme in Weldon's research. This was extended to a consideration of the economic logic of saving, which made use of insights he had obtained in his treatment of intergenerational transfers and public pensions. The subject of public pensions, on which he wrote or jointly authored several papers, provided a bridge between Weldon's interest in the logical foundations of economic theory, and that other overriding theme in Jack's work and life, the very real economic and social concerns of humanity. (A list of Weldon's publications appears at the end of this essay.)

Weldon's rise through the ranks, from lecturer to full professor, was rapid. On his promotion to full professor in 1962, he was immediately named to the vacant Dow Chair of Political Economy, which he held until his death. Weldon's rise to prominence within McGill was paralleled by the high regard of his fellow economists in Canada. In 1975, Weldon became President of the Canadian Economics Association, the same year he was elected to the Royal Society of Canada. The citation, which accompanied his election to the Royal Society, stated in part:

> As a theorist, his insistence on rigour and curiosity about the basis of the theoretical edifice of economics have led him, through his career, into an examination of the logical foundations of economics. This continuing interest has resulted in a number of most perceptive papers on the frontiers of the discipline. Professor Weldon's approach to applied work has been pragmatic. His grasp

of the foundations of the discipline enables him to reduce the issues involved in particular problems to their essentials and thus cut to the heart of the matter. As a major addition to his written work, Professor Weldon has been most effective as a teacher in preparing his students for their own later work in teaching and research.

Jack Weldon's entire academic career was spent at McGill. His intellectual qualities and his genuine concern for students and colleagues made him a natural leader. He was head of the economics section of the Department of Economics and Political Science before it split into separate departments in 1969. He was the obvious and clear choice as the first chairman of the new Department of Economics. In 1970, he began a two-year stint in the demanding post of Secretary for Planning to the Planning and Priorities Committee of the Manitoba cabinet, during the early years of Ed Schreyer's premiership. Weldon returned to McGill in 1972 and served for another two years as chairman of the Department of Economics. Despite growing administrative burdens and a door that was always open to his colleagues, Jack continued to maintain a full teaching load.

It was as a teacher that Weldon left his greatest imprint. Generations of students, some of whom went on to become leading economists, remember him as having had a profound impact on their intellectual development. One of them, now an eminent economist, has written: 'With the exception of Milton Friedman, Jack was the best teacher I ever had, and he probably had the greater influence upon me.'

As a teacher, Weldon was a hard taskmaster, but the care he lavished on his students' work was equal to what he demanded from them. His lectures, full of theoretical insights, were enhanced by irony and wit. He was as expert in reducing the issues involved in particular economic problems to their essentials and communicating his understanding to first-year economics students as he was in teaching 'high theory' to advanced honours undergraduates and to graduate students.

Later generations of his students are the certain beneficiaries of Weldon's most ambitious research project, unfortunately still incomplete at his death. The project, an analytical history of economic thought, occupied Weldon for much of the last decade of his life. There exists an enormous amount of material, well over 1500 typed pages. A mimeographed version was made available to each of the students in his highly regarded History of Economic Thought course, a required and fundamental component of McGill's Honours Economics programme. Just prior to his fatal illness, Weldon had begun to edit for publication this mammoth but still rambling work.

In addition to his classroom teaching, Weldon played a central role in the graduate programme as a supervisor of Ph.D. dissertations. From 1978 until mid-1986, when his fatal illness made further work impossible, Jack supervised thirteen of the forty-one Ph.D. dissertations awarded by the Department of Economics. Moreover, he played the role of second reader in several other doctoral dissertations and supervised a number of M.A. theses. Many a McGill graduate student, whose career was in jeopardy due to dissertation difficulties, owes his or her 'rescue' to Weldon's ability to find a way of reducing a difficult problem to sensible and workable proportions. Weldon's willingness to go far beyond the call of duty in helping graduate students was undoubtedly one of the important factors which prevented the completion of his 'life's work' on the history of economic thought.

Weldon was more than a teacher of university students. His expertness in reducing economic problems to their essentials led to frequent radio, television and newspaper commentaries. He also wrote layman-directed pamphlets on such issues as public pensions and incomes policies. His reputation, both as a theorist and as an expositor, was such that he was often asked to appear as a witness by Royal Commissions.

Weldon's commitment to fairness and social democracy made him a natural supporter of the CCF/NDP and trade unions, to which he acted as an advisor. He was also a deeply committed Anglican, and for many years a fine chorister in the church, St John the Evangelist, which he actively served during his lifetime. Jack's was a religion of social conscience, activism and principle. He was in a real sense a Christian Socialist.

No academic biography of Weldon would be complete without reference to his battles within the university he loved. Throughout much of his thirty-eight years at McGill, Jack had a tendency to regard McGill's administration in 'us' vs 'them' terms. In part, this tendency reflected a departmental tradition with its origins in the 1930s and 1940s. When in his later years an important matter of principle arose in department–university relations, Weldon's call to principle was misunderstood or ignored by McGill's administration and by some of his own departmental colleagues as well. As a result,

Weldon spent most of his last decade at loggerheads with the university his presence graced, and in increasing isolation from several of his colleagues, most of whom he had hired.

Unfortunately, the protracted dispute with the university, in which Weldon's cause was taken up by the Canadian Association of University Teachers, was never resolved. The time and energy consumed, however, were another factor which contributed to Weldon's failure to complete his *magnum opus*. Fatalistically, his last curriculum vitae concludes 'this battle for academic values, I hope, will have been of some use to McGill, but in any event now (1986) seems to me the chief contribution of my academic life'. A few weeks before he died, Jack offered that perhaps he had erred in taking for granted that what he considered fundamental academic principles should have been easily recognised as such by his dissenting colleagues. With Weldon's passing McGill University lost not only one of its outstanding academics, but one of its consciences. He did not always presume that he was right, but he was ardent in his defence of intellectual honesty and integrity.

Nothing written about Weldon would be complete without mention of his unquenchable spirit and sense of fun. There was a special, impish quality to his personality that made him a favourite with a wide range of people – not least among some with whom he disagreed. Those who knew and loved him will never forget him. This *Festschrift* is a testimonial to Jack Weldon the man as well as Jack Weldon the creative and role-model inspiring economist and academic.

The *Festschrift* was to have been presented to Jack's widow, Hazel. Tragically, in January 1989, shortly before the *Festschrift* went to press, Hazel died in her home at the hand of an unknown intruder. All those who knew Jack and Hazel were stricken by this senseless act. With heavy hearts we shall present the volume to Jack's and Hazel's children, John and Susan, and to their grandchildren.

CHRISTOPHER GREEN*

* In preparing this biographical sketch, I have benefited from reading the biographical sketches of J. C. Weldon written by Tom Asimakopulos that have been published in *Canadian Journal of Economics* (May 1987) and in the *Proceedings of the Royal Society of Canada* (1989). I also wish to thank J. R. Mallory, a longtime colleague of J. C. Weldon in the former Department of Economics and Political Science, for his recollections.

The Publications of John C. Weldon

'The Multi-product Firm', *Canadian Journal of Economics and Political Science*, vol. 14, no. 2 (May 1948) pp. 176–90.

'A Note on Measures of Utility', *Canadian Journal of Economics and Political Science*, vol. 16, no. 2 (May 1950) pp. 227–33.

'Preliminary Notes for a Theory of Distribution', *Econometrica*, vol. 19 (January 1951) p. 63.

'On the Problem of Social Welfare Functions', *Canadian Journal of Economics and Political Science*, vol. 18, no. 4 (November 1952) pp. 452–63.

'Economic Effects of Collective Bargaining', *Industrial and Labour Relations Review*, vol. 6, no. 4 (July 1953) pp. 570–78.

(with B. S. Kierstead) 'A Note on the Expectations of Oligopolists', *Economie Appliquee* (September 1955) pp. 425–36.

'Economics of Social Democracy', in *Social Purpose for Canada*, ed. M. Oliver (University of Toronto Press, 1961) pp. 171–97. Reprinted in *The Canadian Economy: Selected Readings*, ed. John Deutsch *et al.* (Macmillan, 1965) pp. 140–72.

(with J. St. Laurent) 'Province of Quebec: Submission to the Royal Commission on Banking' (St. Laurent, chapters I, II, V; J. C. Weldon, chapters III, IV, VI).

(with A. Asimakopulos) 'The Classification of Technical Progress in Models of Economic Growth', *Economica*, vol. XXX, no. 120 (Nov. 1963) pp. 372–86.

(with A. Asimakopulos) 'Sir Roy Harrod's Equation of Supply', *Oxford Economic Papers*, vol. 15, no. 3 (November 1963) pp. 266–72.

'Fairer Competition for Canada's Banks', *The Banker*, vol. CXIV, no. 464 (July 1964) pp. 417–21.

'The Economics of the New Pension Plans', *Proceedings of the C.L.C. Social Security Conference* (1965) pp. 5–24.

'Women Preachers and the Porter Commission', *Queen's Quarterly*, vol. LXXI, no. 4 (Winter 1965) pp. 461–7.

(with A. Asimakopulos) 'A Synoptic View of Some Simple Models of Growth', *Canadian Journal of Economics and Political Science*, vol. XXXI, no. 1 (February 1965) pp. 52–79.

'Consolidations in Canadian Industry, 1900–1908', in L. A. Skeoch (ed.), *Restrictive Trade Practices in Canada* (Toronto, McClelland and Stewart, 1966) pp. 228–79.

'Public Goods (And Federalism)', *Canadian Journal of Economics and Political Science* (May 1966) pp. 230–8.

(with A. Asimakopulos) 'On the Theory of Government Pension Plans', *Canadian Journal of Economics*, vol. I, no. 4 (November 1968) pp. 699–717.

(with A. Asimakopulos) 'On Private Plans in the Theory of Pensions', *Canadian Journal of Economics*, vol. III (May 1970) pp. 223–36.

'Exorcising Inflation and Unemployment', *Labour Gazette* (September 1970) pp. 630–6.

'Theoretical Penalties of Inflation', in *Inflation and the Canadian Experience*, N. Swan and D. Wilton, eds (Industrial Relations Centre, Queen's University, July 1971) pp. 155–63.

'Inflation and Unemployment, Canada', Publication No. 2, Douglas-Coldwell Foundation, 7 pages (November 1975).

'On the Theory of Intergenerational Transfers', *Canadian Journal of Economics*, vol. IX, no. 4 (November 1976) pp. 559–79.

'The Role of Government in the Economy', *Report of the Proceedings of the Twenty-Eighth Tax Conference*, 1976 (Canadian Tax Foundation, 1977).

'A Critique of the Tax Based Incomes Policy Proposed by Sidney Weintraub', Canadian Centre for Policy Alternatives, publication no. 4, 24 pp. (1981).

'Response to Sidney Weintraub's "Prices and Incomes Policy"', in D. Crane (ed.), *Beyond the Monetarists* (Ottawa, 1981) pp. 78–82.

'Une Critique de la privatisation', *La crise economique et sa gestion*. Boreal Express, 2nd trimestre 1982, pp. 201–10.

'Incomes Policies in Canada: Programmes without Theory or Purpose', *Canadian Taxation*, vol. 3, no. 2 (Summer 1981) pp. 76–85.

'Pension Policies: Avoiding Confusion of an Essentially Public Problem', in Canadian Centre for Policy Alternatives, *Pensions: Public Solutions vs. Private Interest*, Conference Proceedings Series No. 1 (1982) pp. 176–98.

'Wage Controls and the Canadian Labour Movement' (one of the Jamieson Lectures given at the University of British Columbia, September 1982), publication no. 10, Canadian Centre for Policy Alternatives, 43 pages (1983).

'Pension Policy: Practice and Positive Theory' (one of the Jamieson

Lectures given at the University of British Columbia, September 1982), publication no. 12, Canadian Centre for Policy Alternatives, 40 pages (1983).

'A Critique of Privatization' (one of the papers delivered in honour of Clarence Barber under the heading 'Economic Policies for Canada in the 1980s'), ISER Monograph Series No. 2, *Macroeconomics: Theory, Policy and Evidence* (University of Manitoba, 1983) pp. 25–49.

'On Social Policies In The Canadian Economy, 1986', in *Christian Dimensions of Social Policy*, by M. Cooke, C. Pratt and R. Hutchison, eds (forthcoming).

'The Classical Theory of Distribution', in *Theories of Income Distribution*, ed. A. Asimakopulos (Boston, Kluwer Academic, 1988) pp. 15–47.

'Economic Processes That Bind Successive Communities', delivered at the *Conference of Anglican Economists*, St John's College, University of Manitoba, 27, 28 May 1986.

'Public Policy and Full Employment in Canada Since 1945', in *Christian Faith and Economic Justice: Toward a Canadian Perspective*, ed. Crawford Pratt and Roger Hutchinson (Burlington, Ontario: Trinity Press, 1988), pp. 55–75.

1 Introduction

Robert D. Cairns*

In a market economy, what is the role of collective efforts to improve social welfare and what does economic theory have to say about it? The chapters in this volume, written by former colleagues and friends of the late Jack Weldon, all touch on this pair of questions in a way that reflects the concerns of Weldon's career. One of my more vivid recollections of Weldon was his continual insistence on 'the essential unity of economics'. Possibly a part of that unity is its consistent attempt to address these two questions. In spite of the jokes about economists' habitual divergence of opinion, that unity comes out in this collection. More to the point, the attempt has not been a labour of Sisyphus, even though the problems have not been and probably cannot be resolved.

The two questions, central to policy analysis today, were a major concern of the classical economists, particularly Adam Smith, and this may in part explain Weldon's explorations of the history of economic thought in the latter part of his life. The themes of the volume are Smith's. We recognise that the State will always be present and must be present to allow for the smooth functioning of the market, but in the end it will often be clumsy. Society must make trade-offs between order and liberty, even between despotism and anarchy. The instability of economic processes sets up an intellectual conflict between analyses of equilibrium and disequilibrium phenomena. A place for 'moral sentiments', which Adam Smith studied before turning to the economy, must be found in a system which appears to neglect them but which relies heavily upon them for its cohesiveness.

In Chapter 2, Kenneth Boulding, one of Weldon's teachers, accords to Adam Smith the central position in the history of economic thought. The reason for this is Smith's insights into the evolutionary nature of the economic system. Boulding notes that information was of great importance in Smith's perception of that system. For

* I am grateful to my co-editors, Tom Asimakopulos and Christopher Green, for comments on an earlier draft.

example, productive techniques are subject to change through changes in knowledge. The political process is a process of learning and adapting through debate as well as of the working-out of immutable interests stressed by public-choice economics.

To Boulding, one way to approach economics is to study the process of exchange. The great virtue of the market is its ability to increase productivity through exchange. But attaining greater productivity through exchange does not entail the inexorable tendency to equilibrium through the striving by economic agents to maximise that is emphasised in contemporary economic theory. Rather, the underlying laws and parameters of the economy are constantly changing, rendering the concept of equilibrium counter-productive to understanding the system. One must also understand that the increased efficiency is not had without a cost: there are also evolutionary *problems* of the market, including the types of positive feedback that created the Great Depression of the 1930s, or that lead to a tendency for wealth to reproduce itself so that the distribution of wealth becomes concentrated.

A second way to approach economics is what Boulding calls provisioning, or what I interpret as the study of incentives and responses to them. Boulding again emphasises the evolution of the system rather than searching for equilibrium. In particular, one cannot assume that preferences, and hence the response to any given incentive, are given. Preferences are learned, and moral sentiments are as important a part of human behaviour as rational maximising.

In Chapter 3 Dan Usher follows Boulding's first approach to economics, the study of the process and efficiency of exchange. He traces the rise and fall in economic thinking of an expanded, activist role for the State, mainly through the writings of four important figures in the history of economics. Adam Smith reasoned that the market required a system of laws, and hence a government, in order to function. Beyond this, Smith noted several departures from efficiency in the public sector which, while they had counterparts in the private sector, appeared to argue for limitations of the powers of the State. In Smith's 'system of natural liberty' there were three legitimate functions of the sovereign, namely, defence, justice and the production of public works.

While Smith was concerned mainly with 'the wealth of nations' and hence with economic efficiency, John Stuart Mill stressed personal liberty as the basis of his advocacy of qualified *laissez-faire*. Still he envisaged a fairly wide range of public sector activities. To his mind the insecurity in a state of anarchy was a great departure from efficiency; he argued that the State was required to resolve disputes and generally to prevent 'predation' by one citizen of another through force, fraud or negligence. Moreover the public sector would have to provide services which the private sector would do inefficiently. Beyond this, Mill feared despotism and advocated restricting the State to the narrowest limits possible.

These two authors, then, drew attention to trade-offs between private and public activities in two dimensions. Smith emphasised their domains of competence in delivering goods and services to society. Mill noted the possible inconsistency between individual security and liberty.

The third author, Sidgwick, did not share Smith's fears of government incompetence nor Mill's of despotism. To him the system of natural liberty involved a third trade-off, between efficiency of the market economy and measures to equalise the disparities it inevitably produced. He advocated a public presence in many activities, despite his admission of several shortcomings of the public sector.

By A. C. Pigou's time, the art of government seemed finely enough developed that he was able to justify State actions that previously were not justified. While some of the public sector's shortcomings were admitted, emphasis was placed on the shortcomings of the market and on the ability of government to correct them for the common good.

Pigou's optimism has not survived to the present day, however. Much of the intellectual justification for 'correction' of market outcomes has disappeared, and scepticism of public activity has led to a re-evaluation of the role of the State. Many economists now advocate limitations for reasons similar to those of Smith and Mill; some advocate a presumption against public solutions except where they are obviously of benefit.

Jack Weldon would have been in full agreement with the observation of Adam Smith and the moderns about the inefficiency of government; one need only recall his report cards on the economic policies of the Trudeau government. He would have been foursquare with John Stuart Mill on the need to be vigilant against potential despotism. The great struggle of his last years was against what he perceived to be a despotic attack on individual freedom in an institution, the university, whose *raison d'être* is to protect individual freedom. Yet he was also firmly a social democrat and a Christian, sensing a profound need for collective correction of the problems of the market, based on moral sentiments.

Gideon Rosenbluth, in Chapter 4, emphasises this theme, which corresponds to Boulding's second approach to economics. He notes that the typical individual is a member of at least one group, and that the group has interests which may conflict with the self-interest of the individual member. Despite this potential conflict the behavioural norm is to cooperate. Furthermore, traditional economic methods, based as they are on rational individual maximisation, are not helpful in explaining this cooperation. For example, game-theoretic models predict reciprocal cooperation only if there is repeated contact among a small number of actors. But cooperation is observed in large groups, where reciprocity cannot be expected to be effective.

Rosenbluth explains the cooperation by social conditioning through, for example, parental example or the inculcation of values in the educational system. These social mechanisms can instil what Rosenbluth calls a 'taste' for whatever cooperative action will benefit the group. Such a taste is similar to an ideology in inducing the individual to act contrary to his self-interest. It depends on social approval (which may be a component of self-interest) but also on internalised aesthetic and ethical senses.

This means that the individual utility function is endogenous to economic conditions and is in fact manipulated by the group, rather than given and immutable. The pervasiveness of cooperative behaviour suggests that exchange based on defined property rights – Boulding's first approach – may not be the only important or interesting device for coordinating economic activity.

The implications of pervasive change for testing economic hypotheses are discussed by Robin Rowley in Chapter 5. He draws our attention to contemporary efforts to reconcile rationality and uncertainty in economic theory and econometrics. Rationality – the consistency or efficiency of choice – is the essential postulate for economics to be able to say anything scientific about reality. Uncertainty, which must be faced in almost any interesting choice situation, is rendered systematic and quantified for decision theory using probability analysis. Probability models are not only a device for making theoretic sense of the world, but are the basis of econometrics, the main source of empirical knowledge in economics.

Often it is assumed in empirical work that the distributions in question are stable. In fact the probability theory on which econometrics is based does assume uniformity, homogeneity and stability through time of the random processes which give rise to the uncertainty. As Boulding observes and as Keynes observed a half-century ago, however, reality cannot be assumed to exhibit these properties.

Therefore, the believability of econometric research and of several types of theoretical model depends on how important one believes the instabilities and non-homogeneities of the probability distributions are through time. The fundamental question of both Rowley and Boulding relates to how confident we can be in assuming that the underlying parameters of the economic system remain constant.

In Chapter 6, Tom Rymes claims that potential instability is a reason for the existence of a monetary authority. Weldon argued that money was inescapably a public good. Against the backdrop of arguments by neoclassical economists that a monetary authority is not necessary, Rymes explores the way in which money can be held to be a public good which should be controlled by the public sector. He presents a simple neoclassical monetary growth model in which the productivities of capital and of real money balances are explicitly taken into account.

If society can be sure that the stability conditions of the model hold, he argues, there is no need for a monetary authority: money can be viewed as a private good to be supplied by the private sector. If, however, the economy is unstable, there may be a role for discretionary monetary policy. This role would be to assure the stability of society's monetary arrangements, and hence the confidence of the public in them. Because money is productive in the sense that it facilitates real economic activity, this is an important role. Therefore, Rymes concludes that Weldon's point about the publicness of money is confirmed even in the context of a neoclassical money growth model.

Serious problems have thus been raised by some contributors to the volume about the possible instability of the economy and the attendant logical difficulties of mathematical modelling. The reader may be inclined to wonder to what use one could put a mathematical economic model and what one could learn from it. Further perspective on the issue may be gained when we note that there are regularities of economic behaviour, and that it is the possibility that insights can be drawn from the observed regularities that motivates a study of economics in the first place. In such study it may be prudent to avoid trying to explain very broad issues but to focus attention on well-defined problems which may permit sharp answers. Rymes's chapter is a case in point, and those by Murray Kemp and Shigemi Yabuuchi (Chapter 7) and John Chipman (Chapter 8), both in the theory of international trade, are also prime examples of such focused attention.

Kemp and Yabuuchi address the problem of the effects on the predictions of trade theory of the possibility that technical information that is available to one producer may not be available to all. They take a very detailed look at the medium-term effects of one of the important factors which, Boulding observes, drives the economic system. Standard trade theory assumes that technical information is freely available to all. Suppose, however, that information is private to one firm. Kemp and Yabuuchi present a model in which one firm produces each of two goods, using both of two factors of production (labour and capital), and each firm operates in both of two countries. Each has private information which prevents entry, and uses this advantage to equate marginal revenue, rather than price, to marginal cost.

Kemp and Yabuuchi examine the effects of private information on the predictions of two of the main theorems of international trade. The Stolper–Samuelson theorem states that an increase in the relative price of one of the commodities raises the real reward of the factor used relatively more intensively in the production of that good, and depresses the real reward of the other factor. Kemp and Yabuuchi find that the Stolper–Samuelson conditions hold under certain restrictions on the utility functions of the citizens of the two countries. The Rybczynski theorem states that an increase in the endowment of one of the factors raises the output of the industry which uses that factor relatively intensively and depresses the output of the other. With private information, a modified form of the Rybczynski theorem also holds, the modification depending on the sign of the determinant of factor proportions in the two industries.

John Chipman explores one of the paradoxes of international trade theory. Metzler's paradox is that under certain conditions, if a country imposes a tariff, the tariff may so improve that country's terms of trade that the relative price of the imported good (on which the tariff is imposed) will fall in its home market. In this situation the tariff does not protect the good on which the tariff is imposed in the home market. Chipman finds an alternative necessary condition for the paradox to hold: it can hold only if a cash transfer from the country exporting the good subject to the tariff to the tariff-imposing country improves the terms of trade of the latter. Also, Chipman shows that a tariff can be decomposed into two policies: an export tax levied by the exporting country followed by a transfer of the tax revenues to the importing country. If each country's export good is non-inferior (an increase in national income does not reduce consumption of the good) then a tariff is superior to an export tax imposed by the foreign country. Moreover, Chipman finds, by the trade-theoretic relationship between a tariff and a quota, that under the same condition an import quota is superior to an export quota. This, of course, has policy implications for US trade policy with Japan.

The nexus between theory and policy in turbulent periods of economic evolution is also the subject of John Dales's chapter on one of the most controversial periods of Canadian economic history (Chapter 9). At the turn of the century the Canadian prairies were opened to settlement. For just over a decade, the government of Canada encouraged prospective immigrants with an aggressive immigration policy which included the Dominion Lands Policy of granting lands to potential farmers. Rapid settlement ensued, as well as a remarkable increase in both absolute and per-capita national income.

Dales evaluates two models of what has come to be known as the period of the Wheat Boom. Chambers and Gordon modelled the growth of productivity in the Canadian manufacturing and agricultural sectors. By assuming constant returns to scale in manufacturing, they allowed that sector to absorb from or to release to agriculture any quantity of labour at a constant wage. On the basis of their model, Chambers and Gordon challenged the prevailing wisdom of the time by concluding that manufacturing accounted for almost all the increase in productivity of the economy during the Wheat Boom, and agriculture almost none. Dales is sceptical of their results, arguing that the assumption about the manufacturing industry simply does not accord with historical fact. Dales goes on to argue that opening up the prairies had a major effect on immigration to and investment in Canada, but only a minor effect on prices.

In the second model evaluated by Dales, Southey argued that the Dominion Lands Policy created a common property resource in prairie farmland. As a result, the potential Ricardian rents from the land were dissipated in the rush to gain them, in a manner reminiscent of a gold rush. That is to say, the rents to the farmland did not show up in the national accounts as rents to agriculture because they were lost through too early a start in taking up the lands. Southey laid the blame for the dissipation upon the Dominion politicians responsible for the Lands Policy. Dales argues that this model is more representative of the period than the Chambers–Gordon one.

Two of the chapters concentrate on macroeconomic policy, the pursuit of which has accounted for much of the growth of the State in western democracies since The Second World War. In Chapter 10, Clarence Barber, like Boulding, takes very seriously the possibility that there are positive feedbacks in the market economy that could lead to serious problems like the Great Depression. Like Boulding, he too is of the opinion that economics has, on balance, made a positive contribution to society. He contends that the western world avoided a depression in the 1980s because of structural changes since the 1930s, and that many of these changes can be attributed to economic policy analysis. Among the resulting policy changes is the larger role of the State in macroeconomic stabilisation. Governments account for a larger share of the economy, and derive a greater share of their revenues from direct taxes which give more built-in flexibility to stabilisation. The public is more willing to accept the use of fiscal and monetary policy and to tolerate the existence of government deficits, which were key factors in avoiding a depression in the 1980s. Also, there have been changes to tariff and other protective measures, and they are more subject to international negotiation.

Thus, Barber takes a traditional Keynesian position on macro policy. He argues that continuing unemployment and slow growth are a result of the fact that investment has not kept up with the savings of society, which have risen with discretionary incomes. The shortfall of investment over nearly two decades has been made up only by government stimulative policies and the automatic stabilisers.

David Schwartzman, on the other hand, takes a more micro approach to these macroeconomic issues. In Chapter 11 he argues that since The Second World War, government stimulative policies have kept the economy growing, and have led to private investment. But the higher relative real wages of unskilled labour have had the effect of inducing investment that has tended to substitute away from unskilled labour, over a fairly long time-period. The decline in wage and price flexibility, also noted by Barber, has maintained real wages in unskilled occupations while the capital stock now in place has been built up. This is the way in which Schwartzman explains his observation of stubborn unemployment of unskilled workers, but low-to-negligible unemployment of skilled workers, professionals and managers. The upshot would seem to be that the very policies which, according to Barber, have prevented a depression on the scale of the

1930s, are contributing to the fostering of a more-or-less permanent underclass of unemployed unskilled workers.

Jack Weldon had a strong interest in the economics of public pension plans, and spent over half his professional career contributing to the analysis of them. It is fitting, then, that three of the papers of this Festschrift discuss economic issues relating to such plans.

Louis Ascah and Tom Asimakopulos in Chapter 12 provide the conceptual background of Weldon's views on pensions and summarise its key elements. In making decisions on pension taxes and benefits, a government is seen as utilising a social welfare function that reflects the collective preferences of the community it represents. The government's concern is with incomes over the lifetimes of its constituents, but it can directly determine only current pension benefits and taxes. To perform its decision-making based on the welfare function, the government must also take into consideration the future pensions of those currently working. Weldon does this by assuming that governments believe that the rules for calculating future benefits will be the ones currently in effect; thus, values for the future pensions can be derived on the basis of current conditions. What a government offers to its constituents who are currently working, then, is a process for determining their pensions which they can expect will have political support in the future. It does not offer a contract for actual values, which will be determined by the future government according to future circumstances. In determining the rules for public pensions, as well as their values, governments will be concerned about saving and investment, because the future pension levels will depend on future economic conditions and hence on present actions. The pension laws and processes are viewed as developing in historical time, where future conditions over the long time-spans involved are highly uncertain. What is assumed is that individuals expect to live into retirement, and what is explained is how public pensions become one of the ways in which members of a community try to provide themselves with income in old age.

Weldon views public pensions as a social response to continuing circumstances where individual efforts to provide an adequate retirement income are often insufficient. He places the focus on social adequacy rather than on individual equity. The rules developed both provide for the current aged and insure the current cohorts of working citizens that they will receive a share of future national income, at least at a basic level. The other economists whose writings on public pensions are reviewed by Ascah and Asimakopulos tend to view public pensions as 'forced' individual saving. They focus on individual equity, and thus on the rate of return obtained on their public pension contributions.

In Chapter 13, Peter Howitt explores how the rules for determining pensions can remain stable over time, when each government acts to promote the welfare of those currently alive and not that of future constituencies. The linkages among governments do not involve contingent promises in any real sense, but do involve strategic anticipation of the reactions of future governments to their own actions. Howitt's game-theoretic analysis of the strategic interactions shows that a government can constrain its successors in their pension choices through its own choice of a pension tax rate on its working generations. The higher the tax rate, the higher the political pressure on successive governments to pay higher pension benefits.

The power of the strategic interactions is illustrated by the fact that the analysis assumes a finite number of periods, or generations, T. What it relies upon at time T for the young to pay the pension benefits when they do not, by assumption, expect to receive any, is the political influence of the old to enable the required redistribution. The only requirement for the existence of the public pension plan is that there be 'weak egalitarianism' (expressed by concavity of the implicit social welfare function maximised by the government). Howitt finds that the redistributions will be Pareto optimal. But, in comparison to the implicit welfare function used by the governments, 'too much' of the national income will be redistributed to the old. An intertemporal 'meta-State' could rearrange the payments to make each government's implicit welfare higher.

John Burbidge, in Chapter 14, carries out a careful empirical study of the pension incomes of elderly women in Canada, and finds that much of the public pension money they receive is saved, rather than spent on current consumption. He considers possible explanations for this behaviour, and tentatively offers a conclusion that the women are satiated in their later old age. The current procedures in Canada may not be Pareto optimal, as *ex post*, at least (and there is anecdotal evidence that the conclusion may be true *ex ante* as well), these women may have preferred to shift some of their real income forward in time, not in response to normal time preferences, but to their capacity to spend and to consume. What Burbidge's findings may suggest is an unrecognised (by present decision-makers) feature of life among the elderly which to date has had no expression in political fora. His study also has important implications for the life-cycle savings hypothesis, which is clearly not consistent with his evidence of substantial saving at the end of the life cycle.

It is fitting that the three chapters on the policy issue of public pensions, which was so important to Jack Weldon, should provide an example of how theoretical and empirical work in economics can both tell us something important about reality and open up new questions of interpretation and measurement. All the papers in this volume give an impression of the steady progress of economics, which in large measure is attributable to its penchant for internal criticism and its openness to developments in the outside world. These are at least some of the attributes of a science. Economics proceeds by small steps. As the criticisms herein show, it has a long way to go to explain the role of the State in improving social welfare, but nevertheless it has taken many steps since Adam Smith's day.

2 Economics: The Trunk and the Branches

Kenneth E. Boulding

Economic thought, as it spreads out through time and space, has some resemblance to a tree. There are roots, some of which may go down a long way, but most prominent, in the seventeenth and eighteenth centuries, are people like Sir William Petty, Richard Cantillon, the Physiocrats like A. R. J. Turgot and Francois Quesnay, and perhaps we should add Thomas Mun and Sir James Steuart on the Mercantilist side, and perhaps even Bernard Mandeville. There is no doubt, however, that the main trunk begins with Adam Smith. Even if he is not the 'Adam' of economics (for he had some forebears), he is certainly the 'Smith', for he forged economic ideas into a remarkably insightful, consistent, and productive structure of theory. *The Wealth of Nations* is still a good book for the teaching of basic economics. Adam Smith not only laid the foundations of equilibrium price theory – which has not really improved much since *The Wealth of Nations*, Book I, Chapter VII – but he also had a theory of economic development and evolution, which stands up very well today. He realised that an increase in productive powers of a system came out of the learning process, that is, a genetic factor of production, which developed partly through what today might be called 'folk learning' of skills and dexterity, but also out of scholarly learning from the 'philosophers' and specialised designers, something which was relatively rare in his own day.[1] This learning of productivity was fostered by the division of labour, which also had some perverse learning effects.[2]

Next up the main trunk, of course, are Thomas Malthus and David Ricardo. It was Malthus who gave Darwin the idea of 'natural selection'. In his famous *Essay on Population*, Malthus developed the concept of the 'ecological niche', though he did not call it that. This was the essence of the subsistence theory of wages, which Ricardo also accepted. Both recognised that this was not a physiological subsistence, but a learned level of income at which population remained constant. Already we see signs of a little branching. From

Malthus comes a sprout in his 1820 *Principles of Political Economy*, which led eventually to Keynes.[3]

After Ricardo, the trunk splits at Karl Marx, going off on a branch that in the eyes of some parts of the world rivals or even exceeds the main trunk, sprouting into Lenin and Marxism-Leninism. The anti-Marxists might well regard this as a graft, coming out of Hegel and Marx's reaction against his Lutheran high school, and certainly there is a lot more to Marxism than economics. On the other hand, it is hard to deny that he is also an economist, springing from Ricardo rather than directly from Adam Smith.

Following Ricardo on the more official main trunk, of course, we have John Stuart Mill, which in turn leads to Alfred Marshall and A. C. Pigou. In Mill's lifetime, however, another branch sprouted off, almost unnoticed at first, with Cournot, in mathematical economics. This then comes out as a main branch with W. S. Jevons, Leon Walras, Vilfredo Pareto, Francis Y. Edgeworth, and so on, to Paul Samuelson. Somewhat parallel to this, though more on the literary side, are the Austrians: Carl Menger, F. von Wieser, Eugen von Böhm-Bawerk, leading up to the neo-Austrians of today. The mathematical branch divides again with Ragnar Frisch, Henry L. Moore, Henry Schultz and others, into econometrics on the one hand, and mathematical theory – Samuelson and so on – on the other. This has developed a lot of foliage, the foliage of this tree, of course, being made of papers. About the time of Marshall, on the other side of the trunk, we get Thorstein Veblen, John R. Commons, Wesley Mitchell and the Institutionalists, leading into the neo-Institutionalists of today.

During Keynes's lifetime there was some tendency for the trunk to split into microeconomics and macroeconomics: microeconomics represented by the theory of imperfect or monopolistic competition (E. H. Chamberlin and the early Joan Robinson); macroeconomics represented by Keynes himself and his followers, such as Roy Harrod and Evsey Domar in development theory. Curiously enough, neither of these seems to be sprouting very much these days. As we get towards the top of the tree, it becomes hard to say where the trunk is.

Then there are some odd branches that don't fit too easily into the scheme, such as Henry George, sprouting off from Ricardo, and the 'funny money school' of Silvio Gesell and Major Douglas. It is a little hard to know where to put Irving Fisher, perhaps the greatest American economist, who represents in one sense a culmination of

Austrian economics in his great book on the theory of interest, but who also is a seed of monetarism in his famous equation of exchange. Monetarism itself – Milton Friedman and his followers – is also hard to put on the tree. Controversies about capital theory have spread among the branches. Perhaps these phenomena might be described as 'Spanish moss'. Supply-side economics might also qualify as Spanish moss, clinging to the main branch of microeconomics, but stretching over to the macro branch. The theory of rational expectations one might also identify as a fungus sprouting out of the micro branch and again, stretching towards the macro in an attempt to create an order that is not really there in the real world.

Another branch that is a little difficult to locate, but which has a good deal of sap flowing through it, might be called 'disequilibrium economics', for which Frank Knight must bear some responsibility, with his emphasis on the importance of uncertainty, ideas which have been developed very beautifully by G. L. S. Shackle. For some reason it does not seem to have produced much in the way of leaves. Other branches can be identified, like the German Historical School, the British Fabians, and so on.

According to scripture, a tree should be known by its fruit, and it is a very serious question as to whether the tree of economics is a thistle or a fig tree, or perhaps a bit of both.[4] It may indeed be an evolutionary curiosity in that both sweet and bitter fruit seem to grow from the branches. Marxism certainly has produced a little seeding of the welfare state, but it also produced the agony of the First Collectivisation under Stalin, the unspeakable tragedy of Kampuchea, and the Cultural Revolution in China, a wide destruction of creativity in art, literature, and so on. Perhaps we should not blame the economic aspects of Marxism too much for this, although economics has some responsibility to bear for the fallacy of the labour theory of value. It is perhaps the Hegelian roots of Marxism that deified dialectical processes and denied the management of conflict, which were responsible for the bitterness. It may be indeed that we are moving into a period of liberal Marxism, as we see it in China, Hungary, and now in Gorbachev's Soviet Union, where the economic sap will rise to counter the bitter poison of dialectics and will foster a greater appreciation of political relaxation and the existence of a benign, if small, invisible hand, even in the partially planned economy.

There is bitter fruit, however, on the capitalist branches as well as some pretty good fruit. On the whole, in my own estimation, economics has done a good deal more good than harm.[5] The free market has very real virtues, especially when compared with a large-scale centrally planned economy. Large parts of the world have definitely become richer than in Adam Smith's day. While he certainly cannot be given all the credit for this – and indeed some of the communist countries have become richer too – there can be little doubt that market processes, by the human productivity increase which they foster, do enrich us. Indeed, one of the strongest cases for the virtues of economics is the contrast between countries like Sweden, which did not bother about being a great power and refrained from using threat systems around the world in the creation of empire, and so got rich quickly, and countries like Britain and France, the development of which was really crippled by the resources which they put into being great powers and using the threat system instead of the exchange system. The economist's beloved hypothesis that exchange is normally a positive-sum game in which both parties benefit, simply because of the veto power which each party has over any particular exchange, is in sharp contrast with the dialectical view that most games are zero-sum and the only way to get richer is to make somebody else poorer. If only economists could take over the departments of defence of the world and make them come up with a 'bottom line', the world would be enormously more secure. There is a high probability that everybody would be better off.

Nevertheless, it is a fundamental principle that something can go wrong with anything and certainly the market, like any complex system, has its pathologies, which economics took a long time to get around to studying with a view to curing. The business cycle creates a good deal of human misery, and from the point of view of the allocational and even distributional results, the market system, beyond a certain point, must be regarded as pathological. Some fluctuations, of course, may be inevitable in any kind of system that has cybernetic processes around a moving equilibrium. But the essence of good cybernetic systems is that these are controlled within tolerable limits. The thermostat is a good example. I once was my own thermostat for a hand-fired furnace. The temperature of the house fluctuated by about 20 degrees. Then we installed an automatic thermostat and the fluctuations were reduced to one degree. There certainly are cybernetic processes in the market, as Adam Smith brings out so well in his price theory. If a price is 'too high', this will produce effects that will tend to make it fall; if a price is 'too low', it will tend to rise. On the other hand, there are positive feedback processes in the market as well. Inflation beyond a certain point is one example, especially an inflation caused by a budget deficit, for the inflation diminishes the 'real' receipts of the tax system and increases the deficit. There can also be purely psychologically inspired market inflations, especially in organised speculative markets, where people interpret a rising price as if it were a trend. Hence, speculators expect prices to rise still further and act to make this come about, and similarly for falling prices.

The Great Depression of the 1930s is an extraordinary example of market positive feedbacks producing a fluctuation of extreme danger, creating great human misery, and all this under a government which was highly friendly to markets and to capital, and yet was quite incapable of dealing with the situation. The Great Depression, however, did produce the Keynesian theory, which at least gave us some inkling as to what was happening and what might be done to prevent it, even though the theory was far from perfect.

It is also widely recognised that a market system can produce pathologies of distribution of both wealth and income, although economists on the whole have tended to shy away from this problem, or tried to dump it in the political scientist's lap. The problem, fundamentally, arises from the dynamics of capital accumulation, in what has been called the 'Matthew Principle': 'For whosoever hath, to him shall be given, . . . but whosoever hath not, from him shall be taken away, even that he hath.'[6] This perverse dynamic is by no means easy to control. There is an inherent instability in equality, in the sense that even if we started off with a situation with everyone having equal net worth, random processes would make some people a little richer than others. Then the principle is bound to come into play that the richer one is, the easier it is to get still richer, simply because it is easier to save, and the poorer one is, the harder it is to get richer, for the harder it is to save. The only unregulated offset for this dynamic is a certain long-run tendency for capitalists to lose their money by unwise investments or to diminish their capital by extravagance – 'the rake's progress'. There is some evidence for the 'shirtsleeves to shirtsleeves in three generations' phenomenon. Grandfather gets rich, father just holds it where it is, and the grandson goes to college and turns into a rake and a spendthrift. There are a good many exceptions to this rule, however, which make it likely that a pure market economy without any public intervention is likely to move towards a distribution of wealth which is perceived by the majority of people in the society as too unequal.

If the wealthy become a very small minority, as they did, for instance, in eighteenth-century France and twentieth-century Russia, it is not surprising that we have revolutions. There is even scriptural recognition of this problem in the concept of the 'year of jubilee',[7] in which all debts were to be forgiven and all properties returned to the descendants of the owners of fifty years before. It is very doubtful whether this was ever carried out. And if it had been, the disorganisation it would have produced would have been horrendous. Nevertheless, the problem remains. Communism derives some of its legitimacy from its professed ability to solve this problem. In practice, however, communist societies have not produced much greater economic equality than capitalist societies, and have produced a very much greater inequality in the distribution of power, which perhaps is even more important than wealth, so that it seems extremely unlikely that communism will prove to be a solution to this problem.

The solution that has been tried in capitalist societies, of course, has been progressive income taxation and inheritance taxation, and at more irregular intervals, land reform, in which large landlords have either been bought out, chased out, or killed off and the land redistributed in smaller parcels to new owners. Another solution has been the direct subsidisation of the poor by the state or other political authorities. Here again, the results are mixed. Japan, for instance, has the most equal distribution of income of all the rich countries, and yet has about the smallest welfare and redistribution programme. Land reforms have been very disappointing, except in a few cases. The political impotence of the poor has sometimes tended to undermine the redistributive system, as it is doing in the United States at the moment. There is evidence for the thesis that the proportional distribution of income is a function of the average level of income, getting more unequal as we move from very poor conditions into somewhat richer, and becoming more equal again as society gets still richer.

Distribution undoubtedly has something to do with the product mix of the economy itself. It is interesting that Adam Smith's first use of the 'invisible hand' was in *The Theory of Moral Sentiments*, where he points out that even though the chief of the highland clan theoretically owns all the food that the clan produces, he cannot possibly eat it all, and so he has to distribute it among the members of the clan. Similarly, once we get to the point where there is one automobile per two people, it is very hard for these not to be distributed very equally. The record in owning automobiles seems to be held by Rajneesh, who was reputed to have owned twenty-seven Rolls

Royces.[8] It is very doubtful whether even the richest person ever owned more than that. With the possible exception of some forms of 'conspicuous consumption', there seems to be a limit of either wealth or income beyond which it is impossible either to enjoy the wealth or consume the income. Hence the establishment of foundations.

Just what economics has contributed to these problems is not wholly clear, but at least it calls attention to the dynamic nature of distribution. In market societies, indeed, there is a constant hurricane of redistribution towards people who are holding assets that are rising in value and away from people who are holding assets that are falling in value in relative terms. In a speculative market in which there is no increase in the overall value of what is being bought and sold, every gain of one person must be offset by the loss of others. Speculation, indeed, has a strong tendency to become a zero-sum game unless the total value of wealth is continually increasing. It is a fundamental principle of economics that in the aggregate people cannot own more net worth than there is.

Even if economics has done more good than harm, the question still arises: How true is it? This is not a trivial question. Economics is an attempt to create images in our mind of a portion of reality which we can call the economy, as a pattern in space-time, such that the image in our minds maps with reasonable accuracy into the real world. I think we can say with moderate confidence that over the centuries the images of the world which economics has produced on the whole have tended to map more accurately into the real world, just as the maps of the geographers have become much more accurate in the last 500 years. Each of us as economists has images in our mind both of the economy and of economics, and it is at least an interesting exercise to try to put these together to see how far they map into each other. We see the economy as a subset of human activity – decisions, images, and learning processes – plus a large subset of human artifacts and organisations. What defines the economy as a subset is not wholly clear, but then no important distinctions are clear. We have to live with fuzzy sets. Still, we do have an image of the economy which consists of people in the acts of producing, exchanging, enjoying, consuming, and managing commodities which are objects, or perhaps sometimes processes, capable of entering into and being evaluated by exchange.

There may be two approaches to the question as to what constitutes an economy, which perhaps are complementary rather than in conflict. The first looks at exchange as the central concept and looks at the economy as how the world is organised through exchange and through exchangeables. This would not exclude the 'grants economy', as I have called it, of one-way transfers of exchangeables.[9] The second might be called the 'provisioning' aspect of the economy, which looks at the structure of goods as they are enjoyed and consumed in the sustaining of the 'good life' and sees exchange, therefore, as only one aspect, though an important one, of the way we are provisioned.[10] The economy may look like a rather larger subset of the world from the provisioning point of view than from the exchange point of view, but the difference is not very large.

It is a very interesting exercise, therefore, as we look at the whole tree of economic thought as it stretches out over the last 300 years or more, to ask whether there are aspects of the economy that economic thought perceived earlier and then lost, which sometimes happens; branches cut off too early. Then one can ask also: Are there misapprehensions, that is, false maps, which have a certain charm and acceptability of their own, even though they may actually mislead us (grafts without fruit)? One can find examples of these phenomena.

We can start with Adam Smith, to whom we owe so much. Is there anything that he understood that somehow we have lost? One thing we have lost perhaps is his very clear understanding of the evolutionary nature of the economic system. In many ways Adam Smith was perhaps the first post-Newtonian thinker who escaped from the trap of determinism and equilibrium, although, of course, coming nearly 100 years before Darwin he did not use the Darwinian terminology. Nevertheless, he sees very clearly that the market is a selective process in which the capacity to satisfy the demand for a commodity, especially the effective demand of those who can afford it, is extremely important in determining what commodities will exist and what will not. He sees also that production is essentially a genetic process constantly subject to mutation, though, of course, again, he does not use these terms. All production originates in human knowledge or in skill and dexterity, which is a kind of muscular knowledge. His factors of production of land, labour and capital are much more factors of distribution than they are of production. I myself have insisted that production, whether of a chicken from an egg or a house from a blueprint or an automobile from the knowledge stored of how to make it, originates with a genetic factor which is described as 'know-how'.[11] This know-how has to be able to capture energy of the right kinds to select, transport, and transform materials of the right kinds into the product. Land, labour and capital are no more factors of production than earth, air, fire and water are elements. This confusion of the factors of distribution with the factors of production has resulted in a long history of futile attempts to find production functions which are somehow independent of human knowledge and know-how. The 'natural price' of a commodity is that which will return to the factors of distribution – in this case, the landlord, the capitalist, and the labourer – a sufficient amount to persuade them to go on providing the know-how, the energy, and the materials, that are necessary to make the commodity. This view is not perhaps explicit in Adam Smith, but it is certainly implicit.

Another aspect of the economy which is clear in Adam Smith, but has tended to be lost in modern economics, is the view of the world of commodities as an interacting ecosystem, each with a population, that is, a stock, occupying a niche determined by the nature of demand, especially effective demand, but also consisting of a 'food chain', a concept much more familiar to ecologists than it is to modern economists. The production of food is fundamental to the economy in Adam Smith. He sees very clearly that it is only what can be spared from food production that is available for the production of other things, for the people who make the other things have to be fed. We could even start off with 'corn', which in Scotland, of course, would be mainly oats. This is grown by the farmer, who eats less than he grows. Therefore, there is a surplus. The surplus is fed into livestock who produce milk and meat. If it is fed into shoemakers along with leather, shoes are produced. If it is fed into carpenters along with wood, furniture and houses will be produced. If it is fed into spinners and weavers along with wool, clothes will be produced, and so on. Furthermore, there is a positive feedback involved, as we would say now. The clothes and the shoes and the farm implements which the oats helped to produce, increase the productivity of the farmer and make more oats. Curiously enough, even Jevons recognised this hierarchy of commodities in the food chain, which is very important in the theory of economic development. But unfortunately one of the side effects of the mathematisation of economics was the loss of this concept. In Walras commodities are just x and y, not corn and meat and clothing, and this really meant a great loss of understanding. Even the input–output analysis of Wassily Leontief does not deal with the crucially important relationships of the 'food chain'.

A legacy of Adam Smith which is not so fortunate is his emphasis on income rather than capital as the measure of the wealth of nations and on consumption as the principal object of economic activity. This ties in also with his dismissal of household capital as not contributing to the 'revenue' of the economy. This point of view, leading to a constant confusion between stocks and flows, goes back to the very first sentence of *The Wealth of Nations*: 'The annual labour of every nation is the fund which originally supplies it with all the necessaries and conveniences of life which it annually consumes.' A fund is essentially a stock. The annual labour is a flow. The fund is the labourers. The most casual observation of economic life would reveal that we get satisfaction not so much from consuming things as from enjoying them. I get very little satisfaction out of the fact that my clothes are wearing out, my car is depreciating, the gasoline in it is being consumed, and so on. We can recognise, of course, that the 'economic welfare' or the 'degree of well-offness' function has in its argument both stocks and flows. We like being well fed, which is a stock, but we also like eating, which is a flow. There are good evolutionary reasons for this: any creature who only liked being well fed, but did not like eating, would not last very long. Nevertheless, it remains that economies in consumption, such as an increase in the length of life of goods, is a gain, and that consumption by itself is a very poor measure of economic well-being. Even people who like eating more than they like being well fed are apt to be gluttons and end up in very bad health.

The throughput from production to consumption is significant mainly because of the stock which it sustains and necessitates. Adam Smith was very clear that if there was to be production, there had to be a stock, which consisted essentially of the pipeline from the food into the labourer and from the raw materials to the finished product. The obsession with income, which has dominated economics now for 200 years or more, perverted our concept as to what really constitutes economic development and led to an extraordinary neglect of such things as maintenance and depreciation, and it has perverted our data system, so that we know far more about income than we know about capital. And yet it is the capital structure and the capital stock which is crucial to the economy, as Adam Smith knew so well. Capital theory is still the more primitive part of economics and the part that has probably caused the most trouble. We see this even in Keynes and the later Joan Robinson and in the so-called Cambridge capital controversy. The Austrians perhaps did a little better on this. They at least were aware that there was a pipeline through which capital was transformed from raw materials into half-finished goods, even into fixed capital, and then to finished goods, and into households. But even Böhm-Bawerk got trapped into too simple a concept of the period of production and tried to interpret what is essentially an endless, ongoing, disequilibrium process as a kind of equilibrium of stationary states, which did not get very far.

This raises another question, which is the devastating obsession with the concept of equilibrium in economics. Adam Smith was very well aware that all equilibria, for instance, of relative prices, were temporary and constantly disturbed by what today we would call mutation. Ricardo was a much less dynamic thinker than Adam Smith was. Marshall to some extent recovered a more realistic view, that all equilibria were transitory, including even long-run equilibria, but was never perhaps able to face up to the consequences of this point of view. Walrasian economics is almost pure equilibrium and can only be described as a catastrophe, diverting economists from the pursuit of evolutionary models into a kind of sterile Newtonianism, which has also greatly afflicted econometrics. I have accused econometrics indeed of being the search for a celestial mechanics of a nonexistent universe. It has had some success in periods where the parameters of the economy have been fairly stable, as they were in the 1950s and 1960s. It is absurd, however, to search for 'laws', by no matter how sophisticated means, if these laws do not exist or are constantly changing. The model of celestial mechanics, indeed, has been disastrous for the social sciences, simply because in the solar system the parameters are very stable, whereas in social systems they are often quite unstable and unpredictably so.

The idea that prediction is a test of human knowledge is only valid as long as parameters are stable. In social systems it is absurd, simply because these systems involve information and knowledge as absolutely essential components. Information has to be surprising. The knowledge that we are going to have in the future cannot be predicted or we would know it now. This does not mean, of course, that the world is random, although it has important random elements in it. Predictions can and should be made, just like plans, but it is very dangerous to believe them in a world of shifting parameters. The economy is an evolutionary system and the history of evolution is dominated by the time at which improbable events happen. The same is true of the economy. It is important to be ready for good luck, but it is disastrous to mistake good luck for good management.

From Adam Smith on, economics has tended to take a rather limited, what might be called a 'first-approximation' view of human behaviour. Adam Smith himself had a much broader view of behaviour than he usually expressed in *The Wealth of Nations*, as reflected in *The Theory of Moral Sentiments*, but economics, unfortunately, did not proceed very much from *The Theory of Moral Sentiments*. What is called 'maximising behaviour', that is, the assumption that people do what they think is best at the time, is indeed hard to deny. But it is at best a static theory. It takes very little account of the human learning process, and historically it has not even taken much account of the 'moral sentiments', which are a very important part of human behaviour. Such things as benevolence, malevolence, pride, shame, and so on, have been almost totally neglected by economists, although there is no great difficulty in putting these into the model. Putting learning into the model is much more difficult, simply because we know so little about human learning. Nevertheless, we cannot simply assume that preferences are given. To some extent preferences no doubt have a genetic base, but in detail they are learned. And just how we learn them cannot be brushed aside in any image of the economy as an ongoing system. Welfare economics, for instance, while in some sense it may have come to a dead end, has done so partly because of its neglect of the 'moral sentiments' and its assumption that social values can be obtained by the sheer summation of individual preferences. Things like the 'Arrow theorem'[12] and the other paradoxes strike me as being remarkable exercises in futility, simply because they neglect the fact that the political process is a process in human learning, especially through debate, not a process in the summation of immutable preferences. I have always thought it odd that economic behaviour assumed that economic persons had none of the seven deadly sins. The Paretian optimum, for instance, assumes that there is no envy. Rationality assumes that there is no lust, gluttony, anger, avarice, or sloth. And I know of virtually no discussion of the economics of pride.[13]

Both the inability of the theory of economic behaviour to go beyond its first approximation, and the obsession with income to the exclusion of capital, has made microeconomics (the theory of the firm and the household, and the economic aspects of other organisations like the state) much less productive than it might have been. The theory of the firm, especially, has been almost a monument to the lack of realism. It has largely failed to recognise, for instance, that the balance sheet is a critical description of the state of the firm at a moment of time, that all events consist of changes within the balance sheet, that cost, for instance, is what goes down in the balance sheet when whatever it is that has cost something goes up, and that profits consist of the revaluation of saleable assets, usually at the moment of sale, which until then are usually valued at cost. It has failed to recognise that the fear of loss may be a much more important motivation than the hope of gain in restricting events, such as purchases, sales, production, and so on, which change the balance sheet in directions that involve more danger, the more things go wrong. The neglect of uncertainty and total neglect of the learning process and of the non-quantifiable aspects of the position statement, of which the balance sheet is simply an inaccurate sample, all suggest that we have arrived at a dead end which it is important to break through. There are not too many signs of this happening, although Simon's efforts in going beyond simple maximisation are at least a step in the right direction.[14]

The obsession with income and the neglect of capital and an inadequate theory of the firm have also led to a tragic neglect of one of the most significant elements in the labour market and a major factor in unemployment, which is the difference between the rate of profit and the rate of interest. Economists, unfortunately, from Adam Smith on, have tended to amalgamate profits and interest, or to suppose that interest automatically is determined by profit, with the rate of interest perhaps two or three percentage points below the rate of profit. This has led to a total neglect of the very obvious fact that when an employer hires anybody, the employer sacrifices the interest that could have been obtained on the money spent on the wage in the hope of profit on the product of the work. The marginal productivity theory, based as it is on income accounting almost to the exclusion of capital accounting, has on the whole neglected this aspect of the problem, assuming that labour will be employed up to the point where the wage of the marginal labourer will equal his/her marginal value product, without recognising that it is expected rates of interest and expected rates of profit which are significant.

The general assumption in the textbook theory of the firm, that only the short-term marginal costs and marginal revenues are significant in determining the level of employment, seems to me quite fallacious and neglects the capital accounting problem. Employing somebody involves diminishing cash and increasing something else, maybe goods in process, finished inventory, or perhaps offsetting depreciation. This is true even when employing a janitor. Suppose the cash paid out in the wage could be used for making a loan or buying a bond at a positive rate of interest, while if it is used for employment it will result in an increase in some inventory item or capital item which is falling in its price, hence resulting in negative profit. Then the 'rational' choice may well be to shut the plant down and use the money derived from the sale of inventory to purchase interest-bearing securities.

Rates of interest and profit are not prices, but rates of growth, and capital markets are so imperfect that there is no guarantee that the rate of interest and the rate of profit will be the optimum distance apart. This imperfection is particularly characteristic of a period of deflation, when 'idle money' bears a positive real rate of interest, with its purchasing power continually increasing, and when similarly the real rate of interest on debt (bonds) will be greater than the nominal rate, again in terms of purchasing power. At the other side of the account, profit is obtained by buying something, say, wheat, at a certain price and selling it later, even when transformed into flour, at a price higher than its cost. If all prices have fallen in the interval between the purchase and the sale, profit will be diminished. The classic example of these principles is 1932–3 in the United States – and in most of the developed capitalist world – when real rates of interest were on the order of 2 or 3 per cent, profit rates were on the order of minus 2 or minus 3 per cent. In those years it is almost literally true that anybody who hired anybody was either a philanthropist or a fool. The amazing thing is that unemployment did not go to 50 or even 75 per cent and the whole society collapse under these circumstances. Probably the only reason why it stayed at 25 per cent was just habit, irrational expectations, and the desire to hold firms together.

A final word may be added on the impact of other disciplines on economics. No tree stands by itself and every tree of learning stands in the forest of other trees. There is a good deal of cross-pollination going on. Economics has been profoundly influenced, for instance, by seventeenth-century mathematics, somewhat I suspect to its detriment, in spite of some significant internal economies. Seventeenth-century mathematics essentially came out of celestial mechanics and is quite unsuitable to deal with a system with changing parameters, sharp discontinuities, cliffs, improbable events, and catastrophes. Furthermore, the real world is essentially topological rather than numerical. It consists of shapes, sizes, structures, fittings, and so on. It is true, of course, that numbers can be translated into topological structures and can be used to explore and interpret them, but economists have done very little of this.

Statistics, likewise, has had some unfortunate effects, as well as some benign ones, on economic study. Its main problem is that it concentrates on the means and on the regressions, and neglects and even tends to throw away the extreme positions of systems. On the other hand, when we have extremely complex systems, we often learn more about them from studying the extremes than we do from studying the means. This is true of the human body, for instance, the patterns of which in some sense reveal themselves only in sickness. Statistics has provided an admirable ritual for the fraternity hazing known as the Ph.D. and nobody can deny it has made some important contributions, but the time has come to take a serious look at the way in which it distorts knowledge. There is a Whorfian principle here,[15] that both mathematics and statistics are languages, and not even languages but jargons, as they can only say certain things, and it is very dangerous to have one's thought determined by the form of the language which one speaks and writes.

The question of what economics and the other social sciences can learn from each other is too large to be considered here and would certainly seem to be an enterprise of great difficulty. Part of this difficulty results from the fact that the other social sciences have also often developed along infertile lines. Psychology, especially, got trapped in the absurdities of behaviourism and the futilities of what might be called 'ritual experimentation'. There is a small subculture of rat economists, but whether they are really learning anything I have not been able to find out. There are some signs of a breakthrough in cognitive psychology, which could have a very fruitful interaction with economics, in terms, for instance, of how we form those images of the future which are the basis of any decisions. Up to now, this potential seems to be something of a vague image of the future itself. There should be a large interdiscipline in economic psychology which hardly exists.

Sociologists rarely study the intricate social relationships that take place in markets, for instance: who knows whom, who believes whom, who operates in what markets, and so on. The sociology of the firm, likewise, would be an enormously fruitful area which has been neglected by both sociologists and economics. Economists like Gary Becker have tried to take over the study of the family, but, here again, their efforts have been ones of economic imperialism rather than of cross-fertilisation. It is clear that there are some empty intellectual niches here which ought to be filled in the future. One only hopes that the young economists of today will take advantage of the enormous opportunities that lie before them and will not remain with their heads buried in the sand like the existing subculture of so many academic economists.

Notes and References

1. Adam Smith, *The Wealth of Nations* (New York: Modern Library) ch. I, p. 10: 'Many improvements . . . to "dissimilar objects"'.
2. Note the famous attack on the division of labour (*The Wealth of Nations*, p. 734) as making people as 'stupid and ignorant as it is possible for a human creature to become'.
3. John M. Keynes, *Essays in Biography* (new edition: London, 1951): 'if only Malthus, instead of Ricardo, had been the parent stem from which nineteenth-century economics proceeded, what a much wiser and richer place the world would be today!'
4. Matthew 7:16–20.
5. K. E. Boulding, 'How Do Things Go From Bad to Better?: The Contribution of Economics' (presidential address to Section F). In: *The Economics of Human Betterment*, K. E. Boulding, ed. (Proceedings of Section F, British Association for the Advancement of Science annual meeting, August 1983) (London: Macmillan Press, 1984) pp. 1–14.
6. Matthew 13:12.
7. Leviticus 25:8–17.
8. Frances Fitzgerald, 'Rajneeshpuram', *The New Yorker*, 22 Sept. 1986, p. 59.
9. Kenneth E. Boulding, *A Preface to Grants Economics: The Economy of Love and Fear* (New York: Praeger, 1981).
10. Adolph Lowe, *On Economic Knowledge: Toward a Science of Political Economics* (New York: Harper & Row, 1965).
11. K. E. Boulding, *Evolutionary Economics* (Beverly Hills, Calif.: Sage Publications, 1981).
12. Kenneth J. Arrow, *Social Choice and Individual Values* (New York: Wiley, 1951).
13. Kenneth E. Boulding, 'The Economics of Pride and Shame' (invited address presented at the Atlantic Economic Society Conference, Boston, 29 August 1986), *Atlantic Economic Journal*, vol. 15, no. 1 (March 1987) pp. 10–19.
14. Herbert Simon, *Models of Man: Social and Rational* (New York: Wiley, 1957).
15. Benjamin Whorf, *Language, Thought, and Reality* (Cambridge, Mass.: Technology Press, 1969; orig. pub. 1956).

3 The Rise and Fall of the Public Sector in the Estimation of the Economists*

Dan Usher

Over the last two centuries, there has been a great cycle of opinion among economists about the sources of inefficiency: from Adam Smith's sharp and unqualified contrast between private sector enterprise and public sector sloth; to Mill's qualified and reluctant allowance of large domains within the economy where the public sector must act because the private sector would not or could not do so; to Sidgwick's concern in the latter part of the nineteenth century with what we would now call market failure and his willingness to trust the public sector to put things right; to Pigou's detailed analysis in the early years of the twentieth century of the defects of the competitive economy coupled with an almost complete disregard of the possibility of public sector inefficiency; to a recent revival of interest in public sector economics and a reassessment of public sector efficiency reminiscent of the views of Adam Smith.

The main texts discussed in this chapter – Smith's *Wealth of Nations*, Mill's *Principles of Political Economy*, Sidgwick's *Principles of Political Economy*, Pigou's *Economics of Welfare*, and several modern works – are chosen to exemplify dominant views of their day. Undoubtedly there were always cross-currents of opinion, but I make no attempt to produce an extensive assessment of the state of opinion at any time.

Our story begins as theology. Before he embarked upon the serious study of economics, Adam Smith, the speculative philosopher, knew that there was a divinely ordained harmony in society. Not benevolence, but the pursuit by each man of his own self-

* With a particular thanks to R. P. Rutherford of the University of Tasmania and E. G. West of Carleton University for helpful comments on an early draft.

interest, leads in the end to best possible state of affairs for society as a whole:

> The idea of that divine Being, whose benevolence and wisdom have, from all eternity, contrived and conducted the immense machine of the universe, so as at all times to produce the greatest quantity of happiness, is certainly of all the objects of human contemplation by far the most sublime . . . The administration of the great system of the universe . . . the care of the universal happiness of all rational and sensible beings, is the business of God and not of man. Man is allotted a much humbler department, but one much more suitable to the weakness of his powers, and to the narrowness of his comprehension; the care of his own happiness, his friends, his country. (Adam Smith, *The Theory of Moral Sentiments*, cited by Jacob Viner in 'Adam Smith and Laissez Faire', an essay in J. M. Clark *et al.*, ed., *Adam Smith 1776–1926*, University of Chicago Press, 1928)

What we have here, as seen from today's perspective, is the fundamental theorem of welfare economics deduced not from a detailed analysis of the interaction of self-interested agents, but as a manifestation of God's purpose on earth.

Smith preserved something of this theological optimism when he turned to the study of the economy in *The Wealth of Nations*, but he had to contract the range of compatibility between private interest and the common good. In principle, a theory that self-interested actions promote the common good may or may not extend to the actions of the government. If public as well as private actions are conducive to the fulfilment of God's plan, then the theory has no economic implications and becomes quite useless as a basis for the reforms Smith wished to advocate. On the other hand, if only private actions are acceptable, there can be no role for government whatsoever, not even the protection of persons and property or the administration of justice. Smith could not subscribe to the latter view, for he believed that a market requires a framework of laws and substantial public expenditure on defence, justice and public works. Smith specified the roles of the public and private sectors as follows:

> All systems either of preference or of restraint, therefore, being thus completely taken away, the obvious and simple system of natural liberty establishes itself of its own accord. Every man, as

> long as he does not violate the laws of justice, is left perfectly free to pursue his own interest his own way, and to bring both his industry and capital into competition with those of any other man, or order of men. The sovereign is completely discharged from a duty, in the attempting to perform which he must always be exposed to innumerable delusions, and for the proper performance of which no human wisdom or knowledge could ever be sufficient; the duty of superintending the industry of private people, and of directing it towards the employments most suitable to the interest of the society. According to the system of natural liberty, the sovereign has only three duties to attend to; three duties of great importance, indeed, but plain and intelligible to common understandings: first the duty of protecting the society from the violence and invasion of other independent societies; secondly, the duty of protecting, as far as possible, every member of the society from the injustice or oppression of every other member of it, or the duty of establishing an exact administration of justice; and, thirdly, the duty of erecting and maintaining certain public works and certain public institutions, which it can never be for the interest of any individual, or small number of individuals, to erect and maintain; because the profit could never repay the expense to any individual or small number of individuals, though it may frequently do much more than repay it to a great society. (p. 651. Except where otherwise specified, all quotations of Adam Smith are from *The Wealth of Nations*, The Modern Library Edition, 1937.)

Notice particularly Smith's uses of the phrase 'system of natural liberty', once to prescribe the proper role of the private sector and again to prescribe the proper role of the public sector. The phrase itself is wonderfully ambiguous, standing halfway between the medieval concept of natural law and the modern concept of economic welfare, with strong overtones of civil rights. It would not be completely wrong to say that Smith advocates what he does because it is right, moral, and in accordance with God's purpose for mankind. Nor would it be completely wrong to say that Smith advocates what he does because it is conducive to economic welfare in the modern sense of the term. Jacob Viner described Adam Smith as the great eclectic. 'Traces of every conceivable sort of doctrine are to be found in that most catholic book, and an economist must have peculiar theories indeed who cannot quote *The Wealth of Nations* to support his special purposes' (Viner, ibid, p. 126). We shall adopt the latter interpretation, not because it is necessarily right, but because it conforms to our special purpose.

By assigning defence, justice and public works to the public sector, Smith, in effect, claims that these activities would not be undertaken by an unfettered private sector or that they would be undertaken inadequately. Smith does not explain why he believes this to be so, why these activities cannot be consigned to the private sector along with the allocation of labour and capital to the production of ordinary goods and services. A defender of Smith's position might say that some things are too obvious to warrant fullblown explanation, but that is no help in our search for a list of actual or potential sources of inefficiency. The matter was only to be sorted out many years after the publication of *The Wealth of Nations*. It will have to do for our purposes to say that there are essential undertakings, justice, defence, and public works, that the private sector will not provide.

Smith wrote extensively and vigorously about departures from efficiency in the public sector, but his argument was developed by precepts and examples rather than by formal theorems, and we can only speculate as to how Smith might have categorised such departures. I suggest a classification under the headings of incentives, corruption, presumption, information, and monopoly.

Under the heading of incentives, I would include a class of problems that have been the object of a great deal of attention in recent economic literature. When two parties engage in a common undertaking and establish an implicit or explicit contract specifying each party's privileges and obligations, it is in the personal interest of each party to shirk his obligations and to slant the enterprise to his own benefit, though both parties would be better off if neither behaved in that way. The worker is less diligent than he might be. The employer skimps on expenditure for the safety and convenience of his worker. The civil servant does not bother to put in the time and effort to perform his duties well. Of course, the incentive problem is not unique to the public sector. It arises whenever performance can only be enforced imperfectly. But it is hardly surprising that Adam Smith paid particular attention to incentives in the public sector. Hierarchy was more extensive in the public sector, and the control over the civil service by Parliament or the King was likely to be looser than the control over the employee by his employer in the private sector where incentives were automatically provided by the options not to buy goods offered for sale, not to employ an unenthusiastic worker, and not to work for an unsatisfactory employer.

> In modern times, the diligence of public teachers is more or less corrupted by the circumstances which render them more or less independent of their successes and reputation in their particular professions . . . A man of real abilities can scarcely find out a more humiliating or more unprofitable employment to turn them to. The endowments of schools and colleges have, in this manner, not only corrupted the diligence of public teachers, but have rendered it almost impossible to have any good private ones. (p. 733)

As a departure from efficiency, corruption is an extreme manifestation of the absence of an incentive to perform work conscientiously. However, the word 'corruption' usually refers to an active, frequently illegal, abuse of authority, while the incentive problem is the passive unwillingness to exert oneself in the interest of one's partners in an enterprise. Smith was particularly indignant about the selling of favours to the private sector and the direct exploitation by the ruler of his subjects. 'The violence and injustice of the rulers of mankind is an ancient evil, for which I am afraid, the nature of human affairs can scarce admit a remedy.' Speaking of bounties from the public sector to particular firms or industries, Smith says, 'though it can very seldom be reasonable to tax the industry of the great body of the people, in order to support that of some particular class of manufacturer: yet in the wantonness of great prosperity, when the public enjoys a greater revenue than it knows what to do with, to give such bounties to favorable manufactures may be natural' (p. 489).

A third departure from efficiency is presumption on the part of the civil servant who comes to believe that he alone knows what is best for the economy and that the businessman who does not willingly accept good advice should be compelled to do so. Smith's views in this matter appear in his discussion of Colbert's system of mercantilism in France:

> The industry and commerce of a great country he endeavored to regulate upon the same model as the departments of a public office; and instead of allowing every man to pursue his own interest his own way, upon the liberal plan of equality, liberty and justice, he bestowed upon certain branches of industry extraordinary privileges, while he laid others under as extraordinary restraints . . . and kept down agriculture of that country very much below the state to which it would naturally have risen in so very fertile a soil and so happy a climate. (pp. 627–8)

Colbert, as Smith describes him, was not corrupt, not dishonest, and not disinclined to serve the King of France with all the ability and energy at his command, but was led by presumption to policies that were in the end harmful to his country.

A fourth source of public sector inefficiency concerns the production and use of information. Only the private sector has the information required to direct the economy effectively. To be sure, no individual in the private sector is as well informed about the economy as a whole as are the servants of the great Ministries. But each manufacturer knows what he needs to know to conduct his business, and prices can be relied upon to co-ordinate decisions. In the summary of the roles of the public and private sector cited above, Smith speaks of public direction of industry and capital as a duty 'of which no human wisdom or knowledge could ever be sufficient'. Elsewhere Smith says that the 'statesman, who would attempt to direct private people in what manner they ought employ their capital, would not only load himself with a most unnecessary attention, but assume an authority which could safely be trusted, not only to no single person but to no council or senate whatever, and which would nowhere be so dangerous as in the hands of a man who had folly or presumption enough to fancy himself fit to exercise it' (p. 423).

A final source of public sector inefficiency is its tendency to support and maintain monopoly. The passage on the system of natural liberty, as quoted above, could be interpreted as including a recognition of the existence of natural monopolies which have to be administered or regulated by the state. Smith's famous invective against monopoly is for the most part directed toward state-created monopoly that could not be preserved without the direct prohibition of potential competitors.

Though Adam Smith had much to say about the effects of public policy on the economy, *The Wealth of Nations* is not a study of government itself. Quite the reverse. One of the great innovations in the book is the study of the economy in isolation from the rest of society. The sub-sections of the book are labour, capital, money, economic growth, international trade and public finance – topics that still constitute the sub-divisions of a textbook of economics – combined for the first time as a separate and distinct field of study. What the book lacked, and what Ricardo was later to supply, was a formal model of the economy in which the central concepts were clearly and forcefully abstracted from the detail of economic life. The formalisation of economic science proceeded throughout the nineteenth century, revealing with ever greater precision the exact sense in which it might be said that one may promote the public interest indirectly by attending to one's own private interest. Intensive study of the competitive economy could not help but focus attention onto a growing list of exceptions, while at the same time diverting attention from the strengths and weaknesses of the public sector.

In *The Principles of Political Economy* published in 1848, John Stuart Mill differed from Smith more in his preoccupations than in his analysis. He was preoccupied, first and foremost, with liberty. His advocacy of *laissez-faire* was no less enthusiastic than that of Smith, but it was as a requirement for personal liberty and not just as a means of generating wealth. Also, as a disciple of Bentham, Mill could hardly avoid being preoccupied with the content of law. Smith was most emphatic about the need for the state to protect the citizen from force and fraud, but he disposed of the matter in a couple of sentences. Mill dealt with the matter at length, adding the definition of property rights, the resolution of disputes, and the specification of the range of permissible contracts to the list of activities that had to be undertaken by the public sector.

It is at least arguable that, to Mill, the great departure from efficiency was predation, the violence and the wastage of labour when one man attempts to take property from another and the other is compelled to divert effort from production to defence. In the closing paragraph of the book, Mill speaks of

> that part of the functions of government which all must admit to be indispensable, the function of prohibiting and punishing such conduct on the part of individuals in the exercise of their freedom as is clearly injurious to other persons, whether the case be one of force, fraud, or negligence. Even in the best state which society has yet reached, it is lamentable to think how great a proportion of all the efforts and talents in the world are employed in merely neutralizing one another. It is the proper end of government to reduce this wretched waste to the smallest possible amount, by taking such measures as shall cause the energies now spent by mankind in injuring one another, or in protecting themselves against injury, to be turned to the legitimate employment of the human faculties, that of compelling the powers of nature to be more and more subservient to physical and moral good. (p. 979. All references are to the 1909 edition of *Principles of Political Economy*, edited by W. J. Ashley, Longmans & Co.)

Though the great departure from efficiency is insecurity and though the ultimate defence against insecurity lies in the public sector, it does not follow that a large and ubiquitous public sector is conducive to liberty or to prosperity. At several critical points in the *Principles*, Mill raises the spectre of despotism which is associated for the most part with the governments of Asia, but is not rigidly or permanently confined there. One gets the impression that Mill, unlike his successors to be discussed below, was not absolutely certain that England would be free of despotism forever. Security . . .

> consists of protection *by* the government, and protection *against* the government. The latter is the more important. Where a person known to possess anything worth taking away, can expect nothing but to have it torn from him, with every circumstance of tyrannical violence, by the agents of a rapacious government, it is not likely that many will exert themselves to produce much more than necessaries. This is the acknowledged explanation of the poverty of many fertile tracts of Asia, which were once prosperous and populous. From this to the degree of security enjoyed in the best governed parts of Europe, there are numerous gradations. In many provinces of France before the Revolution, a vicious system of taxation on the land, and still more the absence of redress against the arbitrary exactions which were made under colour of the taxes, rendered it the interest of every cultivator to appear poor, and therefore to cultivate badly. The only insecurity which is altogether paralysing to the active energies of producers, is that arising from the government, or from persons invested with its authority. Against all other depredators there is a hope of defending oneself. (pp. 113–14)

Like *The Wealth of Nations*, Mill's *Principles* contains no formal list of departures from efficiency, just as it contains no formal proof of a theorem about the efficiency of a competitive economy, but one can easily derive a list of departures from efficiency in the public and private sectors of the economy from the discussion of 'the limits of the province of government'.

The general presumption is

> in favour of restricting to the narrowest compass the intervention

> of a public authority in the business of the community: and few will dispute the more than sufficiency of these reasons, to throw, in every instance, the burden of making out a strong case, not on those who resist, but on those who recommend, government interference. *Laissez-faire*, in short, should be the general practice: every departure from it, unless required by some great good, is a certain evil. (p. 950)

But if *laissez-faire* has the residual authority and each departure from *laissez-faire* has to be justified by some great good, there is none the less a formidable list of justifiable public sector activities. Foremost among these, as might be expected in view of Mill's concern with security, is 'protection against force and fraud' (p. 796). Mill is quick to emphasise that protection against force and fraud is a more extensive responsibility than some proponents of strict *laissez-faire* are inclined to recognise. It entails the establishment of the rules of inheritance, especially when the deceased is of unsound mind or fails to specify the disposition of his property. It entails the establishment of laws specifying what types of contracts 'are fit to be enforced' . . . for 'there are promises by which it is not for the public good that persons should have the power of binding themselves' (p. 798). It entails the drawing-up of rules concerning the non-fulfilment of a contract due to fraud, negligence or occurrences which make the contract impossible to fulfil, as well as the resolution of disputes that 'arise between persons, without *mala fides* on either side, through misconception of their legal rights, or from not being agreed about the facts, on the proof of which those rights are legally dependent' (p. 799). Admissible forms of contracts may be chosen, not so much because one form is intrinsically superior to another, but to minimise the frequency of disputes.

Over and above protection against force and fraud, which is a requirement for the existence of a market, the government, according to Mill, should undertake certain activities which the private sector would attend to inefficiently or not at all:

(i) *The provision of education*: 'any well-intentioned and tolerably civilised government may think, without presumption, that it does or ought to possess a degree of cultivation above the average of the community which it rules, and that it should therefore be capable of offering better education and better instruction to the people, than the greater number of them would spontaneously demand' (p. 953).

(ii) *The protection of lunatics* (p. 957).

(iii) *The protection of children from cruel or uncaring parents*:

> Whatever it can be clearly seen that parents ought to do or forbear for the interests of children, the law is warranted, if it is able, in compelling to be done or forborne, and is generally bound to do so . . . Labouring for too many hours in the day, or on work beyond their strength, should not be permitted to them . . . Freedom of contract, in the case of children, is but another word for freedom of coercion. (p. 958)

Mill would impose no similar restriction on employment of women. He classifies the common subjugation of women to their husbands together with slavery, but goes on to argue that women freed of that burden need no legal restraints and are 'as capable as men of appreciating and managing their own concerns' (p. 959).

(iv) *Natural monopoly*: 'There are many cases in which the agency, of whatever nature, by which a service is performed is certain by the nature of the case, to be virtually single; in which a practical monopoly, with all the power it confers of taxing the community, cannot be prevented from existing' (p. 962). Among these practical monopolies, Mill includes gas and water companies (though these may be local in scope), roads, canals and railways. He adds that 'the state may be the proprietor of canals and railways without itself working them . . . they will almost always be better worked by means of a company renting the railway or canal for a limited period from the state' (p. 963).

(v) *Avoidance of prisoners' dilemmas*:

> The principle that each is the best judge of his own interest, understood as these objectors understand it, would prove that governments ought not to fulfill any of their acknowledged duties – ought not, in fact, to exist at all. It is greatly the interest of the community, collectively and individually, not to rob or defraud one another: but there is not the less necessity for laws to punish robbery and fraud; because, though it is the interest of each that nobody should rob or cheat, it is not any one's interest to refrain from robbing and cheating others when all others are permitted to rob and cheat him. Penal laws exist at all, chiefly for this reason – because even an unanimous opinion that a certain line of conduct is for the general interest does not always make it people's individual interest to adhere to that line of conduct. (p. 966)

(vi) *Provision for the poor*: 'The claim to help, therefore, created by destitution, is one of the strongest which can exist; and there is *prima facie* the amplest reason for making the relief of so extreme an exigency as certain to those who require it as by any arrangements of society it can be made' (p. 967). Mill recognised the force of the standard objection to assistance for the poor, that assistance destroys industry, but he believed that the case for assistance was so strong as to outweigh the cost of the attendant inefficiency and that programmes of assistance could be designed to reduce costs to an acceptable level: 'in all cases of helping, there are two sets of consequences to be considered; the consequences of the assistance itself, and the consequences of relying on the assistance. The former are generally beneficial, but the latter, for the most part, injurious; so much so, in many cases, as greatly to outweigh the value of the benefit' (p. 967).

(vii) *Public goods*: Mill speaks of cases where 'important public services are to be performed, while yet there is no individual specially interested in performing them, nor would any adequate remuneration naturally or spontaneously attend their performance' (p. 975). His examples are 'a voyage of geographical or scientific discovery', maintenance of lighthouses and buoys and 'the cultivation of speculative knowledge' which 'gives no claim on any individual for a pecuniary remuneration' (p. 976).

(viii) *Externalities*: It is arguable, though not beyond dispute, that Mill had a concept of externalities. Part of the difficulty in interpreting the text is that Mill was concerned primarily with the question of what the state ought to do rather than of why the state ought to do it. He comes close to the concept of externalities in a discussion of colonies:

> If it is desirable, as no one will deny it to be, that the planting of colonies should be conducted, not with an exclusive view to the private interests of the first founders, but with a deliberate regard to the permanent welfare of the nations afterwards to arise from these small beginnings; such regard can only be secured by placing the enterprise, from its commencement, under regulations constructed with the foresight and enlarged views of philosophical legislators; and the government alone has power either to frame such regulations, or to enforce their observance. . . . .the removal of population from the overcrowded to the unoccupied parts of the earth's surface is one of those works of eminent social usefulness,

> which must require, and which at the same time best repay, the intervention of government. (p. 970)

The passage (and subsequent discussion) can be interpreted as meaning that the provision of the infrastructure of colonisation is an ordinary public good. The passage can also be interpreted as meaning that each colonist by helping to create a community that others may enter conveys an externality to future colonists and to the mother country where labour becomes less plentiful and real wages rise.

Though Mill does have a considerable list of activities and actions that the public sector does sometimes undertake improperly and to the detriment of society as a whole, his discussion of government places particular emphasis on general problems within the public sector and on reasons why the size of the public sector *per se* may become a matter of concern.

(i) *The risk of despotism*: To Mill, the great and most costly departure from efficiency associated with the public sector occurs when government ceases to be the servant of society and becomes despotic:

> oppression by the government, whose power is generally irresistible by any efforts that can be made by individuals, has so much more baneful an effect on the springs of national prosperity, than almost any degree of lawlessness and turbulence under free institutions. Nations have acquired some wealth, and made some progress in improvement, in states of social union so imperfect as to border on anarchy: but no countries in which the people were exposed without limit to arbitrary exactions from the officers of government ever yet continued to have industry or wealth. (p. 882)

Fear of despotism should constitute a check on the activity of government:

> every increase in the functions devolving on the government is an increase of its power, both in the form of authority, and still more in the indirect form of influence. The importance of this consideration in respect to political freedom, has in general been quite sufficiently recognized, at least in England; but many, in latter times, have been prone to think that the limitation of the powers of government is badly constituted when it does not represent the people, but is an organ of a class, or coalition of classes: and that

government of sufficiently popular constitution might be trusted with any amount of power over the nation, since its power would only be that of the nation over itself. That might be true, if the nation, in such cases, did not practically mean a mere majority of the nation, and if minorities were only capable of oppressing, but not of being oppressed. Experience, however, proves that the depositaries of power who are mere delegates of the people, that is of a majority, are quite as ready (when they think they can count on popular support) as any organs of oligarchy to assume arbitrary power, and encroach unduly on the liberty of private life. (pp. 944–5)

(ii) *Administrative overload*:

Every additional function undertaken by the government is a fresh occupation imposed upon a body already overcharged with duties. A natural consequence is that most things are ill done; much not done at all, because the government is not able to do it without delays which are fatal to its purpose; that the more troublesome, and less showy, of the functions undertaken, are postponed or neglected, and an excuse is always ready for the neglect; while the heads of the administration have their minds so fully taken up with official details, in however perfunctory a manner superintended, that they have no time or thought to spare for the great interests of the state, and the preparation of enlarged measures of social improvement. (p. 945)

(iii) *Technical inefficiency*:

in all the more advanced communities the great majority of things are worse done by the intervention of government, than the individuals most interested in the matter would do them, or cause them to be done, if left to themselves. The grounds of this truth are expressed with tolerable exactness in the popular dictum, that people understand their own business and their own interests better, and care for them more, than the government does, or can be expected to do. (p. 947)

(iv) *Loss of initiative in the private sector*:

Even if the government could comprehend within itself, in each department, all the most eminent intellectual capacity and active

> talent of the nation, it would not be the less desirable that the conduct of a large portion of the affairs of the society should be left in the hands of the persons immediately interested in them. The business of life is an essential part of the practical education of a people; without which, book and school instruction, though most necessary and salutary, does not suffice to qualify them for conduct, and for the adaptation of means to ends. (p. 948)
>
> The only security against political slavery is the check maintained over governors by the diffusion of intelligence, activity, and public spirit among the governed. Experience proves the extreme difficulty of permanently keeping up a sufficiently high standard of those qualities; a difficulty which increases, as the advance of civilization and security removes one after another of the hardships, embarrassments, and dangers against which individuals had formerly no resource but in their own strength, skill, and courage. (p. 949)

Finally, Mill lists a number of activities that governments of his time did undertake, but ought to have avoided because their effects on balance were to discourage industry rather than to promote it: protection of domestic goods against foreign competition, fixing of prices and wages, prohibition of usury, and regulation of forms of partnership. Mill was particularly adamant about the ill-effects of restrictions on the formation of joint-stock companies with limited liability, for, barring outright fraud, persons dealing with such companies would be quite capable of assessing the risks associated with limited liability and of taking whatever steps might be necessary to protect themselves.

The world of Henry Sidgwick's *The Principles of Political Economy* is quite different from that of either Smith or Mill. The book first appeared in 1883 (though all quotations below are from the second edition which appeared in 1887). By that time, England had passed from what Dicey (A. V. Dicey, *Lectures on the Relation Between Law and Public Opinion in England During the Nineteenth Century*) has called a period of Benthamism or Individualism into a period of Collectivism and, though Sidgwick opposed socialism, he did not share Smith's views about the intrinsic incompetence of government or Mill's brooding concern about despotism. The hundred years since the appearance of *The Wealth of Nations* had seen considerable progress in the British economy and in the science of economics. There had also been considerable progress in the art of government, so that, by Sidgwick's time, Great Britain was much farther along the road from absolute monarchy to pure democracy than had been the case in Smith's day, and there had been a radical reform of the civil service. Sidgwick could justifiably assume that some functions of government would be performed well. He may have supposed the liberal society in England to be unshakably secure.

Much of what Sidgwick had to say about the art of political economy – his distinction between the science and art of political economy corresponded more or less to what we would now call theory and policy – was conditioned by his response to socialism. As a contrast and alternative to the ideal organisation of the economy, socialism played somewhat the same role in *The Principles of Political Economy* that mercantilism played in *The Wealth of Nations*. Sidgwick was too ambivalent and too gentle to confront a challenge to the system of national liberty as vigorously or as scornfully as Smith had done. Sidgwick admired the system of natural liberty – he employed Smith's term – but he saw public policy as a trade-off between inequality and efficiency. On the one hand, he could see no moral justification for great disparities of inherited wealth. The '*prima facie* ground . . . on which the interference of government with the distribution of produce that results from the individualistic organisation of industry appears economically desirable, lies in the very great inequalities of income to which this organisation leads' (p. 519). On the other hand, the system of natural liberty is in most circumstances more productive than any other system men knew how to devise. 'I object to socialism not because it would divide the produce of industry badly but because there would be so much less to divide' (p. 517).

Sidgwick's criterion was utilitarian, the maximisation of the sum of the utilities of each person in society on the assumptions that everyone's utility function is, for all practical purposes, the same and that there is a diminishing marginal utility of income. Thus in assessing the system of natural liberty he is on the lookout for inefficiencies that might justify the intervention of government which, once involved in a branch of industry, might use its influence to equalise income somewhat. Sidgwick has a long list of instances in which 'the system of natural liberty would have, in certain respects and under certain conditions, no tendency to realise the beneficent results claimed for it':

(i) *The use of wealth to gratify a lust for power*: Some utilities are not socially desirable; 'among these utilities . . . we must include the gratification of the love of power, the love of ease, and all whims and fancies that are wont to take possession of the minds of persons whose income is far more than sufficient to satisfy ordinary human desires' (p. 404).

(ii) *Misuse of income by the old*: Total utility may not be maximised because the old 'spend larger and larger sums on smaller and smaller enjoyments' or impose 'posthumous restraint on bequeathed wealth [which] will make it less useful to the living' (p. 405).

(iii) *Slavery*: 'If all contracts freely made are to be enforced, it is conceivable that a man may contract himself into slavery; it is even conceivable that a large mass of the population of a country might do this, in the poverty and distress caused by some wide-spreading calamity' (p. 406). The state ought not to permit such contracts. Similarly, the state ought not to uphold contracts agreed to under pressure, as when merchant seamen alienate part of their claims to wages at sea under 'undue influence which the needful discipline of a ship gives to its master' (p. 429).

(iv) *Externalities*: There are 'some utilities which, from their nature are practically incapable of being appropriated by those who produce them or who would otherwise be willing to purchase them' (p. 407). Examples include (a) 'a well-placed lighthouse', (b) 'forests on account of their beneficial effects in moderating and equalising rainfall', (c) inventions where the cost of discovery is greater than the prospective income from a patent but less than the value of the invention to society, (d) education, when the returns are 'more than sufficient to repay the outlay necessary to provide them – while at the same time it would not be profitable for any capitalist to provide the money, with a view to being repaid out of the salary of the laborer educated, owing to the trouble and risk involved in the deferred payments' (p. 408).

(v) *Monopoly, among workers or among firms* (p. 411).

(vi) *Advertising* (p. 412).

(vii) *Balancing of the interests of present and future generations*: The 'purely individualistic or competitive organisation of society . . . does not necessarily provide to an adequate extent for utilities distant in time' (p. 412).

(viii) *Ignorance on the part of the consumer*: 'As the appliances of life became more elaborate and complicated through the progress of invention . . . an average man's ability to judge the adaptation of means to ends . . . is likely to become continually less' (p. 417). 'Our own government does not trust its subjects to find out for themselves and avoid unhealthy food or improperly qualified physicians, surgeons, and apothecaries' (p. 425).

(iv) *Public goods 'which if left to private enterprise . . . would not be provided at all'* (p. 439), or would be provided under conditions of monopoly. Among these are roads, canals, railways, the post office, and, above all, the currency.

Sidgwick does not proceed directly from the identification of what we would now call market failure to the prescription of public policy to set things right. It 'does not of course follow that whenever laissez faire falls short government interference is expedient; since the inevitable drawbacks and disadvantages of the latter may, in any particular case, be worse than the shortcomings of private industry' (p. 414). Thus, parallel to the list of the shortcomings of the market, is a list of the shortcomings of the public sector:

(i) *Corruption*: 'the danger of increasing the power and influence capable of being used by government for corrupt purposes' (p. 415).

(ii) *Special interest politics*: 'the danger . . . that the exercise of [the government's] economic functions will be hampered and prevented by the desire to gratify influential sections of the community – certain manufacturers, certain landlords, certain classes of manual laborers, or the inhabitants of certain localities' (p. 415).

(iii) *Public extravagance*: 'the danger . . . of wasteful expenditure under the influence of popular sentiment – since people, however impatient of taxation, are liable to be insufficiently conscious of the importance of thrift in all details of national expenditure' (p. 415).

(iv) *The social cost of taxation and regulation*:

> when action of the government requires funds raised by taxation, we have to reckon – besides the financial cost of collection and any loss of production caused by particular taxes – the political danger of adding to a burden already impatiently borne . . . where again it requires prohibition of private industry, we must regard . . . the repression of energy and self-help that tends to follow from it; where, on the other hand, the interference takes the form of regulations . . . we may often have to calculate on a certain amount of economic and political evils due to the successful or unsuccessful attempt to evade them. (p. 415)

Speaking particularly of protection, Sidgwick said that the gain 'in particular cases is always likely to be more than counterbalanced by the general bad effects of encouraging producers and traders to look to government for aid in industrial crises and dangers; instead of relying on their own foresight, ingenuity and energy' (p. 489).

(v) *Incentives*: 'the work of the government has to be done by persons who – even with the best of arrangements for effective supervision and promotion by merit – can have only a part of the stimulus to energetic industry that the independent worker feels, who may reasonably hope to gain by any well directed extra exertion, intellectual or muscular, and must fear to lose by indolence or neglect' (p. 416). Similarly, if workers were remunerated by need rather than according to effort, as would be the case under some definitions of socialism, 'we can hardly doubt that the labor thus purchased by the state could not, even by good organization, be made to pay the cost of its support . . . he would have much less motive than at present either for working energetically or for seeking and qualifying himself for the employment in which he would be most useful' (p. 533).

Moving ahead another forty years, we come to A. C. Pigou's *The Economics of Welfare* which first appeared in 1920 and continued to be influential until after the Second World War. Pigou's world – the world of the upper classes of late nineteenth- and early twentieth-century England – was a world free of tyranny and secure for democracy, a world in which, as Yeats expressed it, 'rogues and rascals had died out' or, in so far as they remained here on earth, were confined to the somewhat nasty realm of commerce and were not to be found among the Cambridge-educated gentlemen of His Majesty's civil service. Pigou, quoting Marshall, stated that

> during the past century in England, there has been a vast increase in the probity, the strength, the unselfishness, and the resources of government . . . And the people are now able to rule their rulers, and to check class abuse of power and privilege, in a way that was impossible before the days of general education and a general surplus of energy over that required for earning a living. (p. 333; all quotations are from the fourth edition published in 1932 by Macmillan and Co.)

In fact, Marshall had gone so far as to speak of the civil servants of his time as motivated by an 'economic chivalry' in their concern for the welfare of ordinary people.

Pigou recognised, in principle, that public 'authorities are liable alike to ignorance, to sectional pressure and to personal corruption by private interest' and that 'companies, particularly when there is continuing regulation, may employ corruption, not only in the getting of their franchise, but also in the execution of it'; but the message of the book was that such considerations could well be ignored in practice. The entire subject of misbehaviour in the public sector occupied two pages in an eight-hundred-page book. The only example was where special interests in the private sector exert undue influence on the public sector. There was no mention of the possibility that civil servants might be less diligent than their counterparts in the private sector, and no hint that they might fall victim to 'folly and presumption'.

By implication, if not in so many words, the reader is told that potential defects of government can be safely ignored. 'When there is a divergence between' marginal private net product and marginal social net product 'self-interest will not therefore, tend to make the national dividend a maximum; and, consequently, certain specific acts of interference with normal economic processes may be expected, not to diminish, but to increase the dividend' (p. 172; 'dividend' refers to real national income).

> In any industry, where there is reason to believe that the free play of self-interest will cause an amount of resources to be invested different from the amount that is required in the best interest in that national dividend, there is a *prima facie* case for public intervention. The case, however, cannot become more than a *prima facie* one until we have considered the qualifications which government agencies may be expected to possess for intervening advantageously. (p. 332)

But the 'broad result is that modern developments in the structure and methods of government agencies have fitted these agencies for beneficial intervention in industry under conditions which would not have justified intervention in earlier times' (p. 335). The reader, who is told very little about conditions when intervention is still unjustified, cannot help receiving the impression that the entire question is irrelevant in practice.

Silence in this context is tantamount to bias. One version of the fundamental theorem of welfare economics is that a competitive economy is as efficient as an 'ideal' planned economy – as efficient, but not more so. Hayek has spoken of the ideal as a 'communist fiction', a convenient way of organising one's thoughts about the optimality of a competitive economy. The fiction is harmless as long as it is recognised that an actual planned economy is no more likely to realise the ideal than an actual market economy. Pigou does recognise, in a passage cited above, that no planned economy can measure up to the ideal. But with no systematic attempt to identify the conditions where the actual and ideal diverge, there can be no basis for judging when departures from efficiency in the private sector should not be corrected by the public sector because the cure would be worse than the disease. By specifying in detail the inefficiencies of the private sector, and saying virtually nothing about the inefficiencies of the public sector, Pigou inevitably creates a presumption in favour of the latter.

In fact, the public sector is always preferable when the choice is presented in this manner, for a competitive economy can at best yield one among many possible Pareto optima, while the planner can pick the superior Pareto optimum from a utilitarian point of view. The outcome of a competitive economy depends on the initial distribution of property rights which may be very unequal, while the 'ideal' planner knows no such constraint and can pick the Pareto optimal outcome corresponding to what a competitive economy would yield with a different and presumably more equal distribution of property.

Pigou's list of departures from efficiency in the private sector includes many of the items that we have already seen on Sidgwick's list. There are now four main categories: tenancy, externalities, monopoly and scale.

(i) *The separation of tenancy and ownership*: The tenant may not have a sufficient incentive to maintain the quality of the farm, or to make warranted improvements in drainage, buildings, etc. The landlord may be unwilling to undertake long-term investments when the contract between owner and tenant specifies a fixed rent for a given term of years.

(ii) *Externalities*: Though Pigou does not employ the term 'externalities', he speaks of a class of divergences between social and private net product such that 'one person, A, in the course of rendering some service for which payment is made to a second person, B, incidentally also renders services to other persons . . . of such a sort that payment cannot be extracted from the benefited parties' (p. 183). Here Pigou provides examples that are still the stock-in-trade of welfare economics: (a) the lighthouse, the standard example of a public good carried over directly from Sidgwick; (b) roads, parks, and 'resources invested in lamps erected at the doors of private houses, for these necessarily throw light on the street' (p. 184); (c) research, 'resources, devoted alike to the fundamental problems of scientific research . . . perfecting inventions and improvements in industrial processes . . . of such a nature that . . . that whole of the extra reward, which they at first bring to the inventor, is very quickly transformed from him to the general public in the form of reduced prices' (p. 185); (d) neighbourhood effects, as when a new factory destroys amenities in a residential area; (e) foreign investment when it 'consists in a loan to a foreign government and makes it possible for that government to engage in a war which otherwise would not have taken place, the indirect loss which Englishmen in general suffer, in consequence of the world impoverishment caused by war, should be debited against the interest which British financiers receive' (p. 187); and (f) the injury to the foetus when a pregnant mother works in a factory. Pigou calls this the 'crowning illustration of this order of excess of private over social net product' (p. 187).

(iii) *Monopoly*: Pigou identifies several departures from efficiency that arise when an industry is monopolised or limited to a few firms, each with a large enough share of the market to exert an influence upon the market price. Among the departures from efficiency due to monopoly or oligopoly are: (a) reduction of output to raise the market price; (b) competitive advertisement 'directed to the sole purpose of transferring the demand for a given commodity from one source of supply to another' (p. 196) – Pigou distinguishes between competitive advertising which is socially wasteful and informative advertising which is not; (c) bargaining costs, which arise from the theoretical indeterminateness of bilateral monopoly and 'open up the way for the employment of activities and resources in efforts to modify the ratio of exchange in favour of one or another of the monopolists' (p. 200) – the obvious example is the strike, but negotiation among businessmen over prices and terms of contracts also falls under this heading; (d) deception, as when false weights and measures are employed; (e) the destruction of the 'educative ladder' through the trustification of industry, 'the lessening of the opportunities for training in the entrepreneurial function' when a market consisting of many small firms is cartelised (p. 207).

(iv) *Increasing returns to scale*: 'in a many-firm industry the value of the marginal net product of any quantity of investment is greater than, equal to or less than the value of social net product according as the industry conforms to conditions of increasing, constant of decreasing supply price from the stand point of the industry' (p. 222). There is 'a presumption in favour of State bounties to industries in conditions of decreasing supply price' (p. 224).

The *reductio ad absurdum* of Pigou's reasoning was the economics of socialism as understood by economists in the 1930s and 40s. If every departure from efficiency in the private sector of the economy warrants public activity to set it right, then why not go the whole way with the incorporation of the means of production into the public sector? A central planner would announce prices, managers of publicly owned firms would maximise accounting profits at these prices, temporary shortages and gluts would signify which prices are too low and which prices are too high, and the planner would adjust prices next period, more or less as a competitive economy is supposed to do. Much of the debate centred around the question of whether a planning commission could solve the 'millions of equations' that a competitive economy solves automatically in the determination of prices of all goods and rents of all factors of production. The debate on this point was inconclusive, though the socialists seemed to have the best of the argument since large firms appeared to engage in such planning already and the planning mechanism in the Soviet Union, while hardly ideal in its operation, did not lead to a complete breakdown of the economy and appeared to be amenable to improvement with the advance of statistical and mathematical technique.

Socialism defined as the complete ownership of the means of production by the state, was seen to have two distinct advantages over the private ownership of the means of production. The first is that the national income could be divided equally among citizens except for variations among incomes to compensate for disamenities of certain kinds of jobs. The second is that any departure from efficiency which would arise in a market economy could be eliminated in a socialist economy by means of a compensating divergence between producer price and consumer price. An

> economic system based on private enterprise can take but very imperfect account of the alternatives sacrificed and realized in production. A socialist economy would be able to put *all* the alternatives into its economic accounting. Thus it would evaluate *all* the services rendered by production and take into the cost accounts *all* the alternatives sacrificed; as a result it would also be able to convert its social overhead cost into prime cost. By doing so it would avoid much of the social waste connected with private enterprise. As Professor Pigou has shown, much of the waste can be removed by proper legislation, taxation and bounties within the framework of the present economic system, but a socialist economy can do it with much greater thoroughness.

(Oskar Lange, 'On the Economic Theory of Socialism', originally published in the *Review of Economic Studies*, October 1936 and February 1937, and reprinted with modifications together with an article by Fred M. Taylor in a book with the same title edited by Benjamin E. Lippincott in 1952; the quotation is from page 104. For a contemporary collection of studies generally hostile to socialism, see F. A. Hayek, ed., *Collectivist Economic Planning*, 1935.)

Obviously, socialism is preferable to capitalism if you ignore the innards of the public sector and suppose, implicitly or explicitly, that there is a well-defined common good, and that the public sector can direct the economy accordingly, deploying resources to the production of commodities and distributing commodities to people to maximise social welfare subject only to technical and physical constraints.

It was precisely these assumptions that were about to be abandoned. A disenchantment with the public sector developed gradually but with ever-growing intensity since about the end of the Second World War. The change was no doubt a response to historical events, the growth of the public sector in most countries in the Western World, the absence of severe depressions, the superior economic performance of capitalist countries as compared with socialist countries, and the abundant evidence that extreme socialism was not conducive to justice, prosperity or personal liberty. But it was also a response to two major developments within the science of economics itself: the disintegration of the concept of social welfare as the criterion for public sector intervention in the economy, and the close-study of the economics of the public sector which raised serious doubts as to whether a public sector would in practice act to maximise economic welfare, even if such a thing could be shown to exist.

'During the nineteenth century,' wrote John Hicks in the year 1939,

it was generally considered to be the business of an economist, not only to explain the economic world as it is and as it has been, not only to make prognostications (so far as he was able) about the future course of events, but also to lay down principles of economic policy, to say what policies are likely to be conducive to social welfare, and what policies are likely to lead to waste and impoverishment. (J. R. Hicks, 'The Foundations of Welfare Economics', *The Economic Journal*, 1939, pp. 696–712)

Though the capacity of the economists to 'lay down the principles of economic policy' had been challenged off and on for some time, the decisive challenge in the English-speaking world was the publication in 1936 of Lionel Robbins's *The Nature and Significance of Economics Science*. From our point of view, the essence of Robbins's critique is that principles of economic policy which economists had supposed to be well-grounded in the science of economics were at bottom dependent on ethical premises without which costs and benefits to different people could not be compared. In practice, there can be no economic policy, however beneficial to the greater part of the population, that does not make somebody worse off. If one man's good cannot be balanced off against another's bad, then nothing definitive can be said about economic policy and much of the *raison d'être* of the economist would seem to be lost.

The immediate object of Robbins's attack was the Law of Diminishing Marginal Utility which had been interpreted to imply that 'anything conducive to greater equality, which does not adversely affect production, is said to be justified by the law: anything conducive to inequality condemned' (*The Nature and Significance* . . ., p. 156). The brunt of the attack was not that the law was necessarily wrong, but that it was not economics, and could not be justified by economic reasoning. The Law of Diminishing Marginal Utility is part of the doctrine of utilitarianism, which can be summarised in four propositions: that the satisfaction of different people may be compared on a common scale; that the relation between utility and income is approximately the same for most people; that for any person and at any given set of prices, utility increases with income at a steadily decreasing rate; and that the object of public policy is to maximise total utility. On these propositions, the case for the mitigation of inequality can indeed be established, and Robbins, whose own political philosophy was what he called 'provisional utilitarianism', was prepared to act *as if* they were true in many instances. His argument was that these propositions were ethical rather than scientific. Policy based on the utilitarian calculus is only compelling to someone who accepts the principles of utilitarianism or who can justify such policy by some other ethical principles. Robbins tells the story of a Brahman whose response on hearing about utilitarianism was 'But that cannot possibly be right. I am ten times as capable of happiness as that untouchable over there' (Lionel Robbins, 'Interpersonal Comparisons of Utility: A Comment', *The Economic Journal*, 1938, pp. 635–41, page 636). One may well say in defence of utilitarianism that people should be treated as though they were equally capable of happiness and one may believe it immoral to treat people otherwise, but there is no test, no experiment, no evidence from sample surveys that will demonstrate the Brahman's error, if he persists in his point of view. Nor, for that matter, is there any scientific basis for the view that the object of economic policy is the maximisation of the sum of each person's utility. One either accepts this as a first principle or one does not.

Robbins's critique was to provoke an extensive reformulation of the criteria for the evaluation of economic policy. One response was to reduce the objective from social welfare to Pareto optimality. On the old utilitarian criterion, a policy was said to be desirable if it led to an increase in the sum of everybody's utility (where equality as a component of social welfare could be assigned a greater or lesser weight by increasing or decreasing the curvature of the postulated utility of income function). To replace social welfare with Pareto optimality is to say that a policy is on balance beneficial if it eliminates waste, that is, if it represents a move toward a state of the economy from which no further change can simultaneously make everybody better off. As a criterion for the choice of public policy, Pareto optimality is satisfactory as long as everybody gains or loses together, or the effect of public policy on the distribution of income is irrelevant to the problem at hand. Otherwise Pareto optimality is an inadequate criterion because the efficient outcome is not unique. Pareto optimality provides no basis for choosing between outcomes on the utility-possibility frontier, between outcome A, where Mr. 1 is relatively well off and Mr. 2 is relatively badly off, and outcome B, where Mr. 2 is relatively well off and Mr. 1 is relatively badly off, when both outcomes are such that no improvement in the welfare of one person can be procured without reducing the welfare of the other. Even the substitution of a bundle of goods on the frontier for a bundle of goods below the frontier could not be treated as unambiguously advantageous except in the special case where literally everybody becomes better off. For a time, it looked as though the old certainty could be preserved by what came to be known as 'compensation criteria' according to which there is an unambiguous improvement in the economy as a whole if the gainers can compensate the losers. It turned out after much discussion that the test was internally inconsistent and could not be reformulated to provide an acceptable criterion for deciding when the population as a whole is materially better off. No test could be devised to convey more information than was provided by the utility-possibility frontier. (The original idea is credited to Nicholas Kaldor, 'Welfare Propositions of Economics and Interpersonal Comparisons of Utility', *The Economic Journal*, 1939, pp. 549–52; and its tortuous history is reviewed in E. J. Mishan, 'A Survey of Welfare Economics, 1939–1959', *The Economic Journal*, 1960, pp. 197–256, and S. K. Nath, *A Reappraisal of Welfare Economics*, Augustus M. Kelley, 1969.)

A second and complementary response was to reinterpret the role of the objective function in economic argument. If it is no longer possible to identify an economically given criterion for public policy, it is at least possible to model the logic of public choice. One cannot say that a particular policy is necessarily beneficial, but one can say to the reader that if such-and-such is *your* criterion and these are *your* constraints, then *your* best policy under the circumstances has to be whatever the algorithm decrees. In effect, the economist, as economist, disclaims responsibility for the conclusions of his analysis, so that economics becomes neither positive nor normative in Milton Friedman's sense of these terms but an exercise in the logic of choice in economic matters. The skill of the economist is to represent the essence of a complex situation in a model, and to discover the consequences of the interactions among agents, each doing the best he can for himself with the means at his disposal. Policy implications of economic models are only valid to someone who accepts the ethical premises from which the policies are derived and who agrees that the constraints in the model are a proper representation of the circumstances in which a decision has to be made.

This way of looking at economics was facilitated by the development of the probabilistic interpretation of the utilitarian calculus. Of course the social welfare function need not be utilitarian, but the utilitarian formulation of social welfare is especially simple and attractive. The probabilistic formulation, originally proposed by Harsanyi and then taken up by Rawls (J. C. Harsanyi, 'Cardinal Welfare, Individualistic Ethics, and Interpersonal Comparisons of Utility', *Journal of Political Economy*, 1955, pp. 309–21; and John Rawls, *A Theory of Justice*, Cambridge: Harvard University Press, 1971), is to reinterpret utilitarianism as the doctrine that the right policy is that which I would prefer to see adopted in a society that I am to enter with an equal chance of occupying the circumstances of any of its citizens. One must not claim too much for this prescription. It is still open to me to say that, though I would prefer policy A if I had an equal chance of being anybody in society, I, in fact, prefer policy B because I know perfectly well who I am and I know that I would be best off if policy B were adopted. Furthermore, since I and other likeminded people have the power to effect policy B, we will do so regardless of the interests of the rest of the community. The utilitarian has no response. Either I am persuaded by the ethical argument that I should work for the installation of policy A, or I am not. Uncertainty-based utilitarianism would seem to be particularly appealing in circumstances where the chosen policy will remain in effect for long enough that it becomes difficult for me to predict whether I and my descendants will be among the gainers or the losers from the policy.

The effect of the new welfare economics was probably to swing the climate of opinion away from the more extreme version of interventionism. To be sure, the absence of a clear-cut criterion for economic policy is not an argument for *laissez-faire*. No economic policy can be justified by the absence of a firm basis for the evaluation of economic policy. Nevertheless, the effect of the new welfare economics was probably to inculcate circumspection and modesty on the part of economists, a willingness to let the economy run according to its own laws except where the consequences of intervention seem obviously and overwhelmingly beneficial.

The other major source of the change in the perspective of the economists toward the role of government was the serious study of the mechanism of government itself. If the reformulation of welfare economics showed that economic policy could not be rendered independent of ethical prescriptions, the study of public choice made it clear that governments could not be relied upon to serve the public in a totally disinterested manner. The one knocked away the scientific basis of economic policy while the other cast doubt upon the capacity of government to adopt sound policy, even if such policy could be identified. It is as though Smith's dictum about the folly and presumption of government, after falling out of view for a hundred years, were suddenly thrust back into the centre of economic analysis.

The earliest and perhaps most devastating component of the new study of the economics of government was the analysis of voting. Government can only be presumed to serve the common good if motivated by altruism or if there is a mechanism in society to resolve conflicts of interest among citizens and to induce government to act appropriately. Altruism might take the form of a benevolent dictatorship or of an electorate each member of which is prepared to subordinate his personal interest to the common good. While few would deny the presence of a degree of altruism in society, it is hard to imagine that altruism alone is sufficient to hold modern government in check. Something more than altruism is required. Most people would point in this context to our democratic institutions, an essential component of which is the principle of majority rule in the election of legislators and in voting on bills within the legislature. Yet the closer one looks at the mechanism of voting by majority rule, the more evident it becomes that the outcome in a community of self-interested voters need not correspond to any reasonable conception of the common good. Depending on the constellation of interests among the voters and upon the rules of parliamentary procedure, there may be no equilibrium outcome such that a majority of voters can be found to favour that outcome over all other outcomes, or the equilibrium outcome, if there is one, may be inefficient (Duncan Black, 'On the Rationale of Group Decision Making', *Journal of* Political Economy, 1948, pp. 23–34). The voting mechanism may be employed by a majority coalition based on wealth, race, language or religion to expropriate the property or rights of the minority (Gordon Tullock, 'Problems of Majority Voting', *Journal of Political Economy*, 1959, pp. 571–9). The order of presentation of issues may be manipulated by officers of the legislature to yield an outcome more favourable than otherwise to the officers themselves. A group of legislators may devise voting strategies to procure an outcome more favourable to the members of the group and less favourable to others than the outcome that would arise if all votes reflected the true preferences of the voters on every issue (Robin Farquharson, *Theory of Voting*, Yale University Press, 1969).

The upshot of such theorising was the realisation that voting by majority rule is a less than ideal conduit from the interests of citizens to public policy. Voting may yield an outcome that is more or less satisfactory to most people most of the time. It may be the only mechanism we possess to subordinate the rulers to the ruled, for the alternative may be government by a small, self-interested ruling class. It may be a satisfactory basis for political action to correct for departures from efficiency in the private sector when those departures are large, glaring, and likely to be detrimental to a significant proportion of the population. But it is not guaranteed to produce the appropriate corrective action in every case, and a society might do best to ignore some departures from efficiency for which the social cost is not very large. Recognition of difficulties with voting by majority rule tended to destroy the old confidence that an observed spread between private and social cost is itself sufficient to justify public intervention in the market.

This moral was reinforced by developments in the theory of public finance leading to the realisation that there is typically a very large gap between the dollar value of public expenditure on a project or programme and its full social cost when the response of the private sector is taken into account. There are several components to the gap. On the tax side, the excess cost of public expenditure – over and above its cost as recorded in the public accounts – includes the deadweight loss as tax-payers switch from highly beneficial but highly taxed activities to somewhat less beneficial activities that happen to be less heavily taxed – for example, from taxed purchases of goods and services to untaxed leisure and do-it-yourself activities. Also on the tax side is the social waste of effort and resources on the part of the tax-payer to minimise his tax bill in schemes of legal tax avoidance or outright tax evasion, and the corresponding social waste of effort and resources on the part of the public sector to foil these schemes. To say that these activities are wasteful is not to say that tax-payer and government are acting irrationally under the circumstances; it is merely to assert that the activities neutralise one another and that everyone would be better off if tax avoidance and tax evasion could somehow be costlessly eliminated. (See A. B. Atkinson and N. Stern, 'Pigou, Taxation and Public Goods', *Review of Economic Studies*, 1974, pp. 119–28.) There is a similar problem on the expenditure side of the public accounts. Whenever the government provides a good, service or transfer to any category of firms or people, there is automatically created an incentive for people or firms to devote resources to persuading the government to include them among the beneficiaries; or, if the provision of the good, service or transfer is conditional on misfortune, the perverse incentive is to take less care to avoid the misfortune in the first place. Provision of tariffs or investment subsidies generates 'rent seeking' activity on the part of would-be beneficiaries. (See James Buchanan, Robert Tollison and Gordon Tullock, eds, *Toward a Theory of the Rent-Seeking Society*, College Station: Texas A&M Press, 1980, which contains the seminal articles on the subject.) Provision of support for the unemployed, for single mothers or for the destitute has some effect upon the incidence of these conditions; the argument here is not that support should be denied to those in great need but that the full cost of support should be recognised.

A third development is the theory of predatory government. Regardless of whether a social welfare function exists or can be identified, the government may have objectives of its own that conflict with the good of the greater part of the citizens. Predatory government may be in the interest of one or more dominant groups in the private sector or it may be in the interest of the personnel of the government. The archetype of government as the servant of one class in society is Marx's view of public sector in a capitalist economy as 'a committee for managing the common affairs of the whole bourgeoisie'. On a more modest scale, the view of government as the servant of special interests is reflected in the 'capture' theory of regulation, according to which the regulators of an industry may come to serve the interests of the regulated industry rather than the interests of the public at large. Regulators may allow themselves to be influenced by the prospect of remunerative employment in the regulated industries, or they may, quite innocently, assimilate the attitudes of the industries' representatives. When regulators can be 'captured', it may be best to leave the market alone in many circumstances where the outcome could be improved under an ideal regulatory regime. (On the capture theory, see George Stigler, *The Citizen and the State*, University of Chicago Press, 1980.)

That the government's monopoly of the means of violence may be employed in the interest of the King, bureaucrats, Mandarins or soldiers rather than to maximise the value of a social welfare function is a possibility that was recognised by Smith and Mill, that was subsequently ignored to a great extent, and that is now taken seriously once again by the economics profession. Marx himself allowed that the ruling class may be characterised by a monopoly of the means of violence rather than by a monopoly of the means of production. In an analysis that might have come straight from the pen of John Stuart Mill and can almost certainly be traced to a common source, Marx allowed for the existence of an 'Asiatic mode of production' in which the servants of the emperor constitute a class that rules society in its own interest, without at the same time acquiring a significant amount of property. (The story of the Asiatic mode of production is told in an appendix to Perry Anderson's *The Lineages of the Absolute State* (London: Verso, 1979). It should be noted that, though Mill's *Principles* contains discussions of Asiatic society and communism, and though Mill speculates on 'how far the preservation of "liberty" would be found compatible with the Communistic organization of society' (p. 210), he nowhere associates

Communism with Asiatic despotism and he does not appear to believe that Communism and the preservation of liberty are necessarily and permanently incompatible.)

It has been a perennial criticism of Marx that a communist society instituted by the Party as the vanguard of the proletariat and with public ownership of the means of production would be indistinguishable in practice from the Asiatic mode of production. As early as 1872, the anarchist Bakunin stated that

> This government will not content itself with administering and governing the masses politically, as all governments do today. It will also administer the masses economically, concentrating in the hands of the State the production and division of wealth, the cultivation of land, the establishment and development of factories, the organization and direction of commerce, and finally the application of capital to production by the only banker – the State. All that will demand an immense knowledge and many heads 'overflowing with brains' in this government. It will be the reign of *scientific intelligence*, the most aristocratic, despotic, arrogant, and elitist of all regimes. There will be a new class, a new hierarchy of real and counterfeit scientists and scholars, and the world will be divided into a minority ruling in the name of knowledge, and an immense ignorant majority. . . . for the proletariat this will, in reality, be nothing but a barracks: a regime, where regimented working men and women will sleep, wake, work, and live to the beat of a drum. (Quoted in David Miller, *Anarchism*, J. M. Dent and Sons, Ltd, 1984, pp. 11–12)

This idea was taken up by Karl Wittfogel (*Oriental Despotism: A Comparative Study of Total Power*, Yale University Press, 1958), who argued that the great despotic empires of China and the Middle East were made possible by the development of large-scale waterworks which required an army of administrators who by their numbers and capacity to co-ordinate actions came to dominate the state. At about the same time, the Yugoslavian theorist Milovan Djilas (*The New Class: An Analysis of the Communist System*, Thames & Hudson, 1957) claimed that the Communist Party itself constituted a ruling class with no less capacity or willingness to exploit the rest of society than the property-based ruling classes in the traditional Marxian framework.

Contemporary study of the economics of predatory government is a major preoccupation of the 'public choice' school of economics associated particularly with James Buchanan and Gordon Tullock, whose book, *The Calculus of Consent: Logical Foundations of Constitutional Democracy* (University of Michigan Press, 1962), played a large role in the inculcation of the new, more modest assessment of the capacity of the public sector to promote economic welfare. Their favorite metaphor for the all-encroaching government is the Leviathan, a Biblical beast originally incorporated into the study of government by Thomas Hobbes. What the public choice theorists add, both to the deviant Marxist analysis of the new class and to Hobbes's theory of government, is the close study of the mechanism of predatory government and of means for keeping the Leviathan in check. The ethology of the Leviathan is investigated by James Buchanan in *The Limits of Liberty* (University of Chicago Press, 1975), and by Gordon Tullock in *The Social Dilemma: The Economics of War and Revolution* (University Publications, 1974) and in *Autocracy* (Kluwer Academic Publishers, 1987). Applications to constitutional limits on taxation are discussed in Geoffrey Brennan and James Buchanan, *The Power to Tax* (Cambridge University Press, 1980). These lines of analysis suggest that severe limitations be placed upon use of government as a corrective for the defects of the market, the argument being that if you empower the beast to manipulate the private sector and to redistribute income at will, he will use those powers for purposes of his own and may well leave the ordinary citizen worse off than before.

The study of information and incentives over the forty years since the Second World War has altered the perception of economists about efficiency in the private sector and the public sector of the economy. Traditionally, it had been assumed that buyer and seller in any transaction are both completely informed of the quality of the product or service. Equilibrium changes radically if, for example, the worker knows his level of competence but the employer does not, the insured knows more about his state of health than the insurer can hope to learn until it is too late, or the seller knows more than the buyer about the characteristics of the product. Differential knowledge on the two sides of the market may result in an 'adverse selection' of goods for sale that is always inefficient and sometimes destroys the market altogether.

Though economists have always been aware that one may work more or less diligently according to the probability and severity of punishment for malfeasance, this consideration has usually been ignored in formal economic analysis because it could not be incorporated into well-specified models from which clear propositions may be derived. Only recently have models been developed in which one party acts as the agent of another and the outcome is necessarily less than Pareto optimal, at least by comparison with a world in which effort can be costlessly observed, because resources are used up in monitoring or because too little diligence is applied. Relations between stockholder and manager, manager and worker, landowner and sharecropper, insurer and insured, client and contractor all conform to this general pattern. Agency problems present special difficulties for the study of departures from efficiency because the obvious ideal with which actual behaviour is to be compared – a world in which effort can be costlessly observed and agency problems do not arise – is, almost by definition, unattainable. Hence, evaluation of forms of organisation must be comparative. Output under one set of institutions must be compared not with reference to the ideal, but with reference to other feasible sets of institutions. (A good selection of articles on these matters is contained in P. Diamond and M. Rothschild, eds, *Uncertainty in Economics*, Academic Press, 1978.)

The economics of information and incentives has a natural application to the study of the public sector. There would be no malfeasance if the performance of the agent could be observed costlessly by the principal and if the agent could be appropriately punished for failing to comply with the full terms of his contract. Consequently, one would expect malfeasance to be more prevalent in responsible managerial jobs where the agent must exercise discretion and where effort is not readily observed than in routine work where performance is easier to monitor. The work of the civil servant is usually such that his performance is more difficult to scrutinise than the performance of a manager in a firm in the private sector. Parliament has probably less control over and less power to discipline the bureaucracy than a board of directors has over the executives of a firm. In a sense, the theory of bureaucracy as a ruling-class is the outer edge of the theory of incentives, the extreme where the principal (in this case the citizen as voter) has the least control over his agents.

Surveying the history of the rise and fall of the public sector as a panacea for the undeniable departures from efficiency in the private sector, one can identify two great concepts that have moulded our views about the role of the public sector in the economy. The first of these is the system of natural liberty, a classic juxtaposition between is *is* and an *ought*, for an economy where people are free to follow their own interests is best for the community and ought to be unfettered by public policy. The development of economics after *The Wealth of Nations* might, with some exaggeration, be looked upon as the evolution of the *is* into propositions about the existence and Pareto optimality of the competitive equilibrium together with an ever-growing list of exceptions, and the merging of the *ought* into utilitarianism as a guide for public policy, with the subsequent evolution of utilitarianism into the explicit recognition of the requirement for a strictly ethical social welfare function to which most people subscribe or a rule of procedure that a preponderant majority of the population is prepared to respect and defend for the formation of public policy when peoples' interests conflict. In the course of this transformation, the concentration of economists' attention upon the private sector tended to emphasise its faults and failures, while the faults and failures of the public sector were quietly forgotten. Economists came to look upon government as the self-effacing devotee of the welfare of the governed, anxious to maximise the sum of the utilities of all citizens when informed by the economists how this is best to be done. The second great concept is despotism, a view of government not just as relatively inefficient, but as having a propensity to turn nasty, to become predator, Leviathan or instrument for the exploitation of subjects by a ruling class. Fear of despotism is more evident in the writing of Mill than of Smith, though Mill's preoccupation with security as a requirement for liberty and his rudimentary analysis of society without government led him to see a larger role for government than Smith was inclined to allow. Fear of despotism waned throughout the latter part of the nineteenth and the early part of the twentieth century, primarily, I suspect, because governments in Europe appeared increasingly responsive to the needs and desires of citizens and because of a growing confidence that economic and political progress had become permanent and irreversible. Despotism was mentally relegated to Asia and destined to disappear as European enlightenment spread throughout the earth. That government might have to be designed to minimise the risk of a slide into despotism ceased for a time to be a serious consideration in economic and political analysis. Absence of any real fear of government becoming despotic or even moderately self-serving, tacit acceptance of utilitarian principles for the formation of public policy and the detailed study of market failure characterised the high point of the public sector in the estimation of the economists, just as renewed fear of despotism, the disintegration of utilitarianism as a criterion for public policy and the detailed analysis of self-interest within government, an analysis reminiscent of the strictures of Adam Smith, all contributed to the public sector's decline.

4 Group Self-Interest: The Positive Analysis of Cooperative Behaviour[1]

Gideon Rosenbluth

INTRODUCTION

The axiom of individual self-interest is the source of both the strength and the weakness of economic theory. It leads directly to maximising subject to constraints, that most powerful tool of economic analysis. On the other hand its patent conflict with observed behaviour in many situations means that conventional economic theory does not provide fruitful insights or guides to research on many problems that are reasonably classified as economic.[2]

It is ironic that when economists come to *apply* the axiom of individual self-interest, the 'individual' more often than not turns out to be a small group – the household or the firm. If one asks economists why they persist in treating a group as if it were an individual, they answer that one should read Friedman on positive economics (Friedman, 1953, pt 1, esp. p. 15 ff). The axiom is used because 'it works'. In spite of its patent lack of realism, useful and realistic results are obtained with its aid.

If one wishes to dig deeper and inquire why the axiom of individual self-seeking applied to these small groups 'works' (when it does work), the answer is clearly not to be found directly in the psychology of individual motivation, since the agents to which it is applied are not true individuals. The answer is more likely to be found in the area of social psychology or the sociology of small groups.

In the last thirty years or so economists have begun to trespass into these areas and to examine the inner dynamics of these small groups (Leibenstein, 1960, 1982; Becker, 1981; Simon, 1957, chs 10, 14, 15 and pp. 196–206; Cyert and March, 1963; MacDonald *et al.*, 1988). The guiding assumption in these developments has been that individuals within the group pursue individual self-interest subject to institutional constraints imposed by the structure of the group, which is treated as exogenous. This research has made it easier to distinguish problems for which the household or the firm are usefully treated as self-seeking 'individuals' from those for which this is not the case.

In this chapter I consider the relation between individual and group self-interest in larger groups, such as the industry, the occupation, the ethnic or religious group, the class, or even the 'economy'. When economists consider larger groups their attention is focused on the *market relations* among the members of these groups, the members being either individuals or the artificial individuals we have just discussed – the firm and the household. The corner-stone of microeconomic theory is the proposition that given suitable conditions (not generally encountered in actual economies) market relations produce a coincidence between individual self-interest and the self-interest, suitably defined, of the largest group – the 'economy'. This is the message of Adam Smith's 'invisible hand' (Smith, 1776, book 4, ch. 2).

But the economic activities of members of these larger groups are also governed by non-market relations, and these are the focus of this chapter.[3] It deals with situations in which it would be more accurate to say that it is the group rather than its individual member that pursues self-interest. These are situations in which individuals act so as to benefit a group to which they belong, even when this conflicts with maximising their individual benefit. I cite examples of such phenomena, discuss their distinguishing characteristics, and survey attempts to explain their causes and their consequences. Finally there are brief discussions of the methodological and policy implications of viewing the economy as containing such self-centred groups.

EXAMPLES OF GROUP SELF-INTEREST SERVED BY INDIVIDUAL BEHAVIOUR IN MODERN CAPITALIST ECONOMIES

Cartels

An example well known in economic analysis is 'joint monopolisation'. The individual benefits most when he chisels while the others maintain the monopoly price, but the group benefits most when all maintain discipline. Oligopoly theorists and empirical investigators have tried to pinpoint the conditions conducive to chiselling and to analyse the institutional devices for maintaining discipline. In this example it is not clear when chiselling is 'deviant' rather than 'normal', but it is agreed that chiselling is more likely when the number of firms is large.

Separation of Ownership and Control

A second example is the behaviour of management in firms in which there is effective separation of ownership and control. It has astonished some economists to find that there is little difference between the performance of firms in which ownership and control are separated and that of owner-controlled firms. These results suggest that even when owners are not in control, managers strive to maximise owner benefits rather than their own. An explanation that has been offered by sociologists is that managers are members of the propertied class, and the interest of that class as a whole is served better when firms are run for maximum profit than when firms are run for the maximum personal benefit of the management (Mills, 1956, pp. 100–6). A hypothesis more appealing to many economists is based on management fear of hostile take-overs (Marris, 1964).

Strikes

A third example is the behaviour of union members who stay out on strike even when their individual income would be higher if they went back to work as strikebreakers.

Racial and Religious Discrimination

From the standpoint of standard economic theory racial discrimination by a competitive employer seems irrational since it restricts his range of choice of employees and thus may prevent him from employing those who would contribute most to his profit. Discrimination becomes rational, however, if one views the 'white' employer who refuses to employ 'blacks' as maximising the collective real income of 'whites' as a whole rather than his own. The effect of withholding from 'blacks' the well-paying jobs in 'white' industry is to create a pool of very cheap labour to provide cheap goods and services for 'whites'.

If the labour supply is exogenous, discrimination against 'blacks' favours 'white' employees as a group but is unfavourable to 'white' employers who discriminate, since they would have a larger potential labour supply and could pay a lower wage if they did not discriminate.

But no employers lose if the 'black' workers who are victims of discrimination constitute a net addition to the labour supply which would not be tolerated by the 'whites' in the absence of discrimination. This is the typical situation where the victims of discrimination are 'foreign' – guest workers, immigrants, or ethnically distinct – a very frequent occurrence. North America, South Africa, Israel, England, and other European countries provide examples.

An analytically distinct aspect of racial discrimination is the theft (in the widest sense) of natural resources by 'settlers' from 'natives' (North America, Latin America, Africa, Australia, Israel, etc.). While analytically distinct, this phenomenon is linked to employment discrimination since it creates a class of landless cheap labour.

Becker (1971) attempted to rescue the application of conventional theory to this problem by throwing a 'taste for discrimination' into the employer's utility function and those of his employees. This device is used as a framework for discussing the consequences of discrimination, but it can tell us nothing about the causes. As suggested below, any human, or indeed animal, behaviour can be viewed as maximising an individual's utility function, given a suitable definition of tastes and constraints.[4]

Collective Invention

Allen (1983) describes a process of technological innovation in two nineteenth-century industries (pig iron and steel) that involved a surprising degree of cooperation among competing firms. Firms did not devote resources specifically to research, but freely exchanged and published information on the specifications of new capital equipment, the associated processes, and the results in terms of output and costs. On the basis of such information, other firms undertaking new investment could experiment by, for example, building higher blast furnaces than the existing ones or raising the temperature of the blast. Since the information was made public, a firm could gain by becoming a free rider and not divulging its own data, but this did not, typically, happen. Allen conjectures that this process of 'collective invention' occurs in situations where a regime of free exchange of information is more advantageous to all participants in the industry than a regime of trade secrets. There is a clear analogue with the cartel phenomenon discussed above.

Class Conflict

The Marxian theory of class conflict is a theory of group self-interest. The worker who is prepared to risk his livelihood on the picket line or even his life on the barricades is, according to this theory, acting in the interest of his class.

Patriotism

An individual who complains about every dollar of taxation levied on him by the state is ready to lay down his life for that same state.

COMMON CHARACTERISTICS OF THESE EXAMPLES

The common feature of the examples is that there is a potential conflict between group and individual self-interest. We are dealing with situations in which Adam Smith's 'invisible hand' does not operate within the group. The individual pursuing strictly his own interest would become a 'free rider' benefiting from the activity of the group without making any sacrifices himself, but if many members of the group attempted to become free riders, none would benefit. Typically in such situations free riding is not unknown, but it is regarded as deviant, and the individual acting in the group interest rather than directly maximising his own benefit is regarded as the norm.

Such a structure can be analysed as a variant of the well-known 'prisoner's dilemma' game, played by each member of the group against all the others. The exact nature of the game varies, depending on the number of members of the group and other factors. For example, the problem of cooperation in a cartel with a large number of members can be illustrated by the payoff matrix below:

Per capita payoff*

		Individual	
		Cooperate	Non-cooperate
Others	Cooperate	5, 5	4.99, 7
	Non-cooperate	2.01, 1	2, 2

*The figures in each cell show payoff to 'others' followed by payoff to the 'individual'.

If all members maintain price and output discipline the desirable outcome in the top left-hand corner is obtained. If one cuts price, he gains at the expense of the others (top right), but when the individual's market share is small, as is the case when the number of members is large, the loss to the others is trivial. If all cut price, the all-round low payoffs of the bottom right are obtained, and if all but one cut price, their profits are almost as low, and the single 'cooperator' is left with very little business (bottom left).

The matrix does not look like that of a prisoner's dilemma game, but that is nevertheless the game, because of the special feature that the payoffs shown for the 'individual' in the matrix apply to each member of the group. If the members of the group pursued their individual self-interest, each would reason: If others co-operate (top row) my best strategy is not to cooperate (i.e. be a free rider, top right), and if others do not cooperate (bottom row) that is also my best strategy (bottom right). What is true of each is true for all, and the resulting equilibrium is the non-optimal bottom right. Pure competition can be regarded as the bottom-right solution to this cartel game.

In a cartel with fewer members the top right sector would show a more substantial loss to the 'others' resulting from the chiseller's defection, and this would both improve their ability to detect the chiseller and increase their incentive to punish him when the game is played repeatedly.

Analagous versions of the game apply to the other examples we have cited. If the costs and benefits of cooperation and non-cooperation were adequately caricatured by the payoffs we have postulated, and if individual self-interest prevailed, one would expect the non-cooperative bottom-right solutions to be typical. The observed normal behaviour in the examples we have cited is, however, the superior outcome described in the top left sector. The members of the group cooperate in the interest of the group as a whole. What are the mechanisms by which group self-interest comes to control individual conduct?

THE SOURCES OF COOPERATIVE CONDUCT

Schotter (1981), developing a theory of social institutions at a somewhat higher level of generality than is our purpose, states (p. 24):

> If societies face prisoner's dilemma games recurrently, it would be efficient for them to evolve some regularity of behavior that would avoid the repeated use of equilibrium, but inefficient, strategies . . . Such a regularity would be a social convention that would prescribe behavior for the agents in this recurrent situation and would be adhered to . . . However, since the game is of the prisoners' dilemma type, at each iteration there is an incentive to deviate from the institutional rule. The consequences of such deviation must be spelled out in the definition of the institution itself.

So the questions arise, what is the nature of these institutions? and how do they originate? In reviewing the answers to these questions attempted by economists and others it is useful to keep in mind some distinctions not commonly made in economic literature. Confining our attention for the moment to natural persons, and at the risk of being pilloried as an amateur psychologist, I want to distinguish between the sources of motivation, the motivation itself, and the resulting conduct.

In terms of the jargon of the utility function, I mean by the sources of motivation whatever determines the shape of the utility function and its arguments. In less technical language I mean whatever determines human motives. For the present purpose it is sufficient to distinguish two types of sources: 'natural' and 'social'. By 'natural' I mean whatever we mean by 'human nature' when we say that it is human nature to be selfish, want sex, love one's children, etc. By 'social' I mean social conditioning of individual motivation through parental and school education, religious preaching, peer group pressure, advertising, propaganda, brain-washing, and so on.

The motivation itself is, in economists' jargon, the maximisation of a specified utility function. In less technical language I mean the individual's objectives. For the present purpose it is necessary and sufficient to distinguish two types of motivation: selfish, that is aiming at one's own benefit, and altruistic, aiming at benefits for others.

Between motivation and conduct there stand the economist's 'constraints': limited resources, but also the host of social institutions that determine the limits of feasible conduct. The translation of motivation into conduct is also governed by rationality and its limits, joined with imperfect knowledge and understanding in an uncertain world. For the present purpose we distinguish two classes of conduct: cooperative and non-cooperative.

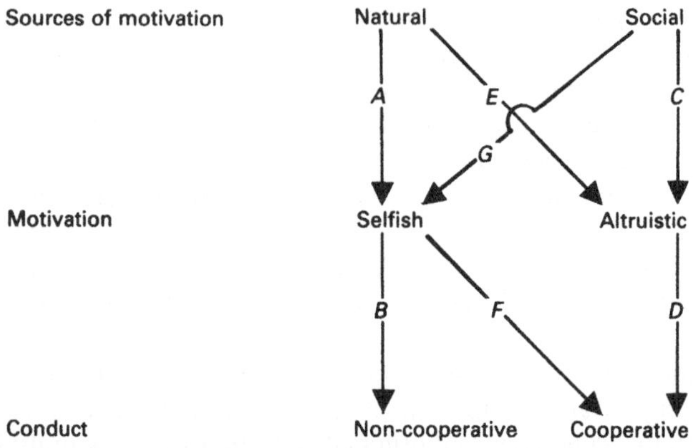

Figure 4.1

Possible causal connections between sources, motivation, and conduct are shown as arrows in Figure 4.1. The figure might be criticised as lacking in sophistication because of the absence of feedback. Nevertheless it is very useful as a means of organising the discussion of the sources of cooperative conduct.

Common observation suggests that causal links *B*, *F* and *D* between motivation and conduct are all important aspects of social life and that *F* and *D* can be found operating jointly in many instances of cooperative conduct. Theories that focus on one of these and neglect the other have been found useful, but are necessarily limited in their useful application.

It is notoriously difficult to distinguish between nature and nurture as sources of motivation, so that theories concerning causal links *A*, *C*, *E* and a possible *G*, are highly speculative.

Mainstream economic theory has concentrated on link *B* between selfish motivation and non-cooperative conduct, with implicit reliance on 'human nature' as the source of selfish motivation as indicated by link *A*, and an institutional setting of law-and-order, property, and markets, that prevents economic collapse.

In this chapter I suggest that links *C*–*D* are important, and concentrate on link *C*. Much of the specialised economic literature on the sources of cooperative conduct deals with link *F*, and the new field of 'sociobiology' has much to say about link *E* as well as *A*. Link *G* represents ideological conditioning favouring capitalism, pro-capitalist tax structures, and other institutions promoting self-centred motivation.

SELFISHLY MOTIVATED COOPERATIVE CONDUCT

Compulsion

The simplest institution by which a group can induce cooperative and even self-sacrificing behaviour in its members is compulsion: commands and rules backed by force. The use of compulsion is not confined to the state, but in modern civilised society its use by other groups is exceptional. The law and its enforcement mechanisms can be seen as an institution of this type, limiting non-cooperative behaviour such as cheating, theft, or assault against other members of the group, and enforcing cooperative behaviour such as paying taxes and assaulting members of other groups.

North (1981) points out that compulsion is a very costly way of securing cooperation, unless it is supplemented by ideological conditioning that predisposes the individual to cooperate. 'Very costly' is a way of saying 'impossible' that reflects the economist's preference for continuous functions. The force-based regimes that are weak in the propaganda department, such as the military regimes of less developed nations, exhibit a high degree of instability. Ideological conditioning is at the core of link C in our diagram and is discussed below.

Reciprocity

The derivations of cooperative conduct from self-centred motivation that are most appealing to the economist's mind-set are those that produce cooperative solutions to prisoner's dilemma games with a minimal addition of institutional structure.

One of the best known of these is Axelrod (1984) which, although it is entitled *The Evolution of Cooperation*, is of only limited use in uncovering the sources of cooperative conduct in our examples. Axelrod views the group as consisting of a set of two-person prisoner's dilemma games played by each member of the group separately against each of the other members. The games are played repeatedly with an unpredictable number of repetitions. In this framework a non-cooperative move by one player is easily detected by the other, unlike the game with a large number of players discussed above, where the lone free rider is not easily detected, since his behaviour makes practically no difference to the payoff received by the others. Moreover in Axelrod's game a non-cooperative move can be 'punished' by a non-cooperative response, and a cooperative move 'rewarded' by a cooperative response, the strategy of 'tit-for tat'. Such a cooperative response is not feasible in the large numbers game (without added institutional structure) because it would require the coordination of the activities of a large number of group members.

Axelrod shows that if a number of members of the group employ the 'tit-for-tat' strategy, a very plausible assumption given the conditions he sets, the cooperative solution is likely to emerge in the long run for all or nearly all games. Selfishly motivated cooperative conduct emerges because of reciprocity. It is reasonable to expect cooperative conduct on the part of others in response to and conditional on one's own cooperative conduct.

This theory can be applied to cooperative conduct in small groups such as oligopolies, partnerships and cooperative enterprises, clubs, small communities, or extended families. But it does not provide a convincing explanation of collusive conduct in professional associations with hundreds of members, or of 'responsible' management of manager-controlled corporations, or joint employment discrimination by hundreds or thousands of employers, strikes of hundreds or thousands of workers, class conflict, or patriotism.

Akerlof's (1983) theory of 'loyalty filters' also resorts to reciprocity to explain certain forms of cooperative conduct, such as honesty and loyalty to one's class both in the narrow sense of a graduating class and in the wider (but not widest) sense of an elite social group. When dealing with others *within the group* on an individual basis, reciprocal niceness pays off better than reciprocal nastiness.

Akerlof's formal models are examples of selfishly motivated cooperative conduct (link *F* in the diagram), using the technique of utility maximisation. The informal discussion, however, views parents and the elite academy as inculcating appropriate values in the young, namely a high regard for honesty and class loyalty. 'Children are taught to be honest, even to their own detriment' (p. 54). In terms of our diagram this is an example of link *C*, socially conditioned unselfish motivation designed to elicit conduct that favours the interest of the group.

A theory relying on both links *F* and *C* implies that the child or academy graduate is myopic or not totally rational. If he were rational and informed he would know that honesty and loyalty pay off via reciprocity, and would not need to be indoctrinated with values that make these lines of conduct desirable in themselves. In Akerlof's world the parent knows that honesty pays, but the child does not and even the child grown to adulthood does not, but acts honestly because he has been indoctrinated.

As we shall argue below, social conditioning through parents, school, and other channels is certainly of major importance in accounting for cooperative conduct, but it derives its importance from the prevalence of 'large' groups in which, as already indicated, reciprocity cannot operate to assure co-operation.

Other Rewards and Penalties

Olson (1965 and 1982) has made a major contribution to the analysis of cooperative behaviour. His interest centres on lobbies and cartels, and he advances a number of hypotheses to explain when and how the free rider problem is avoided and cooperative behaviour secured. In his model the group benefit is a 'public good' for the members, such as favourable legislation or a monopoly position. He develops the proposition discussed above, that it is easier to avoid free riding in small groups than in large ones. However the main institutional device by which, he suggests, free riding is held in check, is what he calls 'selective incentives'. These are rewards to group members contingent on their cooperation or penalties for not cooperating. Examples are participation in farm cooperatives or group insurance schemes contingent on membership in the lobby group, group air fares and other special deals. As examples of negative selective incentives Olson cites the union shop or its forerunner, 'dues picketing' with the aid of pick-handles.

Olson's description and analysis is confined to groups and activities that are motivated by 'rent seeking' or monopolising. But there are important cases of cooperative groups outside this range, as indicated by our examples of managerial behaviour, patriotism and collective invention, as well as the existence of producer and consumer cooperatives. Moreover, Olson's hypotheses, like the others in this section, do not seem to allow for 'selflessly' motivated cooperation.

'Tastes' for Conformism, Discrimination, and Doing Good

Jones (1984) explains group loyalty by assuming that the human utility function includes a taste for conformism, and then applying the standard economist's maximisation-of-individual-utility analysis. He uses a supplementary assumption to derive the persistence of particular patterns of conformity over several generations. He assumes that conformism includes respect for seniors. Becker (1971), as mentioned above, analyses discrimination by assuming that the utility function includes a 'taste for discrimination'.

Thus both Becker and Jones attempt to model particular types of cooperative behaviour by adding arguments of unanalysed origin to the individual person's utility function and without requiring any special institutions. This approach does not help us to understand the origins of cooperative behaviour. Postulating that x, y or z are arguments of the individual's utility function does not tell us why this is so. It cannot therefore throw light on the causes of cooperative conduct, though it can be of some use in analysing its consequences. However, it fails to explain a most important set of consequences: the benefits to the group resulting from cooperation.

Becker (1976a) goes further and attempts to model *altruism* by adding still more arguments to the utility function. The welfare of the beneficiaries of the altruist's cooperative conduct is defined as an argument of the altruist's utility function. This is a way of *defining* altruism, one that comes naturally to economists, and cannot explain its origin. Becker, however, deduces a *consequence* of altruism which, in his view, suggests that altruism may have originated by natural selection. He shows that altruism can pay in terms of income, because (unless the beneficiary's welfare is an inferior good for the altruist) the beneficiary may be induced to engage in conduct that raises the altruist's income and to refrain from conduct that lowers it. The altruist is truly casting his bread upon the waters.

The problem with this analysis is that it views altruism as another example of Axelrod–Akerlof reciprocity, and the comments made above apply. Its relevance is limited to pairwise interactions, and to special cases within that class. The altruism has to be person-specific, the beneficiaries must know who their benefactors are, and the dependence of A's income or welfare on B's actions has to be just right. Moreover exactly the same 'altruistic' conduct would be exhibited by a rational egotist who was aware of all the consequences of his actions. The altruism embedded in the utility function by some process of natural selection is therefore implicitly viewed, like Akerlof's value creation, as a substitute for fully informed rationality. The analysis cannot help us understand large-group cooperative conduct by fully rational individuals.

As already suggested, it is possible to throw everything but the kitchen sink into the individual's utility function so that any human, animal, or even plant behaviour can be represented as maximising the utility of individual agents subject to a constraint. When a mugger says to me: 'Your money or your life' and I hand over my wallet, I am indeed maximising my utility subject to a constraint, but little useful insight is gained by this way of looking at the situation. By extending the range of arguments included in the utility function one dilutes the concept of utility, extending its meaning from well-being or satisfaction to anything that motivates action. Whether this is worth doing in a particular case depends on whether useful propositions about the consequences of the conduct under investigation can be derived.

There are two methodological dangers in this procedure. One is that the economist or his audience may forget that utility is no longer coextensive with welfare or satisfaction, thus, for example, wiping out the distinction between self-seeking and altruism.[5] This is a common problem in welfare economics.

The other methodological danger is that the investigator may think that he has explained a particular type of motivation, when what he has done is to define it. If one defines motivation in terms of the language of the utility function, explanation requires a model in which the utility function and its arguments are endogenous. That is a type of theorising that does not come easily to economists, but it is required for progress in the analysis of cooperative conduct, and we turn to it in the next section.

COOPERATIVE CONDUCT DUE TO SOCIAL CONDITIONING

Social Conditioning is a focal point of the model proposed by North (1981). The groups with which his analysis is concerned are, on the one hand, society as a whole, the 'established system', and on the other hand, groups aiming at its overthrow:

> Something more than an individualistic calculus of cost/benefit is needed in order to account for change and stability. Individuals may ignore such a calculus, in an attempt to change the structure, because of deep-seated ideological convictions that the system is unjust. Individuals may also obey customs, rules, and laws because of an equally deep-seated conviction that they are legitimate. Change and stability in history require a theory of ideology to account for these deviations from the individualistic rational calculus of neoclassical theory. (p. 12)

Ideologies are an amalgam of theories of how society works and 'values inculcated by the family and by schooling that lead individuals to restrain their behavior so that they do not behave like free riders' (p. 46).

> Any successful ideology must overcome the free rider problem. Its fundamental aim is to energize groups to behave contrary to a simple, hedonistic, individual calculus of costs and benefits. (p. 53)

> The educational system in a society is simply not explicable in narrow neoclassical terms, since much of it is obviously directed at inculcating a set of values rather than investing in human capital. (p. 54)

North's object is to develop a theory of economic history, rather than an analysis of cooperation. Nevertheless in stressing ideology he points to a major source of cooperative behaviour.

But the processes by which the individual is conditioned to cooperate without compulsion go beyond what is comprehended in North's concept of ideology. In terms of the models of the preceding section they include all the social influences on the individual's utility function. Most economists are not disposed to analyse these social conditioning mechanisms because, as our review above has suggested, so much of their modelling relies on the convenience of exogenously given utility functions that are stable over the period to which the model is applied.[6] Group influence on individual thought and action is, however, the staple diet of sociologists, psychologists, and social psychologists (see, for example, Brown, 1985).

The relevant processes include parental influence, peer group influence, schooling, religious activities, club and association activities, propaganda, rallies, pep talks, etc. These processes determine the individual's ethical values and aesthetic judgments, and both strengthen and exploit the individual's need for social approval. They produce the 'taste for conformity', 'taste for discrimination', and concern for the welfare of others which Jones and Becker assume in their models. Social conditioning develops three types of motivation that can operate jointly. The individual is made to feel that non-cooperative pursuit of self-interest is unethical, that it is unaesthetic, and that it leads to social disapproval.

The importance of instilling the appropriate ethical values explains why those who participate in professional organisations or cartels seem to the economist to have mental blocks that make it impossible for them to distinguish between the interest of the public and the interest of their association or cartel. Conversely the participants in these groups are astonished at economists' inability to understand that chiselling or even advertising one's price is unethical.

For the analysis of economic problems it is probably not necessary to have good models of these social conditioning processes, but it is vitally important to recognise their existence. Many major economic phenomena are not usefully analysed by assuming exogenous personal utility functions.

The hypothesis proposed here is that the personal utility function is endogenous to a model in which a suitably defined group objective function is maximised or at least satisficed. The individual's utility function is manipulated by social conditioning to serve the interest of the group by inducing the individual to cooperate.

SUBGROUP FORMATION AND EXPLOITATION

When cooperation-inducing institutions exist, those who can control their operation can use them to induce higher degrees of cooperation in others while becoming something like free riders themselves. In the state those who control the use of force can tax and conscript others. Those who control the family, the schools, the media of communication, and the religious institutions can induce subservience in others (obedience, respect for elders, respect for authority, patriotism, loyalty, fear of God, and so forth). Generals and televangelists get rich, and it now turns out that they have their counterparts in the Soviet Union. Similar opportunities exist in smaller groups: the self-enriching union boss is a well-known figure in the history of industrial relations. More generally and less dramatically, the opinion-makers in small communities, clubs, interest groups, political organisations, obtain benefits for themselves by virtue of their control of the agenda, since they can lead the group's activities to reflect their own interests more closely.

Since control of the cooperation-inducing institutions is worth striving for, coalitions of group members struggle to gain control and retain it with greater or lesser stability. In this way subgroups tend to be formed within the group and it may develop a hierarchical structure.

Marx's account of the class struggle and exploitation was incomplete, since the power to exploit was in his model based entirely on control of the means of production, production being narrowly defined to exclude services. Control of the non-market cooperation-inducing institutions was ignored as a source of exploitation, or more precisely, regarded as an appendage of control of the means of production. As a result Marx formed an essentially utopian view of the development of a classless society once the means of production fall into the hands of 'the workers'. The actual development in the Soviet Union and other socialist countries has seen a struggle among various groups for control of the cooperation-inducing institutions: the armed forces, the party, the government, and leading positions in economic management. It has also seen the exploitive use of such control, though on a scale that is no doubt dwarfed by exploitation in the non-socialist world.

EVOLUTION OF COOPERATION-INDUCING INSTITUTIONS

How do cooperation-inducing institutions originate? To this question social scientists and biologists have answered: natural selection. Groups develop a great variety of institutions, and both groups and institutions are transient. But institutions that promote the strength and survival of groups tend to be more durable than others, and the cooperation-inducing institutions are of this type.

While the idea of natural selection is derived from biology, it has been extensively applied to social groups. In economics it has been put forward as an answer to the question why firms seek profit: one does not need to analyse motivation within the firm; those that survive in a competitive world do so because they act like profit maximisers (Alchian, 1950).

The most extreme form of the natural selection hypothesis applied to social institutions has been summarised by E. O. Wilson in his famous work on 'sociobiology' (Wilson, 1980, p. 4):

> Natural selection is the process whereby certain genes gain representation in the following generation superior to that of other genes located at the same chromosome positions . . . The individual organism is only their vehicle, part of an elaborate device to preserve and spread them with the least possible biochemical perturbation.

> In the process of natural selection, then, any device that can insert a higher proportion of certain genes into subsequent generations will come to characterize the species. One class of such devices promotes prolonged individual survival. Another promotes superior mating performance and care of the resulting offspring. As more complex social behavior by the organism is added . . . altruism becomes increasingly prevalent . . . This brings us to the central theoretical problem of sociobiology: how can altruism, which by definition reduces personal fitness, possibly evolve by natural selection. The answer is kinship: if the genes causing the altruism are shared by two organisms . . . and if the altruistic act by one organism increases the joint contribution of these genes to the next generation, the propensity of altruism will spread through the gene pool.
>
> . . . The hypothalamic-limbic complex of a highly social species such as man . . . has been programmed to perform as if it knows that its underlying genes will be proliferated maximally only if it orchestrates behavioral responses that bring into play an efficient mixture of personal survival, reproduction, and altruism.

In support of this hypothesis Wilson describes the well-known patterns of cooperative and even self-sacrificing conduct of individual members of insect and animal societies, followed by a survey of cooperation in human societies.

In describing cooperative behaviour among the social insects (ch. 19) Wilson suggests something similar to our proposal that the self-seeking unit of analysis should be the larger group (p. 190):

> It is useful to think of an insect colony as a diffuse organism . . . possessing from about a hundred to a million or more tiny mouths. It is an animal that forages amebalike over fixed territories a few square meters in extent.

A reading of *Sociobiology* suggests that the theories set forth by Wilson are provocative but highly speculative conjectures. We may not buy the genetic explanation of altruism but can still regard the theory of biological natural selection as a useful *analogy* for a theory of the evolution of social institutions. This is how Alchian (1950) views his use of natural selection in the theory of the firm (see Alchian, 1953). It seems highly plausible that cooperation-inducing institutions evolve and survive because they contribute to the survival of the groups to which they pertain.

Is Cooperation 'Natural'?

We have not analysed link *A* of Figure 4.1, implicitly following the economist's assumption that the axiom of individual self-seeking does not require any special justification or explanation, because self-seeking is 'natural', inherent in human nature. Unselfishly motivated cooperative behaviour on the other hand, we have implicitly assumed, does require an explanation, and we have furnished explanations that assume that such conduct is *not* inherent in human nature.

When one makes statements of this sort one is implicitly claiming to be able to distinguish nature from nurture – a notoriously difficult undertaking. We recall that Adam Smith, in his advocacy of free markets, asserted that the 'propensity to truck and barter' was inherent in human nature (Smith, 1776, book 1, ch. 2), a proposition that many today would question.

A perusal of Wilson's book must make one question whether 'nurture' is in fact the main source of cooperative behaviour. Wilson documents what every university graduate knows in any case: there are (at a rough count!) at least as many examples of cooperative conduct in animal and precapitalist human socities, as there are of non-cooperative self-seeking, or self-seeking linked only by markets. The recognition that cooperative conduct is pervasive in animal and human life goes back at least to the 1890s when Kropotkin published the papers later collected in his book on *Mutual Aid* (Kropotkin, 1902).

To what extent this widespread cooperative conduct reflects nature rather than nurture is still a matter of debate among social scientists, psychologists, and biologists (see, for example, Campbell, 1975). A 'natural' source of cooperative conduct is of course supplied by the reciprocity theories of Axelrod and Becker (linkage *A–F* in Figure 4.1). An entirely different hypothesis is favoured by Wilson and other sociobiologists, as indicated by the quotation above (linkage *E–D* in Figure 4.1). In Wilson's examples the 'natural' cooperative groups are based on kinship, and it is the gene rather than the individual organism that behaves, metophorically speaking, in a self-seeking manner. One does not, as we have said, have to buy Wilson's explanations, but one must acknowledge the possibility that cooperative behaviour is at least in some circumstances no less 'natural' than non-cooperative behaviour.

We have argued above that reciprocity theories, whatever their validity, are relevant to cooperation in small groups, and the same may be said of gene-based theories. Cooperation in large groups is more reasonably explained by social conditioning and compulsion. Whether the source be nature or nurture, however, Kropotkin, Wilson, and others remind us of the frequency of cooperative interaction of individuals in economic life in both the past and the present. It seems surprising, then, that mainstream economics should view exchange based on property rights as the only important or interesting device for coordinating economic activity.[7]

METHODOLOGICAL IMPLICATIONS

Economists have only recently begun to join other social scientists in the analysis of cooperative conduct, and it would be premature to make more than tentative suggestions regarding analytical methods likely to be useful.

In this Chapter we have emphasised the inadequacy of traditional economic methods of analysis for understanding the sources of cooperative conduct. But paradoxical as it may seem, a suggestion that emerges from our discussion is that the realm of traditional economic analysis might fruitfully be extended. Once it is appreciated that cooperative conduct serves a suitably defined group interest, the group interest can be taken as the driving force, and for many applications it is not necessary to have a well-defined model of just how the group interest induces cooperative conduct. Models based on maximising an objective function subject to constraints can be applied to larger groups, just as their application has been extended from the individual person to the family and the firm.

In some fields of application this has already been done. In the theory of industrial relations the modelling of unions as maximising an objective function subject to constraints is common. Farber (1986) reviews the controversy between Dunlop (1944) who advocated this type of theory, and Ross (1948) who opposed it. Farber concludes that this type of modelling is fruitful, but that it should be supplemented by an analysis of the determinants of the objective function. These determinants include the internal structure of the union and its political processes, the factors stressed by Ross. In this context Farber discusses the conditions under which the union leadership may exploit the members, and the formation of coalitions vying for control of the leadership. These trends are examples of the subgroup formation we have discussed above.

It is likely, then, that when modelling based on maximising an objective function is extended to larger groups, the interactions among the individuals in these groups will not long remain a 'black box' despite the proven payoff to such simplification at the level of the firm and the family. Researchers seeking the determinants of the objective functions will delve into the structures and processes we have discussed: the inducement of cooperative conduct and the formation of coalitions and hierarchical structures. We have already seen such methodological development from the simple to the complex at the level of the family, the firm, and the union.

SOME NORMATIVE IMPLICATIONS

Wilson's picture of gene-driven human motivation producing the mix of selfish and cooperative behaviour that best serves the gene pool has been attacked as providing a rationale for fascism and racism. Marten (1983) has documented this use of the theories of sociobiology and its forerunners at (possibly excessive) length. Such derivation of normative propositions from positive hypotheses in the field of genetics involves, *inter alia*, the assumption that what is 'natural' is *ipso facto* good for society, an axiom that is clearly preposterous. It would, for example, dictate the repeal of most of the criminal code and the dismantling of health services.

One can, however, discuss normative implications of our analysis once a set of values has been introduced. From the point of view of the liberal-social-democratic values to which (nearly) all who discuss public policy in Canada profess to subscribe,[8] the recognition of cooperative behaviour in the pursuit of group self-interest means that free markets cannot be relied upon to achieve policy goals.

Cooperative behaviour of interest to the economist can be viewed as a *consequence* of 'market failure' within the larger group, and a *cause* of market failure 'between groups'. Within the group, markets cannot bring about a coincidence of individual and group interest because of the free rider problem. The solution of the problem by cooperation suppresses competition within the group and thus tends to lead to monopolistic competition in the economy composed of a set of such groups.

'Market failure' is the somewhat weird policy-oriented term invented by economists to describe the failure of markets to conform to their unrealistically optimistic expectations. If the policy-maker is motivated by the liberal-social-democratic values we have postulated, he is compelled to judge case-by-case whether cooperative conduct is nasty (racial discrimination, oligopoly), nice (responsible corporate management, labour unions), or of debatable niceness in a federal state (Quebec patriotism), and to legislate and (dare one say it?) regulate accordingly.

Our discussion of subgroup formation and exploitation points to a concomitant public policy danger: the policy-maker may not be adequately motivated by the liberal-social-democratic values he professes, and may assert a group interest as a tool of exploitation. He may even do so without consciousness of insincerity. 'What's good for General Motors is good for the country.' Examples abound.

CONCLUSIONS

This somewhat rambling essay has been concerned with pre-research discussion of an important topic. Such rambling discussion is a necessary step in the progress of our discipline, and this contribution is not the first, nor, I presume, the last, in its field.

For individuals, households, and firms, cooperative behaviour is no less 'natural' or plausible than non-cooperative self-seeking behaviour. *A priori* there is no more justification for the axiom of self-seeking by these entities than for an axiom of self-seeking by larger groups. There are important economic problems that may be more usefully investigated by adopting the latter axiom.

Cooperative behaviour as a solution to a prisoner's dilemma game is induced by processes of socialisation and group pressures that are imperfectly understood, that involve the formation of hierarchies and exploitation, and that may result from an evolutionary process of natural selection.

Contemplation of the importance of cooperative behaviour in economic life must make one sceptical of the reliance on free markets as a solution to problems of fairness and efficiency.

Notes

1. I am indebted to Bob Allen, Chris Archibald, David Donaldson, Bob Evans, Chris Green, and Tony Scott for helpful comments.
2. Most of the bricks and mortar of this essay are not new, though I believe the structure is. For similar views of the strength and weakness of economics see North (1981), Hirshleifer (1985), Coleman (1988). For a vigorous denial of weakness see Becker (1976b).
3. I include non-market relations governing the collective behaviour of sellers or buyers in a market.
4. I am indebted to David Donaldson for reminding me that to cover *all* behaviour, the utility function must be thought of as exogenously variable.
5. Richler (1969, pp. 102–3) describes a TV host who torments a missionary nun by forcing her to agree that helping the poor and disabled 'affords you pleasure', leading his studio audience of slobs to yell in unison that she is 'as shitty as we are'. Hirshleifer (1985, p. 54) remarks: 'After all, men and women do sometimes seek the welfare of others, and they are sometimes led astray by thoughtlessness and confusion. How should our profession respond . . . A kind of answer, one with which I have little patience, is to use a verbal trick so as to redefine all goals as self-interested, and all choice of means as rational'.
6. Economists with interdisciplinary interests are notable exceptions to this rule. They include Marx, Veblen, Galbraith, Hirschman (1982, pp. 9–10), and H. A. Simon (1957, chs 6, 7, 8, 10).
7. Friedrich Hayek, that champion of free markets, contended that cooperation is natural and 'adapted to the hunting and gathering life of the small bands' that characterised prehistoric man. Man's 'innate instinct to pursue common perceived goals' had to be suppressed, and institutions fostering non-cooperative conduct – 'freedom' – had to emerge, in order for civilised life in large societies to develop (Hayek, 1979, pp. 159–65). This point is discussed in Hirshleifer's interesting survey of non-mainstream economics (Hirshleifer, 1985, p. 58).
8. Not, I suppose, in the United States where 'liberal' has now become a term of abuse.

References

Akerlof, G. A. (1983) 'Loyalty Filters', *American Economic Review*, 73, pp. 54–63.

Alchian, A. A. (1950) 'Uncertainty, Evolution and Economic Theory', *Journal of Political Economy*, 57, pp. 211–21.

Alchian, A. A. (1953) 'Biological Analogies in the Theory of the Firm: Comment', *American Economic Review*, 43, pp. 600–3.

Allen, R. C. (1983) 'Collective Invention', *Journal of Economic Behavior and Organization*, 4, pp. 1–22.

Axelrod, R. (1984) *The Evolution of Cooperation* (New York: Basic Books).

Becker, G. S. (1971) *The Economics of Discrimination*, 2nd edn (Chicago: University of Chicago Press).
Becker, G. S. (1976a) 'Altruism, Egoism, and Genetic Fitness: Economics and Sociobiology', *Journal of Economic Literature*, 14, pp. 817–26.
Becker, G. S. (1976b) *The Economic Approach to Human Behavior* (Chicago: University of Chicago Press).
Becker, G. S. (1981) *A Treatise on the Family* (Cambridge, Mass: Harvard University Press).
Brown, H. (1985) *People, Groups, and Society* (Milton Keynes: Open University Press).
Campbell, D. T. (1975) 'On the Conflicts between Biological and Social Evolution and between Psychology and Moral Tradition', *American Psychologist*, 30, pp. 1103–22.
Coleman, J. S. (1988) 'Social Capital in the Creation of Human Capital', in C. Winship and S. Rosen (eds), *Organizations and Institutions* (Chicago: University of Chicago Press) pp. S95–S120.
Cyert, R. M. and J. G. March (1963) *A Behavioral Theory of the Firm* (Englewood-Cliffs, NJ: Prentice-Hall).
Dunlop, J. T. (1944) *Wage Determination under Trade Unions* (New York: Macmillan).
Farber, H. S. (1986) 'The Analysis of Union Behavior', in O. Ashenfelter and R. Layard (eds), *Handbook of Labor Economics*, vol. 2 (Amsterdam: North Holland) pp. 1039–89.
Friedman, M. (1953) *Essays in Positive Economics* (Chicago: University of Chicago Press).
Hayek, F. A. (1979) *Law, Legislation and Liberty. Volume 3: The Political Order of a Free People* (London: Routledge & Kegan Paul).
Hirshleifer, J. (1985) 'The Expanding Domain of Economics', *American Economic Review*, 75, 6, pp. 53–68.
Hirschman, A. O. (1982) *Shifting Involvements* (Princeton: Princeton University Press).
Jones, S. R. G. (1984) *The Economics of Conformism* (London: Blackwell).
Kropotkin, P. (1902) *Mutual Aid* (reprinted, New York: Garland, 1972).
Leibenstein, H. (1960) *Economic Theory and Organizational Analysis* (New York: Harper).
Leibenstein, H. (1982) 'The Prisoners' Dilemma in the Invisible Hand', *American Economic Review (Papers and Proceedings)*, 72, pp. 92–7.
MacDonald, G. M. *et al.* (1988) 'Symposium on New Directions in the Economic Analysis of Organizations', *Canadian Journal of Economics*, 21, pp. 441–91.
Marris, R. (1964) *The Economic Theory of 'Managerial' Capitalism* (New York: Free Press).
Marten, H. G. (1983) *Sozialbiologismus* (Frankfurt: Campus).
Mills, C. W. (1956) *White Collar* (New York: Oxford University Press).
North, D. C. (1981) *Structure and Change in Economic History* (New York: Norton).
Olson, M. (1965) *The Logic of Collective Action* (Cambridge, Mass.: Harvard University Press).

Olson, M. (1982) *The Rise and Decline of Nations* (New Haven: Yale University Press).
Richler, M. (1969) *Cocksure* (New York: Bantam).
Ross, A. M. (1948) *Trade Union Wage Policy* (Berkeley: University of California Press).
Schotter, A. (1981) *The Economic Theory of Social Institutions* (Cambridge: Cambridge University Press).
Simon, H. A. (1957) *Models of Man* (New York: Wiley).
Smith, A. (1776) *An Inquiry into the Nature and Causes of the Wealth of Nations* (reprint of 1812 ed, London: Ward Lock).
Wilson, E. O. (1980) *Sociobiology*, abridged (Cambridge, Mass: Harvard University Press).

5 Probability and Rationality in Economics

Robin Rowley

Many years ago, Knight (1921) insisted that 'if we are to understand the workings of the economic system we must examine the meaning and significance of uncertainty; and to this end some inquiry into the nature and significance of knowledge itself is necessary'. He provided a simple distinction between risk and uncertainty, in which the former was identified with the existence of probability distributions, but this distinction proved inadequate as probabilistic concepts were expanded and as their connections with knowledge were clarified. Further the vagaries of individual decisions produced a conflict between views that the axioms of probability were descriptive and those that stressed rationality, sometimes in a prescriptive sense. Other conflicts emerged as important qualifications to the application of probability were ignored and as the number of different conceptions of probability grew. Qualifiers such as objective and subjective lost their meaning.

Rationality can involve consistency, optimality and efficiency of choices by individual economic agents or the outcome of a collective of such choices. It can also refer to the progress of economic science in the sense of a widely-based, moving forward in the accumulation of relevant information and the understanding of economic phenomena. Concern for such rationality re-emerged with special force in the 1960s as economists became aware of the efforts of Popper, Lakatos, Kuhn and others to characterise scientific activity and to assess criteria for validating or dismissing theories. Here economists inevitably turned to statistics and probabilistic methods of testing. Unfortunately they were insufficiently sceptical of significance tests and other statistical diagnostics. Econometrics became entrenched in training programmes for economists while the evident failure of many econometric models produced some unease with this development.

In the three sections of our discussion in this chapter, we seek to clarify difficulties for the reconciliation of rationality and probability.

We begin by recognising potential instabilities in the economic context and the subsequent dangers of presuming strong properties for probabilities. Then we look at the problem of choosing between abstraction and reality which has often led to a mixing of probabilistic concepts. Finally we discuss the progress of economic science by looking at the conflict between an encompassing-testing paradigm and criticism. We point to the iterative nature of theory construction, reliance on instrumental assumptions, the lack of firmness of many economic hypotheses, and the general problem of finding appropriate rules for research in non-experimental environments.

1 PROBABILITY AND THE ECONOMIC CONTEXT

Almost a half century has passed since Keynes reviewed a book prepared by Tinbergen for the League of Nations. His adverse response to Tinbergen's econometric methods appeared in the *Economic Journal* (1939). It is reprinted with a comment, rejoinder and other contemporaneous correspondence in Moggridge (1973). For Keynes, the central question for econometric methodology was the 'logic of applying the method of multiple correlation to the unanalysed economic material, which we know to be non-homogeneous through time'. He insisted, in similar vein, the 'main prima facie objection to the application of the method of multiple correlation to complex economic problems lies in the apparent lack of any adequate degree of uniformity in the environment'. Keynes sought to elaborate questions which the economist 'is bound to ask' in deciding whether the econometric method is applicable, for he was troubled by the non-compliance of the economic context with the conventions of the classical linear model and other statistical frameworks.

Non-uniformity, non-homogeneity and other instabilities weaken the realism and practical value of postulated covariance-stationarity and ergodicity. Indeed any prior matching of statistical assumptions with accurate perceptions of economic conditions presumes the existence of an instructive standard of sufficient realism to guide the choice of assumptions. However, an alternative empirical criterion has often been proposed to avoid the prior consideration of the economic context by focusing instead on post-model evaluations of empirical findings. This criterion is illustrated by Minford and Peel (1983):

> [The] linchpin of the whole edifice of econometrics is the postulate of regularity in aggregate behaviour by individuals faced with regularities in economic nature. That postulate in turn justifies the assumption that they face regularities. Whether this postulate is 'true or false' can only be settled empirically, by evaluating the success and failure of econometrics in attempting to apply this basic assertion.

Clearly pragmatism prevails here rather than realism and we have only weak linkages with the axioms of probability, which are thus difficult to justify except on the basis of mathematical convenience or fashionable convention.

Similar issues of abstraction, realism and pragmatism occur in economic theory at the level of individual agents. A counterpart of the Keynesian perspective is provided by Hicks (1966), who points out that economics as a social science is concerned with the activities of human beings who are 'not omniscient, and are not wholly rational' and who have 'diverse, and not wholly consistent, ends'. Knight (1921) was even more severe when he pointed to economic behaviour as 'more or less impulsive and capricious', which 'raises the fundamental question of how far human behaviour is inherently subject to scientific treatment'. These distinguished economists responded to potential irrationality and informational deficiencies in different ways. Hicks avoided statistical analysis and chose to express himself primarily in literary terms rather than mathematical ones. Eventually he gave a forceful account of his position in 1984. Knight chose instead to identify himself with a method of successive approximations in theoretical economics, subject to 'empirical correction' in real situations. Neither of them gave us much hope of elucidating the character of appropriate probabilistic concepts, especially with respect to the convergence of individual probabilities, their measurability, potential mathematical properties, and coherence or rationality.

Recent proponents of subjective concepts of probability have sought much more for economic theory. Thus we find Lindley (1984) insisting that 'probability is the only adequate description of uncertainty' and Smith (1984) noting the subjectivist conviction that 'quantified individual degrees of belief are inescapably the starting point for any systematic study of human scientific response to an uncertain world'. Their notion of uncertainty is markedly at odds with that put forward by Knight. Yet another view is found in Keynes's logical theory of probability, which failed to elicit much direct support but stimulated later attitudes to the integration of uncertainty in economic models. Braithwaite (1973) reflects a general assessment when he notes 'Keynes's thesis that some probability relationships are measurable and others unmeasured leads to intolerable difficulties without any compensating advantages.' Non-comparable probabilities and their incomplete ordering do not preclude modelling but they make it much more difficult and less comprehensive in scope. Keynes shared with Knight the view that probabilities are conditioned on knowledge, which varies across individuals and affects applicability in economics. Overall, he opted for a realist bias in arguing that 'as soon as mathematical probability ceases to be the merest algebra or pretends to guide our decisions, it immediately meets with problems against which its own weapons are quite powerless'. We find him persistently stressing historical developments, which weaken assumptions of stationarity and relative frequencies, and incompleteness so mathematical expectations are not numerically measurable. Perhaps it is appropriate here to give the last word on realism, non-repetitive or unstable economic phenomena, and economic science to Hicks (1984):

> Economics is 'on the edge of science and on the edge of history'. It is on the edge of science; because it can make use of scientific, or quasi-scientific, methods; but it is no more than the edge, because the experiences that it analyses have so much that is nonrepetitive about them . . . Economics is in time, and therefore in history, in a way that science is not.

2 THE MIXING OF PROBABILISTIC CONCEPTS

For two decades, the success of econometric modelling has been actively criticised and new research programmes proposed. The new level of scepticism is illustrated by Thurow (1983) when he argues economic evidence 'is often contradictory, and even where it is consistent, the conclusions have been wrong so many times that the credibility of even consistent results is suspect and can be ignored by those who want to'. The emergence of new research programmes, briefly described in Rowley and Hamouda (1988), brought forward two special problems: namely, whether models are intended to display theories or to test their validity, and whether theories or data should take precedence if they are apparently incompatible. These problems reflect a research environment characterised by ignorance, wishful thinking and methodological imprecision – not least in areas where probability and rationality are both invoked. This can be illustrated by consideration of approaches using 'rational' expectations (RE-models). These reveal a curious mixing of probabilistic concepts, more awkwardness for the choice between reality and abstraction, and a shift to simulative models from confirmatory ones.

The present RE-theory is a culmination of research on optimal predictors for realisations of covariance-stationary, stochastic processes or, more loosely, on certainty equivalents. This began when Muth (1961) introduced a market-level hypothesis that equated anticipated values of some economic variables with their conditional expectations after elimination of deterministic and non-stationary components. All variables in his framework were assumed to be generated by linear normal processes; that is, by stationary moving-averages of normally distributed, white-noise sequences. The rhetoric of present RE-theory links the subjective probability distributions of anticipations with objective distributions of market outcomes so a mixing of probabilistic concepts is involved. This complication has been explored by Swamy, Barth and Tinsley (1982), who demonstrate the 'impossibility' of interpretation of the theory due to the mixing of frequentist and subjectivist notions of probability. Models are highly aggregated with few variables and they contain an implicit assumption that processes are recurrent and identifiable so their parameters are constant and known – a far cry from the economic context described by Keynes. Clearly the framework is unrealistic. This is of little relevance if RE-models are simply fables since then any assumption is acceptable if it facilitates the telling of a good story. Difficulties arise when we want to go beyond this position and seek means of evaluating statistical assumptions and their underpinnings in probability or when we attempt to associate the theoretical variables with realistic counterparts.

Reconciliation of subjective probabilities with real behaviour is especially difficult if we do not specify whose probabilities are involved or rely on those attributed to a mythical typical individual. The Bayesian approach, as Smith (1984) insists, is 'predicated on the primitive notion of individual preferences' while the formal argument 'uses a single decision-maker and it is not possible, at the moment, to extend the ideas to more' (Lindley, 1984). Further, the existence of different knowledge and non-shared experiences among economic agents must lead to discrepant probabilities and create difficulties for measurment. Lindley, Tversky and Brown (1979) point to two sources of such difficulties:

> First, subjective probability is a measure of degree of belief, which reflects one's state of information. It is not only subjective but also variable since it can change from one situation to another. Second, it is not possible in general to obtain independent measurements of subjective probability from the same individual because he is likely to remember his previous thoughts and responses.

Clearly real heterogeneity, intertemporal variation and learning diminish the attractiveness of subjective elements in RE-models. With this background, what is the subjective probability at a market level of aggregation or for a representative participant in any market?

Turning to the use of evidence, many proponents of RE-models argue that their lack of realism is not a major deficiency if they provide suitable forecasts and satisfy a rather vague empirical standard – such as crude conformity with some 'stylised facts' drawn from an inspection of NBER chronologies or a similar source. Note this standard has nothing to do with probabilistic ingredients of the models. In practice, what matters is the preparation of 'mimic cycles' from stochastic difference equations, which are tuned rather than estimated. At the stage of validation for the models, the rhetoric of the initial models with its probabilistic tone has no significance. Similarly data have reduced status so the qualitative dynamics of the models can be displayed. The primitive notion of confronting the predictions of theory with evidence is distorted, for tuning is unprincipled if we cannot find 'realistic' values for the parameters of the difference equations. How can such values be integrated with models as abstract as these?

3 THE PROGRESS OF ECONOMIC SCIENCE: ENCOMPASSING OR CRITICISM

The interpretation of RE-models as fables is consistent with views that much of economic theory is 'little more than a plausible story' (Granger, 1981) which gives modest guidance to the specification of econometric equations and the choice of appropriate probabilistic structures. Theoretic models are excessively simple and unrealistic so they provide only vague hypotheses for empirical testing. Further, the analytical complexity of statistical procedures restrains their application beyond models of very small size and econometricians have been satisfied with impure procedures 'for they are evidently not justified in deforming the reality of complex phenomena in order to force it to fit into overly simplified specifications' (Malinvaud, 1981).

In recent years, the apparent lack of progress in empirical research stimulated a pronounced shift toward issues of specification and methods for enhancing the rationality of research procedures. The iterative and sequential nature of much research, its dependence on particular conventions of limited value, and the lack of continuity across research efforts received attention. Data-analytic methods were supplemented and the term 'criticism' came to represent a major aspect of statistical modelling with the role of facilitating effective iteration between theory and practice. In a series of papers, Box (1976–80) reveals the nature of criticism including the interplay of induction and deduction, the amending of models as knowledge evolves, and the use of diagnostic checks.

The role of probability in the multi-stage research strategies of criticism is complex. Potential errors of specification and consideration of alternative distributional assumptions can guide the search for robust procedures and robust samples, but sensitivity analyses are not simple to evaluate and the habit of reliance on exact probability distributions is difficult to resist. Moreover, our experience with diagnostic checks is limited and we need reassurance that particular checks will permit timely convergence of iterations to appropriate inferences. Hendry (1979) illustrated potential convergence to a mis-specified model due to a simple-to-general element that is often part of criticism. He chose an alternative approach relying on 'intended overparameterisation with data based simplification'. This came to be embedded in the paradigm of 'encompassing-testing' as Hendry, Mizon, Richard and others addressed the rationality of empirical economic science with a general-to-specific element, influenced by awareness of power considerations in the nesting and non-nesting of hypotheses. Not surprisingly, Hendry (1980) launched his advocacy of this paradigm by reappraising the Keynes–Tinbergen exchange.

Neither criticism nor the encompassing-testing paradigm presume models are true and their proponents share recognition of the subjectivity of research choices, the theory-dependency of observations, and other difficulties, but there are important differences between the two schools of thought with respect to probability. Criticism makes far less use of formal tests of the Neyman–Pearson type and it need not be preoccupied with normality. Encompassing-testing, on the other hand, generally seems overdependent on such tests and normality. See, for example, the accounts provided by Hendry and Richard (1982–3) and Mizon (1984), which demonstrate their distance from the Keynesian perspective on measurability for probabilities, fulfilment of instrumental conditions permitting familiar tests, and overall stability. Keynes would certainly not have accepted the feasibility of finding a common distributional basis for rival models. From his perspective, the suggestions of Hendry that 'the three golden rules of econometrics are test, test, and test', and that 'rigorously tested models, which adequately described the available data, encompassed previous findings and were derived from well-based theories would greatly enhance any claim to be scientific', seem ill-conceived and misleadingly naive given the strictures on probability concepts and the awkwardness of economic situations. Quite apart from such opposition, this approach depends critically on the validity of tests which again hinges on the reconciliation of probability and rationality. How should we test? Are the bases of tests adequate for the task they are being given? Are the outcomes of tests sufficiently definite or must they also be affected by 'provisionality' (Braithwaite)? Do economists use tests in a manner that permits them to have substantive significance as well as statistical significance?

Such questions are important so we need to address the nature of some common tests. It seems sensible to begin with what economists do – as reviewed, for example, by McCloskey (1985) and Zellner (1980). The former found that about three-quarters of the contributors to the *American Economic Review* misuse tests of significance when they present them! Zellner found little awareness of any relationship between the choice of a significance level and sample size; power considerations are not generally discussed; the rationale and meaning of *p*-values are seldom explained; little use is made of prior parametric information in testing; non-sharp hypotheses are not utilised very well; and almost no attention is given to the problem of pre-test biases and the lack of test statistics. This is not a promising background for basing the perceived rationality of economic science on multiple tests in iterative and sequential modelling procedures.

The self-deception of researchers is obviously troublesome not least because it weakens the attention given to any search for better probabilistic structures. Leamer (1983) provides a clear picture of the present situation where inference is whimsical and we are the prisoners of our heritage. Indeed, as argued by Lindley (1984), most of our conventional methods were developed in the 1930s before the computer existed and thus their present form is essentially determined by earlier limitations on calculating power. The pressure of tradition is also reinforced by our methods of communication, which caused Berkson (1980) to complain that the chief reason for the persistent advocacy of any maximum likelihood criterion was 'the academic and editorial establishments hold it to be virtually sacrosanct in principle'. Tests of significance and maximum likelihood ratios remain evidence but they are inadequate for decisions.

The encompassing-testing paradigm is also adversely affected by data deficiencies. Decisions made in any sequence of confrontations with tests may depend on the data being employed. Since these are seldom satisfactory and economists tend to use the data at hand, rather than search for better (but more remote) data, the outcome of a testing paradigm is always potentially corrupt. Another difficulty stems from the common reliance on asymptotic theory for test statistics. Much of the time, referential statistics have only asymptotic support although economic samples are very limited in size. Recently econometricians have realised that asymptotically equivalent testing procedures (usually various maximum likelihood procedures) can produce conflicting results when they are used with finite samples and fixed nominal significance levels. Our overall impression is that reliance on asymptotic validity for tests substantially distorts the reconciliation of probability and rational economic science.

Finally, in connection with testing and criticism, we should ask what questions motivate research and how they are related to the environment in which research efforts occur. There are obvious dangers of putting myopic academic interests before practical ones. As Box (1984) reveals with examples drawn from the lives of Fisher, Yates, Yule, Wald, Barnard, Page, Finney, Daniel and Tukey, progress often arises from the responses of an original mind to a challenging environment that is conducive to discovery. Much of our debate on alternative scientific programmes is quite remote from the practical functioning of economic life and it tends to be focused on highly stylised issues such as can be represented in the familiar confines of aggregate econometric equations. This leads to somewhat sterile academic debates rather than scientific advance. It also leads to the use of familiar conventions whereas real advance may require changes in rules that initially seem 'little short of cheating' (Box). Further, in contrast to the encompassing criteria which seem to be backward-looking, science needs a forward vision. As forcefully expressed by Tukey (1980), this forward element means finding questions to address since science 'does not begin with a tidy question' and does not end in a tidy answer. The encompassing-testing paradigm is just too 'neat'! Economic research may be disorderly and progressive just as it can be orderly and irrational.

4 CONCLUDING REMARKS: NORMAL SCIENCE

Our discussion has identified some obstacles that inhibit the reconciliation of probability and rationality within RE-models and in the research practices of economists. The crucial assumptions of market-level rationality in RE-models and existence of moving-average representations provide a convenient framework for deriving simple analytical results but they also result in an awkward situation. Different concepts of probability are mixed and subjective notions are attached to markets rather than to individuals! Further, the focus on certainty equivalents or conditional expectations that pervades these models must impose excessive constraints on the probabilistic character of economic variables. We know the stochastic processes for variables cannot all be linear, normal and covariance-stationary so the practical relevance of the models is somewhat limited. Generally this means RE-models are simulated and their parameters are tuned rather than estimated and their realism refers to the mimicry of qualitative dynamics. Simulative experiments, however, redirect attention away from probability. Thus RE-models yield interesting fables but the status of their probabilistic ingredients remains either instrumental to this story-telling or ill-defined.

Turning to criticism and the encompassing-testing paradigm, both are cited as suitable means for guiding the progress of multi-stage research programmes. They invoke probability in different ways. Criticism in its search for robustness considers alternative probability distributions to determine choices that might reduce the adverse consequences of mistaken assumptions but, otherwise, makes only modest demands on probability. The encompassing-testing paradigm, however, requires rival theories to be expressed within a comprehensive distributional framework, which is indeed a major burden. It also needs the full apparatus of statistical tests and the fulfilment of environmental conditions that these entail. Advocacy of bases for rational conduct of research ultimately has to be judged against the background of 'normal science', which was described by Popper (1970) as the activity of 'the non-revolutionary, or more precisely, the not-too-critical professional: of the science student who accepts the ruling dogma of the day; who does not wish to challenge it, and who accepts a new revolutionary theory only if almost everybody else is ready to accept it – if it becomes fashionable by a kind of bandwagon effect'. Criticism can be readily assimilated into normal science when its diagnostics are integrated in software packages and when our statistical textbooks become more balanced in their treatment of exploratory and confirmatory criteria. Clearly successful criticism will also depend on more appreciation of practical imperatives.

In contrast to the full assimilation of criticism, the acceptance for the encompassing-testing alternative seems likely to be both less extensive and more distorted. Any shift away from asymptotic validity to finite modifications, for example, can only be pursued by a few scholars for a limited number of smooth probability distributions. The habitual reliance on tests of significance and normality suggests we should not be too optimistic about reducing the widespread confusion of substantive significance and its statistical counterpart. The paradigm is also weakened by the vagueness of theories and the frequent disjointedness of theory change. Comparisons are often adversely affected by topic incommensurability, dissociation and meaning incommensurability, which reflect science as firmly grounded in history. These perhaps explain the controversies and non-resolution of disagreements among economists just as easily as does the suggestion of unsystematic procedures. We should also note the belt of auxiliary hypotheses that accompany most contentious theories and the way in which the momentum of a research programme often overshadows anomalies, statistical or otherwise, to the detriment of effective rules for their rejection.

Where does this discussion leave us? Obviously the search for better procedures is valuable. It must not be curtailed too soon by choosing just one of the two approaches that we have noted and ignoring its major flaws. For encompassing and testing, much remains to be done in developing constituent elements (especially the probabilistic ones), in adding appropriate qualifications for the application of test statistics to economic environments, and in teaching economists to be more aware of these qualifications. So far, as we found with RE-models, the reliance on probability seems both incomplete and perhaps insincere.

References

Berkson, J. (1980) 'Minimum Chi-square, Not Maximum Likelihood', *The Annals of Statistics*, 8, pp. 457–87.

Box, G. E. P. (1976) 'Science and Statistics', *Journal of the American Statistical Association*, 71, pp. 791–9.

Box, G. E. P. (1979) 'Some Problems of Statistics and Everyday Life', *Journal of the American Statistical Association*, 74, pp. 1–4.

Box, G. E. P. (1980) 'Sampling and Bayes' Inference in Scientific Modelling and Robustness', *Journal of the Royal Statistical Society*, A143, pp. 383–430.

Box, G. E. P. (1984) 'The Importance of Practice in the Development of Statistics', *Technometrics*, 26, pp. 1–8.

Braithwaite, R. B. (1973) 'Editorial Foreword', *The Collected Writings of John Maynard Keynes. Vol. VIII: A Treatise on Probability* (London: Macmillan).

Granger, C. W. J. (1981) 'The Comparison of Time Series and Econometric Forecasting Strategies', in *Large-scale Macro-econometric Models*, (eds) J. Kmenta and J. B. Ramsey (Amsterdam: North Holland) pp. 123–8.

Hendry, D. F. (1979), 'Predictive Failure and Econometric Modelling in Macroeconomics: The Transactions Demand for Money', in *Economic Modelling*, (ed.) P. Ormerod (London: Heinemann) pp. 217–42.

Hendry, D. F. (1980) 'Econometrics: Alchemy or Science?', *Economica*, 47, pp. 387–406.

Hendry, D. F. and J.-F. Richard (1982) 'On the Formulation of Empirical Models in Dynamic Econometrics', *Journal of Econometrics*, 20, pp. 3–33.

Hendry, D. F. and J.-F. Richard (1983) 'The Econometric Analysis of Economic Time Series', *International Statistical Review*, 51, pp. 111–63.

Hicks, J. R. (1966) 'Linear Theory', in *Surveys of Economic Theory, 3* (London: Macmillan) pp. 75–113.

Hicks, J. R. (1984) 'Is Economics a Science?', *Interdisciplinary Science Reviews*, 9, pp. 213–9.

Knight, F. H. (1921) *Risk, Uncertainty and Profit* (New York: Houghton Mifflin).

Leamer, E. E. (1983) 'Let's Take the Con Out of Econometrics', *The American Economic Review*, 73, pp. 31–43.

Lindley, D. V. (1984) 'Prospects for the Future: The Next 50 Years', *Journal of the Royal Statistical Society*, A147, pp. 359–67.

Lindley, D. V., A. Tversky and R. V. Brown (1979) 'On the Reconciliation of Probability Assessments', *Journal of the Royal Statistical Society*, A142, pp. 146–80.

Malinvaud, E. (1981) 'Econometrics Faced With the Needs of Macroeconomic Policy', *Econometrica*, 49, pp. 1363–75.

McCloskey, D. N. (1985) 'The Loss Function has Been Mislaid: The Rhetoric of Significance Tests', *The American Economic Review* 75, pp. 201–5.

Minford, P. and D. Peel (1983) *Rational Expectations and the New Macroeconomics* (Oxford: Martin Robertson).

Mizon, G. E. (1984) 'The Encompassing Approach to Econometrics', in *Econometrics and Quantitative Economics*, (eds) D. F. Hendry and K. F. Wallis (Oxford: Blackwell).

Moggridge, D. (ed.) (1973) *The Collected Writings of John Maynard Keynes. Vol. XIV: The General Theory and After. Part II. Defence and Development* (London: Macmillan) pp. 285–320.

Muth J. F. (1961) 'Rational Expectations and the Theory of Price Movements', *Econometrica* 29, pp. 315–35.

Popper, K. R. (1970) 'Normal Science and its Dangers', in *Criticism and the Growth of Knowledge*, (eds) I. Lakatos and A. Musgrave (Cambridge: The Cambridge University Press) pp. 51–8.

Rowley, R. (1987) *The Way the Cook Chooses: A Modern Reassessment of the Keynes–Tinbergen Exchange*, Paper presented at the Conference of the Eastern Economic Association, Washington.

Rowley, R. and O. Hamouda (1988) *Expectations, Equilibrium and Dynamics* (Hemel Hempstead and New York: Harvester-Wheatsheaf and St. Martin's Press).

Smith, A. F. M. (1984) 'Present Position and Potential Developments: Some Personal Views', *Journal of the Royal Statistical Society*, A147, pp. 245–59.

Swamy, P. A. V. B., J. R. Barth and P. A. Tinsley (1982) 'The Rational Expectations Approach to Economic Modelling', *Journal of Economic Dynamics and Control*, 4, pp. 125–47.

Thurow, L. C. (1983) *Dangerous Currents: The State of Economics* (New York: Random House).

Tukey, J. W. (1980) 'We Need Both Exploratory and Confirmatory', *The American Statistician*, 34, pp. 23–5.

Zellner, A. (1980) *Statistical Analysis of Hypotheses in Economics and Econometrics*, Paper presented at Annual Meeting of the American Statistical Association, Houston.

6 On the Publicness of Fiat Money

Thomas K. Rymes

INTRODUCTION

Jack Weldon[1] wrote on money as a public good.[2] Peter Howitt, in the *New Palgrave*, addresses the problem.[3] Ten years before Howitt, David Laidler had also turned to the same theme.[4] Like them, I take up Weldon's question.

In Weldon's writings there were a number of subdivisions of the central theme. He argued, first, that money exists only as a public good and that, appearing as 'real' balances, it is subject to change by public contrivance; second, that money so interacts with the rest of the monetary technology that private valuation of welfare gains or losses owing (say) to inflation are inadmissible; and, third, distributional considerations also render the private welfare calculations suspect. There is also a fourth subdivision, namely, optimum money supply policies are not feasible. The argument is that the interest payments on money balances must be 'real' and that it might be difficult, if not impossible, for such payments to be other than a mere shifting of the decimal place on fiat money – so assuring superneutrality and ridding the policies of any operational content.[5] I shall make no direct comment on this fourth subdivision in this chapter.[6]

The question I seek to answer is: In what sense is fiat money, or its services, or the services of the Monetary Authorities, public goods? I shall argue that it is the services of monetary stability, provided by the Authorities, which is the public good, and it is one of the determinants of the 'real' value of, and the real rate of return to, fiat money.

A SIMPLE MODEL

While Professor Weldon did not have much sympathy with such work,[7] I use the neoclassical monetary growth model[8] to understand his criticisms of the neoclassical welfare economics of inflation. There are deemed to be two assets: goods and money. The goods are representable by the usual one commodity, whereas the money is fiat, created by Monetary Authorities, costlessly in the sense that it costs nothing (or negligible amounts) in the way of real resources to reproduce[9] but not costless in the sense that it may cost real resources to maintain the confidence of the public in the real value of the stocks of money through, for example, enforcement against counterfeiting. Private persons in the economy acquire the services of money or the services of the monetary arrangements brought about by the Monetary Authorities through holding and using money balances.

Individuals will be content with the proportions held of these two assets, stocks of commodities and stocks of money, only when additional amounts of each, acquired by giving up equal quantities of present consumption, are expected to be equally fruitful in adding to their permanent streams of consumption. When the money price of the commodity stock is such that the individual is content with the proportions of wealth being held, the price is a temporary equilibrium price. When the money price is such that the individual is content with the absolute amounts of capital and real money balances being held, the price is a full equilibrium price.[10] I focus then on the sequence of temporary equilibria and study as well the steady state to which it is assumed the sequence converges.[11]

Given the nature of technology, the holding and use of fiat money is less costly than the holding and use of commodity capital for transactions purposes. From the basic model, one develops two portfolio equations showing real net rates of return to the two assets, commodity capital and money, as

$$R_k = c_k(k, m) - \delta \gtreqless (\varrho + n + n')$$

and

$$R_m = c_m(k, m) + i - p - \delta_M \gtreqless (\varrho + n + n')$$

where c_k represents the marginal physical product of capital, c_m represents the marginal physical product of the services of real money balances, with both capital and real money balances, expressed in Harrod-augmented units, contributing to consumable output, i is the nominal rate of interest the Authorities may pay on fiat money balances, p is the perfectly anticipated rate of inflation in the level of commodity price, P, δ and δ_M are the carrying cost associated with the holding of capital and the service charge, expressed as a rate, which the Authorities may charge for the measurable services being provided by fiat money balances, ϱ is the rate of time preference, and n and n' are the rates of growth of the population, in natural and Harrod-augmented units.

When the two real rates are equal, that is, $R_k = R_m$, commodity capital and fiat money balances are equally satisfactory routes between present and future permanent consumption streams. When the real rates are equal to the steady state rate, $\varrho + n + n'$, the individuals will be content with their consumptions streams and will not be seeking to augment or reduce future consumption streams relative to present consumption.

Equalisation of the two rates of return occurs in each period of time. Suppose 'today' there exists a certain stock of capital, as determined by history, K_0, and a given stock of nominal money balances determined by the Authorities, M_0. Individuals take as given the carrying costs of the stock of capital, the rate of interest paid by the Authorities on nominal money balances, the service charge levied for the use of the services of money balances and form identical expectations as to the rate of change of prices which will hold in the steady state by assuming the validity of the underlying optimal monetary growth model. The model entails that the rate of change of prices, given the rate of growth of output, will be determined by the rate of growth of the nominal money stock engineered by the Authorities. If the Authorities are confidently expected to produce a steady state rate of growth of the nominal money supply of $\dot{M}/M$, then the expected steady state rate of change of prices will be $p = \dot{M}/M - (n + n')$. Consider a particular initial price level, P. Could any arbitrarily chosen price level exist? A price level immediately implies a certain stock of 'real' money balances which, given the stock of capital, entails the gross marginal physical products of the services of capital and the services of 'real' money balances. Given the knowledge of δ_M, i, and p, and the validity of the optimal neoclassical monetary growth theory, then the expected net rates of return to capital and to money balances are determined. A price level is said to be a temporary equilibrium price level if and only if the two rates of return are the same.[12] There exists, then, a temporary equilibrium price level, P_0, such that rates of return to the two assets are momentarily equalised.[13] The temporary equilibrium price level is assumed to be unique.[14]

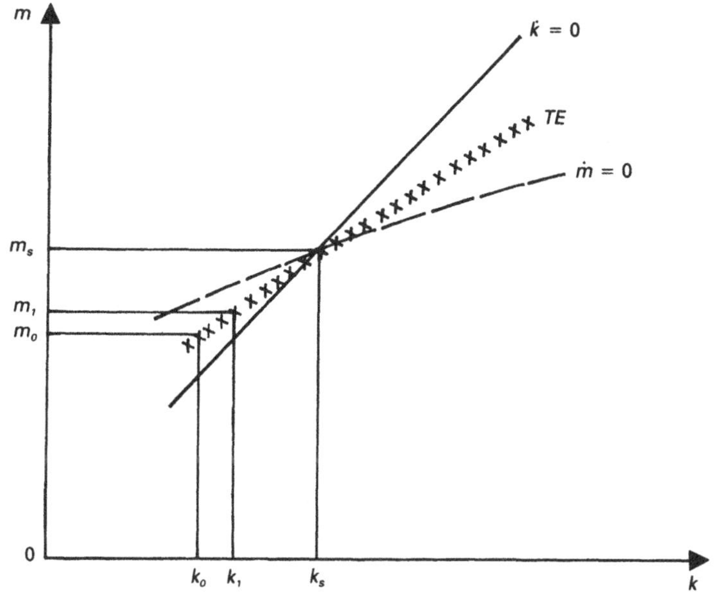

Figure 6.1

The argument may be better understood by means of Figure 6.1. The vertical and horizontal axes of Figure 6.1 are in terms of 'real' money balances and capital in Harrod-augmented terms, that is, $m = M_t/[P_t L_0 e^{(n + n')t}]$ and $k = K_t/[L_0 e^{(n + n')} t]$. The solid line in the diagram, designated $\dot{k} = 0$, is the set of all *m*s and *k*s such that the rate of return to capital is equal to the steady state rate of return, the rate of time preference, ϱ, plus the steady state rate of growth of output, $n + n'$, at which there will be no net capital accumulation. All pairs of *m*s and *k*s to the right of the solid line entail rates of return to capital below the rates of time preference and growth, so that there would be net capital *de*cumulation. All pairs of *m*s and *k*s to the left entail rates of return above the overall rates of time preference and growth so that net capital *ac*cumulation would be undertaken. The dashed line, designated $\dot{m} = 0$, is the set of all *m*s and *k*s such that the rate of return to 'real' money balances is also equal to $\varrho + n + n'$ so that no 'real' money balance net accumulation would occur. All pairs above the dashed line would entail rates of return below the steady state rate of return on 'real' money balances so that individuals would attempt to reduce their 'real' balances; such attempts would be associated with higher price levels and lower 'real' balances. All pairs below would entail rates of return below the steady state rate, attempts by individuals to acquire more 'real' balances, lower price levels and hence greater 'real' money balances. The pair, m_s and k_s, where the two lines intersect, constitute the steady state pair, where there is no further growth, in Harrod units, in either the stock of physical capital or the stock of 'real' money balances.

Consider the point k_0 on the horizontal axis, representing some initial stock of capital. Given the nominal stock of money, there will exist some initial price level, P_0, such that the rates of return to physical capital and 'real' money balances are equal. That price level, associated with the stock of 'real' money balances m_0, is called the temporary equilibrium price level. The pair, k_0 and m_0, is on the temporary equilibrium locus, *TE*, represented by the line of crosses.

At k_0, m_0, the equal rates of return exceed the steady state rate of return and therefore individuals will attempt to accumulate more capital and 'real' money balances. Suppose the extra physical capital accumulation resulted in a stock in the next period equal to k_1. A similar argument would entail the existence of a new price level, P_1, such that the stock of 'real' money balances would be m_1 and a new temporary equilibrium would prevail on the locus *TE* with again equal but lower rates of return to capital and 'real' money balances. The analysis implies that one would observe only pairs of physical capital and 'real' money balances associated with the *TE* locus consistent with a sequence of temporary equilibria, the sequence terminating in the steady state pair, m_s and k_s. At the steady state, the rates of return to capital and 'real' money balances will equal the rates of time preference and growth of output and net capital and 'real' money balance accumulation in Harrod units will have terminated. One could start with whatever physical capital and nominal money stocks history dictates and apply the same analysis of a sequence of temporary equilibria terminating in the steady state.

The steady state values m_s and k_s are determined by the real rate of interest on money, $i - p$, dictated by the Authorities together with the price, δ_M, which the Authorities charge for the measureable services of the fiat money balances held by the individuals.

EFFICIENT MONETARY ARRANGEMENTS

How would the economy capture the full benefits of the Monetary Arrangements? I take as given the standard proposition in the quantity theory of money that an once-over change in the nominal quantity of money will have no 'real' effects.[15]

Whereas once-over changes in the nominal money supply are deemed to be neutral in the sense of having no real effects, differences in the steady rate of growth of the nominal money supply will have 'real' effects and are said therefore to be supernonneutral.

To consider the argument in its simplest guise, ignore for the moment the interest payments by the Authorities on money balances. Consider now a rate of growth of the nominal money supply which is equal to the steady state rate of growth, that is, $\dot{M}/M = n + n'$. In the steady state, the rate of change of prices, p, would be zero and the steady state rate of return on money balances would be

$$R_m = c_m(k, m) - \delta_M = \varrho + n + n'$$

The value of the gross marginal physical product of 'real' money balances would exceed the service charge levied by the Authorities for the measureable services of 'real' money balances. Efficient equilibrium in the Paretian sense requires, however, the service charge levied by the Authorities for the use of such services of 'real' money balances should equal the value of the gross marginal product of such services. If, however, $c_m(k, m) = \delta_M$, then the net rate of return on money would be zero, and portfolio disequilibrium would prevail. Agents would seek to hold less money, the price level would be higher, 'real' money balances lower, and the value of the gross marginal physical product of money balances higher.

Though portfolio equilibrium exists, with the value of the gross marginal physical product of money balances greater than the service charge levied by the Authorities, the observed steady state equilibrium would be inefficient in the Paretian sense.

Imagine now the Authorities pursuing a higher rate of growth of money so that a steady *positive* rate of change of prices, or inflation, occurs. Then, the rate of return to holding money is lower, including as it now does the real capital loss owing to the 'inflation tax'. Portfolio disequilibrium implies individuals would seek to hold lower 'real' money balances and a once-over rise in the level of prices above that associated with the on-going inflation would occur. A reduction in 'real' money balances and a rise in the gross marginal physical product of 'real' money balances occurs until once again portfolio equilibrium holds. This case is illustrated in Figure 6.2.

The dashed $\dot{m} = 0$ line in Figure 6.2 is the locus of m's and k's

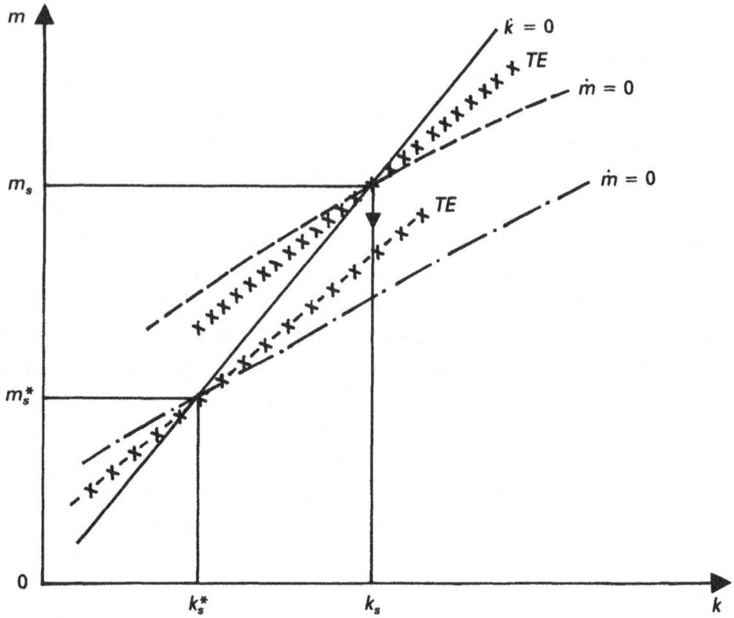

Figure 6.2

which holds when the Authorities are pursuing zero inflation. The dashes-dotted locus is that which pertains when the Authorities are pursuing an inflationary monetary growth policy. It is lower than the dashed line because in order to offset the capital loss associated with inflation, 'real' money balances must be lower entailing a higher gross marginal physical product of money. There are two Temporary Equilibrium schedules: the crosses line is associated with the dashed $\dot{m} = 0$ schedule, the dotted-crosses line with the dashes-dotted $\dot{m} = 0$ schedule. When the Authorities switch from a regime of $\dot{M}/M = n + n'$ to a regime of $\dot{M}/M > n + n'$, people correctly believe that the Authorities are now following an inflationary monetary growth policy. The immediate impact on the economy occurs through the overall level of prices because individuals seek to hold lower 'real' money balances and there will be a temporary equilibrium increase in the price level until 'real' money balances are lower to a point where, on the dotted-crosses *TE* locus, rates of return are again equalised. With lower 'real' balances, however, the equalised rates of return are lower than the steady state rates. Decumulation begins. The economy moves through a sequence of temporary equilibria along the dotted-crosses *TE* schedule until a new steady state equilibrium is reached with 'real' money balances and capital stocks m_{s^*} and k_{s^*}. A measure of the loss in wealth associated with the inefficiency of the inflationary monetary policy is the reduction in the stock of the primary inputs in the Harrod-efficient sense $[m_s - m_{s^*} + k_s - k_{s^*}]$ and the loss measured in permanent streams of consumption would be $(\varrho + n + n')\ [m_s - m_{s^*} + k_s - k_{s^*}]$.[16] It would appear that inflation is a costly monetary policy.

It is not, however, the inflation per se which is the problem. It is, rather, the failure of the Authorities to pay the competitive steady state 'real' rate of return on money balances. In the case illustrated in Figure 6.2, the rates of return on money balances in the two steady states were respectively $R_m = c_m(k_s, m_s) - \delta_M$ and $R_{m^*} = c_m(k_{s^*}, m_{s^*}) - p - \delta_M$. The inefficiency involved in c_m exceeding δ_M is enhanced by c_{m^*} exceeding δ_M by p, the rate of inflation. All this could be resolved by the Authorities paying a nominal rate of interest on fiat money such that $i - p$ was equal to $\varrho + n + n'$, the steady state rate of return. If the Authorities can pay interest on money[17] then they could pick a nominal rate $i = \varrho + n + n'$ and control the rate of growth of the money stock through lump sum taxes or transfers such that p, the rate of inflation, would be zero. It is the supposed failure of the Authorities to pay the steady state rate of return on money balances and not necessarily an 'inflation tax' which leads to the nonoptimality of the arrangements. The Authorities, by the lump sum rule, might ensure that inflation was zero but might not pay any interest on money balances. The monetary arrangements would continue to exhibit non-optimality even if there were no inflation.

If the Monetary Authorities have the capacity to affect the real capital and 'real' money balances of the economy which will be held in the steady state – if supernonneutrality exists – then they have the capacity to bring about optimal Monetary Arrangements. They have, moreover, the capacity to determine not just the steady state outcome to which the economy is heading but as well the particular Temporary Equilibrium path to that outcome.

If the Authorities pay the steady state rate of return as the real rate of interest on money balances, then the real money stock in steady state equilibrium will be such that $R_m = c_m(k, m) - \delta_M + i - p = \varrho + n + n'$, or $c_m(k, m) = \delta_M$. The price paid for the measureable services of fiat money balances will then equal the value of marginal product of such services and Paretian efficiency prevails.

WELDON'S QUESTIONS: INITIAL CONSIDERATIONS

Given the standard supernonneutrality result that Monetary Authorities, by paying the competitive rate of return on costless fiat money balances, generate Paretian efficient Monetary Arrangements in the steady state,[18] we are now able to dismiss some of Weldon's concerns. Alteration of the Monetary rule clearly has effects on the capital and 'real' balance intensities but they are captured by our admittedly crude standard general equilibrium results so that private valuations of the welfare gains associated with the optimum money supply policy rule are not rendered incalculable, as Weldon suggested, by the interaction of money and the monetary technology.[19] If we introduce different agents so that the relative distribution of capital and real money balances will differ among them, we may still be able to calculate steady state individual demand functions for the services of real money balances across the different individuals. Other than the relative positions of the individuals changing from the nonoptimum to the optimum steady states, I cannot see why distributional considerations, multiple equilibria aside, make the welfare calculations here any more suspect than is usual in economics.[20]

Weldon's fundamental objection – the publicness of money – has yet to be addressed. In the neoclassical monetary growth theory, there is simply no justification for the existence of the Monetary Authorities. The literature suggests that the Authorities will not follow the optimum monetary supply rules because they will try to impose inflation taxes,[21] or that they will succumb to the temptation of trying to do 'real' things such as reduce the level of unemployment and will therefore impose welfare losses associated with inflation on the economy.[22] The Monetary Authorities should be constrained to follow optimum money supply rules since there would seem to be no other role for them to perform. It is also argued that, with *laissez-faire* banking, the rate of interest being earned on bank monies would be the competitive real rate of return and therefore the optimality of monetary arrangements would be arrived at by free banking systems. Central Banks or Monetary Authorities are, therefore, so many fifth wheels whose only real role would appear to be to impose welfare losses on the community.

It is the principal characteristic of almost all of this literature, as was the characteristic of the neoclassical monetary growth model, that stability is assumed! Yet Weldon, Laidler and Howitt observe that any individual's demand to hold money balances in order to obtain the services of money balances is predicated on the assumption that other individuals will be holding and using the services of money balances.[23] The greater the holdings of money balances by other individuals the greater, apparently, is the productivity of one's own money balances. I am, however, unable to see why such optimum holdings of money balances would not be brought about by a competitive banking system.[24] The 'network' externality, the proposition that the marginal physical product of one individual's 'real' money balances, is affected by the extent of the use of money balances by others, could be, I should argue, appropriately taken into account by competitive producers of the services of 'real' money balances. Competitive producers of bank notes, for instance, accepted each other's notes at par.[25] *The externality, the publicness of Weldon's money, must be sought elsewhere. I believe it is to be found in the problem of the stability in the 'real' value of money.* In this chapter, I shall focus on the problem of the stability in the general price level, given the nominal money supply, rather than instability in the nominal money supply (for example, the phenomena of bank runs), given the price level. In the literature there are arguments that, under *laissez-faire* banking, stability in the price level would follow if there was convertibility[26] or, more radically, that the question of the price level would simply not arise.[27] What if, however, the problem of instability in the price level in a world of costless fiat money is a matter of concern not to be just assumed away?

No assumption is made that the economy is inherently unstable or stable; rather, the assumption is made that the economy *may* be unstable so that a role for discretionary policy and therefore the public good nature of the service of the Authorities *may* be developed. By instability I do not mean the economy is globally unstable such that, regardless of the initial conditions, the economy is off into ever accelerating upward spiralling prices (hyperinflation) or ever accelerating downward spiralling prices (hyperdeflation). Rather I shall mean that there are some particular initial conditions from which the economy will tend to its steady state while from all other initial conditions the economy will exhibit hyperinflations or deflations. I shall investigate the conditions under which the Authorities can play a role in determining initial conditions which ensure stability, the real consequences, that is, of the problem of saddlepoint instability.

SADDLEPOINT INSTABILITY

I shall ignore instability in the sense of ever accelerating changes in price levels arising because Authorities impose higher and higher 'inflation' taxes[28] or because individuals form their expectations myopically.

Consider the monetary technology. The returns to scale assumption employed so far is contained in slopes given the $\dot{k} = 0$ and $\dot{m} = 0$ schedules in Figures 6.1 and 6.2. Those slopes imply that

$$\frac{c_{kk}}{c_{km}} > \frac{c_{mk}}{c_{mm}} > 0$$

or that the technology, while exhibiting constant returns to scale in labour, capital and real balances, will exhibit decreasing returns to scale in terms of Harrod-augmented capital and real money balances.

The underlying technology might exhibit non-constant returns to scale. In such a case, it is possible for the slopes of the $\dot{k} = 0$ and $\dot{m} = 0$ schedules to be reversed, as in Figure 6.3. The consequences for the stability of the economy and monetary policy are most interesting.

In Figure 6.3, consider an initial capital stock k_0. Given the expectations of the individuals with respect to the real rate of interest on money, which is determined by the Authorities, there will exist a price level, P_{01}, such that real money balances will be m_{01} so that the rate of return to capital will equal $\varrho + n + n'$, so that there will be no additional accumulation of capital. On the other hand, there is a *higher* price level, P^{02}, such that real money balances will be m^{02} so that the real rate of return on money balances, including the real rate of interest paid by the Authorities, will equal the steady state rate of return and there will be no further accumulation of real money balances. As the price level is moved higher from P_{01} to P^{02}, real money balances are made smaller so that the real rate of return to capital is made lower. There exists a temporary equilibrium price level, P_0, such that real money balances are m_0 and real rates of return to capital and money balances are equalised. The equalised rates of return are, however, at a level which is below the steady state equilibrium level and real money balance and capital *decumulations* are set in motion. With the next sequence of capital at k_1, as in Figure 6.3, the new temporary equilibrium price level must be higher at P_1 such that real money balances will m_1. The economy is on a path of

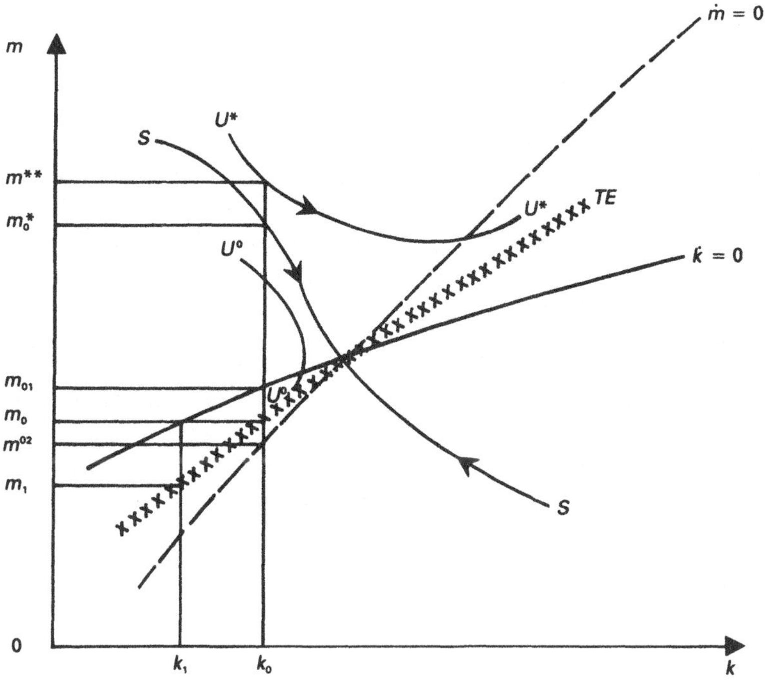

Figure 6.3

decumulation with higher and higher price levels and is further and further away from the steady state.

Inspect Figure 6.3 even more carefully. When the price level was P_{01}, people were content with their holdings of capital but because the rate of return to real money balances was below that being earned on capital they would be trying to get rid of real balances, which is what prevented P_0 from being a temporary equilibrium price level and resulted in the price level rising as people tried to shift out of holding money balances and to consume more. What would happen if, in fact, the price level were even lower than P_{01}, so that real money balances, given k_0, were even greater? Persons would be even more desirous of shifting out of money balances since the rate of return on money balances would be even lower, but they would be desirous of accumulating more capital since the rate of return on capital would now be above the steady state rate of return. If such a price level could be made to exist then some accumulation of capital would take place while some decumulation of real money balances would occur as the price level moved higher. The economy would quickly return, however, to its unstable path, as the curve labelled U^0U^0 illustrates. The temporary equilibrium locus labelled *TE* in Figure 6.3, unless there is some other reason so far unspecified, will attract all price levels to it and will lead to the problem of instability.[29] There will exist a lower price level, P_{0*}, however, such that the economy will have real money balances m_{0*}, so that capital accumulation and real money balance decumulation will take place along the 'stable arm' path labelled *SS* in Figure 6.3. There could exist a sequence of price levels starting off with P_{0*}, getting higher and higher such that the process of capital accumulation and real money decumulation leads the economy to the steady state. If somehow the price P_{0*} could be brought about, the economy could exhibit stability rather than instability. Notice however that if an even lower price level, P_{0**}, had somehow been brought about so that the economy had initial real money balances of m_{**}, as labelled in Figure 6.3, the process of capital accumulation and real money balance decumulation would revert to real capital and real money balance accumulation with the initial rise in the price level being replaced by ever lower price levels occurring in an unstable way. The path of the economy in this case is illustrated by the curve U^*U^*. The special temporary equilibrium price level, P_{0*}, is unique. Any higher price level leads the economy to follow a path eventually entailing ever higher and higher price levels. Any price level set lower leads to ever lower and lower price levels. The important point is clear. Given some initial capital stock there does exist, however, a special temporary equilibrium price level which ensures the economy may track its way to the steady state equilibrium. There is, therefore, a sequence of temporary equilibrium price levels which ensures stability and prevents the economy from exploding into ever higher or ever lower price levels and ever lower or ever higher amounts of capital and real money balances.

The price level which will hold in the initial temporary equilibrium is, as we have seen, not independent of the monetary rule the Authorities are following. Should the individuals believe the Authorities will adhere to a rule which entails a rate of interest less than the steady state rate, then, if the initial k is less than the steady state k_s, the history of the economy will entail a higher sequence of temporary equilibrium price levels than otherwise. Suppose therefore that the Authorities have set the optimum money supply rule and the individuals form their expectations about the rates of change of prices in a rational rather than myopic way. The problem is that under the assumption that monetary technologies exhibit non-constant returns to scale the problem of saddlepoint instability may hold. What can be done? Does a role for discretionary policy by the Authorities remerge?

Suppose the Authorities are aware of the instability problem. In the situation just described, the Authorities can announce that, either immediately or at some time in the future, the real rate of interest on fiat money will be increased in an once-over way. The once-over or discretionary increase in the real rate of interest on money, it will be appreciated, must be quite distinct from the rule with respect to the real rate of interest. Consider now the temporary portfolio equilibrium. The price level, P_0, which resulted in the portfolio equilibrium which led to instability will no longer be the temporary equilibrium price level because, given that individuals believe that the Authorities will be successful in raising the real rate of return on money immediately or in the future in a discretionary way, the expected rate of return on money balances will be greater. Individuals would seek to hold more money. The temporary equilibrium price level will be lower at P_{0^*} such that the economy, initially at least, is on a stable path to the steady state equilibrium as dictated by the optimum money supply policy rule. The Authorities have assured stability, however, by superimposing on the rule an element of discretionary policy.

The basic problem which the Authorities confront is that, given the initial stock of capital and the expectations of the individuals with respect to the real rate of interest on money as determined by the Authorites seeking to implement a monetary rule, the temporary equilibrium price level which brings about portfolio equilibrium does so at the cost of causing the real rates of return to be below the steady state level and the economy begins a process of capital and real money balance decumulation manifested in the form of ever higher and higher price levels. The very existence of Authorities, however, would belie such a scenario. The problem is that the temporary equilibrium price level involved rates of return which caused individuals to attempt to get out of *stocks* of goods, and real money balances which led, as the individuals pursued higher current consumption, to the sequence of ever rising prices. If individuals could be persuaded by the Authorities, however, that their views about the rates of return on money were ill-founded and that the Authorities will offer either immediately or in the future a once-over higher real rate of interest on money, then it is the essence of the existence of saddlepoint equilibrium analysis under rational expectations that individuals will believe in effect that the Authorities will so act in a discretionary way to ensure monetary stability.

The essential argument is that if the Monetary Authorities should continue to pursue a rule, then the system would exhibit instability. However, should individuals believe that the Authorities will act with discretion to pursue stability, their confidence in the Authorities will enhance the possibility of stability.

One cannot say that stability will be ensured. One sees this by noting that the Authorities must pursue a sequence of discretionary acts to ensure the possibility of stability. The requirement is very severe. For the Authorities to be successful in ensuring the economy ends at the optimal monetary steady state equilibrium, a sequence of discretionary real rates of interest on money balances must be paid, all rates higher than the rule rate but the difference will be diminishing as the economy approaches closer and closer to the optimal solution. When the economy reaches the optimal state then the real rate will be back down to the rule rate but not before! Should any of the fundamental conditions, such as the rule rate of interest on money, require to be changed, then, of course, the Authorities must start a new sequence of real rates of interest on fiat money balances in order to ensure that the economy tracks its way to the revised optimal steady state solution.

The point remains. The role of the Authorities is to preserve the confidence of the community in the stability of its monetary arrangements, that is, in the continued usefulness of a monetary technology. The Authorities may have to give up the optimum rule and follow a policy of discretion with respect to the real rate of interest on money. Given the usefulness and resource savings involved in a costless-to-produce and to-augment fiat money, the community will select Authorities not governed entirely by rules but required possibly to act with discretion. I have not argued that the economy *must* exhibit instability, rather I assume the economy *might* exhibit instability. If the Authorities and individuals are confident the economy is stable, then the Authorities must leave well enough alone. They must continue with the welfare-maximising optimal monetary policy of setting the real rate of interest on money balances equal to the steady state real rate of return. If, however, there is a doubt, if the Authorities believe the economic system might be characterised by instability, then, to preserve the confidence of the community in the monetary arrangements, the Authorities must act with discretion, they must change the real rate of interest on money, they must abandon the rule of the optimum real rate of interest over the sequence of the temporary equilibria.

WELDON'S BASIC QUESTION: CONCLUSION

If the provision of measureable monetary services such as clearing arrangements could be privately produced, there would be no rationale for the existence of Monetary Authorities. Their mere existence might well involve the community in welfare losses. Under *laissez-faire*, the monetary arrangements would be efficiently produced. Central Banks or Monetary Authorities would exist only to impose non-interest bearing reserves or inflation taxes on the community, either deliberately or because of the delusion that Authorities can determine natural rates of growth, employment and real rates of return. Welfare losses of the type calculable in the standard way would result. Monetary Authorities should be wound up or constrained to follow rules which ensure optimality or which mimic the private provision of monetary arrangements. If the problem of instability exists, however, and if the Monetary Authorities can make a contribution to the control of such instability, then the Monetary Authorities provide a service which enhances the monetary arrangements of the community. People hold and use the services of money because, lying behind such services, which could be privately produced, they know there are the services of the maintenance of monetary stability provided by the Monetary Authorities. It is these services which are the public good associated with fiat money. Not only that but, as we have shown, in order to provide such services, the Monetary Authorities must be constrained to abandon monetary rules since maintenance of those rules might exacerbate rather than reduce the instability of the monetary arrangements. Under such conditions, therefore, the standard calculations of the welfare losses associated with so-called inefficient monetary arrangements imposed upon the community by the Authorities fall to the ground and Weldon's basic point is reaffirmed. He (Weldon, 1973) argued that

> money exists only as a public good, and in its consequent form, real balances, is changed only by public action, that is, any exogenous action in the monetary parables must be conceived of as a publicly determined contrivance to change real balances.

With the understanding that it is the provision of stability in 'real' balances which constitutes the public good, I conclude that Weldon's basic point that the publicness of money renders standard calculations of the theoretical penalties of inflation suspect is fundamentally correct.

Notes and References

1. Professor J. C. Weldon supervised my McGill thesis, submitted in the summer of 1968 as 'On the Theory and Measurement of Capital' and subsequently published as *On Concepts of Capital and Technical Change* (Cambridge: Cambridge University Press, 1971). He ran faculty seminars on monetary theory which I attended while a visiting lecturer at McGill from 1972 to 1975. The seminars, led by Weldon with brilliance and wit, were a great delight, where the freest and sharpest exchange of scholarly views could occur without being accompanied by the vicissitudes which sometime mar academic life. This chapter is written, then, in memory of Jack Weldon, the scholarly guidance he provided, and the monetary seminars he led at McGill.

   I am grateful for comments on an earlier draft by Jack Galbraith, John Smithin and the editors of this volume.
2. His first work was published as 'Theoretical Penalties of Inflation', eds N. Swan and D. Wilton, *Inflation and the Canadian Experience* (Kingston: Industrial Relations Centre at Queen's University, 1971) [Weldon, 1971]. The second was 'On Money as a Public Good' (McGill University, mimeo 2 June 1973), a paper presented to 1973 meetings of the Canadian Economics Association [Weldon, 1973]. In the second paper, Professor Weldon allowed as how it was the third version of the theme, the first 'tentatively offered to a seminar at Carleton, in 1968 I think'. Alas, there is no trace of Weldon giving the seminar at Carleton nor of the paper he gave at the time.
3. Peter Howitt, 'Optimum Quantity of Money', *The New Palgrave Dictionary, III* (London: Mcmillan, 1987).
4. David Laidler, 'The Welfare Cost of Inflation in Neoclassical Theory – some unsettled problems' ed. E. Lundberg, *Inflation Theory and Anti-Inflation Policy* (Boulder, Colorado: Westview Press, 1977). Professor Laidler has returned recently to the problem. See D. Laidler, 'Taking Money Seriously', *Canadian Journal of Economics*, 21 (November 1988) pp. 687–713, and 'Monetarism, Microfoundations and the Theory of Monetary Policy', University of Western Ontario Working Paper 8807C.
5. See Weldon, 1973, pp. 12–13, especially footnote 24, and, in particular, his discussion with Professor Robert Mundell in the section on interest-yielding money in 'Inflation, Saving, and the Real Rate of Interest', in Mundell's *Monetary Theory* (Pacific Palisades: Goodyear Publishing Company, 1971).

6. See, however, Thomas K. Rymes, 'The Logical Impossibility of Optimum Money Supply Policies', Carleton Economic Papers 72–15; Jon Harkness, 'The Neutrality of Money in Neoclassical Growth Models', *The Canadian Journal of Economics*, 11 (November 1978) pp. 701–13; and John N. Smithin, 'A Note on the Welfare Cost of Perfectly Anticipated Inflation', *Bulletin of Economic Research*, 35 (May 1983) pp. 65–9.
7. See A. Asimakopulos and J. C. Weldon, 'A Synoptic View of Some Simple Models of Growth', *Canadian Journal of Economics and Political Science*, 31 (February 1965) pp. 52–79.
8. For an example of such a model, see R. Dornbusch and J. Frenkel, 'Inflation and Growth: Alternative Approaches', *Journal of Money, Credit and Banking*, 5 (February 1973) pp. 141–56. For an earlier version of part of the argument of this paper, see Thomas K. Rymes, 'Keynes and Stable Money', ed. O. Hamouda and J. Smithin, *Keynes and Public Policy After Fifty Years, II* (Aldershot, Hants: Edward Elgar, 1988), and for an extension of the argument to include banking see my 'The Theory and Measurement of the Nominal Output of Banks, Sectoral Rates of Savings and Wealth in the National Accounts', eds. Robert Lipsey and Helen Stone Tice, *The Measurement of Saving, Investment, and Wealth* (Chicago: University of Chicago University Press for the NBER, Inc., 1989).
9. The Bank of Canada reports (See Bank of Canada, Press Statement, 14 March 1986, contained in its *The Story of Canada's Currency* (Ottawa, 3rd ed 1981)) that one of its bank notes costs in the order of six cents to produce and handle. If one were talking about the production of a $1.00 bank note then a production cost of six cents is in no way negligible. If it is assumed, however, that the cost of a $10.00 bank note is also six cents then the cost of increasing the nominal stock of bank notes from one $1.00 note to one $10.00 note is zero. Thus, if the nominal stock of bank notes were increased in Canada by replacing one-dollar notes with ten-dollar notes, two-dollar notes with twenties, fives with fifties, and so forth, the reproduction cost of the stock of bank notes would remain unchanged while the nominal value of the stock of fiat currency would have been increased tenfold.
10. Such propositions were discussed by Marshall in his Essay on Money when he wrote (circa 1871) about an individual choosing between holding horses and money. See the Essay on Money in ed. J. K. Whitaker, *The Early Writings of Alfred Marshall 1867–1890, I* (London: Macmillan for The Royal Economic Society, 1975, p. 167) and were developed further by Keynes, under the influence of Sraffa, in 'The Essential Properties of Interest and Money', in his *The General Theory of Employment, Interest and Money, Collected Writings of John Maynard Keynes, VII* (London: Macmillan for the Royal Economic Society, 1973). See Carlo Panico, 'Sraffa on Money and Banking', *Cambridge Journal of Economics*, 12 (March 1988) pp. 7–28, for a discussion of Sraffa's influence on Keynes.
11. Lucas argues (S402) 'Technically, I think of economics as studying decision rules that are steady states of some adaptive process, decision rules that are found to work over a range of situations and hence are no

longer revised appreciably as more experience accumulates.' Robert E. Lucas, Jr., 'Adaptive Behaviour and Economic Theory', *Journal of Business*, 59 (October 1986) pp. S401–S426.

12. Consider a lower price level which will be associated with a larger stock of 'real' money balances and a lower gross marginal physical product of the services of such 'real' money balances. Since the stock of 'real' money balances is greater, with the stock of capital unchanged, the gross marginal physical product of the services of capital will be greater. The lower price level will be associated with a lower rate of return on money balances and a higher rate of return on capital. The lower price level cannot, then, be consistent with portfolio balance temporary equilibrium.
13. The lower price level, by seemingly making the representative individual wealthier, may result in a change in the supply of labour and flow of saving, so that the equality of the two rates of return brought about by the equilibrating price level must also take into account such effects.
14. If there are different individuals with different preferences, then it is possible that there will be multiple temporary equilibrium price levels.
15. If one doubled M, all that would occur would be a doubling of the price level, P, and, since $m = M_t/[P_2L_0e^{(n+n')t}]$, nothing 'real' would follow. This result is based on the temporary equilibrium line of reasoning set out above so that if history dictates a particular k and M, temporary equilibrium entails a P such that portfolio equilibrium holds. Should history dictate a different nominal stock of fiat money, the initial temporary equilibrium would entail a proportionately different price level.

    The Authorities, considering once-over changes in the nominal money supply, will not do so in an unexpected or surprising fashion. I assume that the community, having seen its Monetary Arrangements evolve to the point where the real resources involved in the production and maintaintence of those Arrangements are at a minimum, will not countenance Authorities, supposedly the caretakers of such Arrangements, behaving in unpredictable, random and idiosyncratic fashions nor will the Authorities, in the confines of this model, be deemed to be behaving in a manner inconsistent with the underlying monetary theory. I do not consider at this stage, then, the Authorities acting in a discretionary way.
16. For a discussion of the welfare losses associated with inflation, see Martin J. Bailey, 'Welfare Cost of Inflationary finance', *Journal of Political Economy*, 64 (April 1956) pp. 93–110; Milton Friedman, 'The Optimum Quantity of Money', in *The Optimum Quantity of Money and Other Essays* (Chicago: Aldine-Alberton, 1969); and three papers by Harry Johnson, 'Problems of Efficiency in Monetary Management', 'Inside Money, Outside Money, Income, Wealth and Welfare in Monetary Theory', and 'Is There an Optimum Money Supply?' in his *Further Essays in Monetary Economics* (London: George Allen & Unwin, 1972).
17. It is the difficulty of paying interest on circulating bank notes and coin that leads to the adoption of a deflation monetary growth rule as the device for 'paying' a real rate of interest on money balances. Interest can be paid on bank notes but it probably would be too costly to pay interest on circulating coin. See Harry G. Johnson, *Further Essays*.

It will be remembered that I am not discussing Weldon's point about the impossibility of such supernonneutral monetary policy.

18. The reader will note that I have *not* said that the payment of the steady state net rate of return in the form of the real rate of interest on money balances will be an optimum monetary policy all along the sequence of temporary equilibria.
19. See Bailey's comment in Weldon, 1971, in which he makes the point 'that one needs a general rather than a partial equilibrium demand' schedule for the services of real money balances to measure the Bailey trapezoids. In the simple general equilibrium model I set out, adoption of the optimum money supply rule leads to greater capital and real money balance intensities in the steady state. One could introduce Sidrauski results so that only real money balances would be greater, or Tobin results so that, though total wealth would be greater, the greater real money balances would be accompanied by reduced capital intensity. Cambridge capital theoretic results might entail that, in the steady state with the optimum money supply policy in force, it could be that real capital intensities might be sufficiently lower so that overall wealth would also be lower, suggesting very damaging ambiguity with respect to the optimum rule. (See David Laidler, 'Notes for a Panel Discussion on the Relevance of the Work of the Stockholm School for Modern Economics', mimeo, n. d.) Laidler argues that adoption of the monetary rule alters the real rate of interest and relative prices setting in motion the whole problem of capital aggregation. It should be noted, however, that what is altered is the real rate of interest on money balances and *not* the steady state real rate of return to capital. It is changes in the monetary and capital intensities which take place owing to change in the real rate of interest on money balances which requires investigation. I have not explored the possibilities of 'perverse' changes in such intensities in this chapter.
20. See D. H. Robertson, 'Utility and All That', *Utility and All That and Other Essays* (London: George Allen & Unwin, 1952).
21. Some argue that the inflation tax is not necessarily nonoptimal. See E. Phelps, 'Inflation in the Theory of Public Finance', *Swedish Journal of Economics*, 75 (March 1973) pp. 67–82, and A. Drazen, 'The Optimal Rate of Inflation Revisited', *Journal of Monetary Economics*, 5 (1979) pp. 231–48.
22. See M. Feldstein, 'The Welfare Cost of Permanent Inflation and Optimal Short Run Economic Policy', *Journal of Political Economy*, 56 (August 1979) pp. 745–68; Finn E. Kydland and Edward C. Prescott, 'Rules Rather than Discretion: The Inconsistency of Optimal Plans', *Journal of Political Economy*, 85 (June 1977) pp. 473–91; R. J. Barro, 'Recent Developments in the Theory of Rules versus Discretion', *Economic Journal*, 96, Conference Papers 1986, pp. 23–37; and Nicholas Rowe, *Rules and Institutions* (Deddington, Oxford: Philip Allan, 1989).
23. In an addendum to his 1971 paper, Weldon refers (p. 163) to a remark by Professor Kaliski of Queen's University that a 'private valuation of an extra 'phone misses the improved worth of all existing phones', a point Weldon subsequently reiterated (Weldon, 1973; p. 22) and to which

Laidler refers (Laidler, 1977, p. 333, and Laidler, 1988 and 1988a). The analogy between the service of a telephone and a bank deposit is apparently the reason for the externality associated with money, over and above that associated with the externality discussed by Friedman (Friedman, 1969) in discussing there the difference between the private and social marginal cost of acquiring extra 'real' money balances.

24. In the text, for instance, it was alleged that the Monetary Authorities could provide a clearing system more efficiently than could be privately provided. No rationale for the assumption was given. Indeed, the assumption is much questioned in the literature. See, for example, Richard H. Timberlake, Jr., *The Origins of Central Banking in the United States* (Cambridge, Mass.: Harvard University Press, 1978), and 'The Central Banking Role of Clearinghouse Associations', *Journal of Money, Credit and Banking*, 16 (February 1984) pp. 1–15.
25. See George Selgin, *The Theory of Free Banking*: Money supply under competitive note issue (Totowa, N. J., USA: Rowan Littlefield, 1988).
26. See Selgin, *ibid.*
27. See E. Fama, 'Financial Intermediation and Price Level Control', *Journal of Monetary Economics*, 12 (July 1983) pp. 1–28.
28. See Harry G. Johnson, 'A Note on the Dishonest Government and the Inflation Tax', *Journal of Monetary Economics*, 3 (July 1977) pp. 375–77.
29. If one assumes an initial capital stock which exceeds the steady state level, then the reader can understand Figure 6.3 by tracing out a process of ever lower prices and unstable capital and real money balance accumulation. One starts the analysis by showing that the initial temporary equilibrium price level entails that the equal rates of return to capital and real money balances exceed the steady rate of return.

7 The Role of Information in Trade Theory[1]

Murray C. Kemp and Shigemi Yabuuchi

1 INTRODUCTION

In the conventional theory of international trade it is assumed that, world-wide, technical information available to one producer is freely and completely available to every other actual or potential producer; this is the assumption of *open access*. Evidently the assumption lies at one extreme of a continuum of possibilities. At the other extreme, world-wide, technical information is available to only one producer in each industry; this is the assumption of *closed access*.

When combined with the assumption of constant returns to scale, open access implies a perfectly competitive relationship of producers, whereas closed access implies a strategic relationship, at least in commodity markets. Thus market structure is highly sensitive to a change of assumption about the availability of information. One wonders, then, how robust the principal propositions of conventional theory are to such a change.

In the present chapter we examine the robustness of the familiar Stolper–Samuelson and Rybczynski theorems which form the core of modern international economic theory. Both theorems relate to a single national economy in which two goods are non-jointly produced by two primary factors of production under conditions of constant returns to scale. According to the Stolper–Samuelson theorem, any sufficiently small increase in the relative price of the ith commodity ($i = 1$ or 2) raises the equilibrium real reward of the factor employed relatively intensively in the ith industry and depresses the equilibrium real reward of the other factor; and, according to the Rybczynski theorem, any sufficiently small increase in the endowment of the jth factor ($j = 1$ or 2) raises the output of the industry which is relatively intensive in its use of the jth factor and depresses the output of the other industry. It is shown that each theorem survives a change from open to closed access, not exactly but in slightly modified form. This suggests that, in general, the theorems are robust to changes of assumption about the availability of technical information.

We are not the first to have looked into these questions. The pioneers were Melvin and Warne (1973) and Batra (1972, 1973). However, Melvin and Warne did not consider the Rybczynski theorem and contented themselves with the negative remark that 'the Stolper–Samuelson results cannot be proved in a monopoly situation' (Melvin and Warne, 1973, p. 132), while Batra relied on the special *CES* utility function in arguing for the continued validity of both theorems.

2 THE MODEL

Two countries (the home and the foreign) trade two consumption goods, each produced under conditions of constant returns to scale with the aid of two primary factors of production. In each industry there is a single firm. Following Stolper, Samuelson and Rybczynski, it is assumed that each firm produces in both countries.

Let x_i be the home output of the ith commodity, v_j the home endowment of the jth factor, and w_j the home reward of the jth factor; and let asterisks indicate variables of the foreign country. Then the ith unit-cost functions of the home and foreign countries may be written $c^i(w_1, w_2)$ and $c^i(w_1^*, w_2^*)$, respectively.

The same homothetic preferences prevail everywhere. Hence the marginal revenue m_i derived from sales of the ith commodity depends only on the *ratio* of the aggregate amounts consumed and produced of the two commodities. Thus if d_i is the amount of the ith commodity consumed at home, then

$$m_i = m^i \left[\frac{d_1 + d_1^*}{d_2 + d_2^*}\right] = m^i \left[\frac{x_1 + x_1^*}{x_2 + x_2^*}\right]$$

It is assumed that each producer behaves competitively in the factor markets. The assumption is traditional. It has been defended by Melvin and Warne (1973, p. 119) as an implication of multi-plant production, with each plant hiring independently, and as an implication of the identification of the two firms as marketing boards; by Batra (1973, p. 286) as an implication of unionisation of the factor markets; and by Helpman (1984, p. 350) on the ground that each of the two commodities may be viewed as a proxy for many commodities. Nevertheless, it would be better to dispense with it.

Each Cournot producer equates marginal revenue to marginal cost at home and abroad:

$$m^i \left[\frac{x_1 + x_1^*}{x_2 + x_2^*}\right] = c^i(w_1, w_2) = c^i(w_1^*, w_2^*) \tag{7.1}$$

The equilibrium system is completed by adding the conditions of factor-market balance:

$$\sum_i a_{ji}(w_1, w_2)x_i = v_j \tag{7.2}$$

$$\sum_i a_{ji}(w_1^*, w_2^*)x_i^* = v_j^* \tag{7.3}$$

where a_{ji} (w_1, w_2) is the cost-minimising input of the jth factor per unit of the ith output. The system (7.1)–(7.3) contains eight equations in the four outputs and four factor rentals. It will be assumed that it has a unique and positive solution.[2]

From (7.1) we see at once that, in the absence of factor-intensity reversal, factor rewards must be everywhere the same.[3]

3 THE STOLPER–SAMUELSON THEOREM

In system (7.1)–(7.3), the allocation and pricing of factors of production are determined by the ratio of marginal revenues, not by the ratio of commodity prices. It is not to be expected, then, that the Stolper–Samuelson conclusions will survive the switch from public to private information. In this section we formulate additional restrictions which ensure that the Stolper–Samuelson conclusions do survive.

Let p_i be the price of the ith commodity in terms of any unit of account, and let $p \equiv p_2/p_1$ be the price of the second commodity in terms of the first. It is well known that

$$m_i = p_i\,(1 - 1/\eta_i)$$

where

$$\eta_i(p) \equiv -\frac{p_i}{d_i + d_i^*}\frac{\partial(d_i + d_i^*)}{\partial p_i}$$

is the partial elasticity of demand for the *i*th commodity and, from the homotheticity of preferences, depends on relative prices only. Defining

$$\pi_i \equiv p_i/\eta_i$$

therefore, we can write

$$m_i = p_i - \pi_i \tag{7.4}$$

or, making use of (7.1),

$$\sum_i a_{ji}(w_1, w_2) = p_i - \pi_i \tag{7.5}$$

Differentiating (7.5), we find that

$$\sum_j \theta_{ji}\,\hat{w}_j = \hat{p}_j\,(1 - \theta_{\pi i}) + \theta_{\pi i}\hat{\eta}_i \tag{7.6}$$

where $\theta_{ji} \equiv w_j\, a_{ji}(w_1, w_2)/p_i$, $\theta_{\pi i} \equiv \pi_i/p_i$ and, for example, $\hat{w}_j \equiv dw_j/w_j$. Moreover,

$$\hat{\eta}_i \equiv \varepsilon_i \hat{p} \tag{7.7}$$

where $\varepsilon_i \equiv (p/\eta_i)\,(d\eta_i/dp)$. Finally, from (7.6) and (7.7),

$$\begin{bmatrix}\theta_{11} & \theta_{21}\\ \theta_{12} & \theta_{22}\end{bmatrix}\begin{bmatrix}\hat{w}_1\\ \hat{w}_2\end{bmatrix} = \begin{bmatrix}(1-\theta_{\pi 1}) - \theta_{\pi 1}\varepsilon_1 & \theta_{\pi 1}\varepsilon_1\\ -\theta_{\pi 2}\varepsilon_2 & (1-\theta_{\pi 2}) + \theta_{\pi 2}\varepsilon_2\end{bmatrix}\begin{bmatrix}\hat{p}_1\\ \hat{p}_2\end{bmatrix}$$

Let the lefthand square matrix be denoted by Θ, the righthand square matrix by Ω. Then it can be verified that if $\varepsilon_1 \leqslant 0$ and $\varepsilon_2 \geqslant 0$ then either $\Theta^{-1}\Omega$ or $-\Theta^{-1}\Omega$ is a Minkowski matrix with unit row sums, implying that either

$$\hat{w}_2 > \hat{p}_2 > \hat{p}_1 > \hat{w}_1$$

or

$$\hat{w}_2 < \hat{p}_2 < \hat{p}_1 < \hat{w}_1$$

respectively.

Proposition 1: If $\varepsilon_1 \leqslant 0$ and $\varepsilon_2 \geqslant 0$, the Stolper–Samuelson conclusions survive.

It is known that if preferences can be represented by a *CES* utility function then $\varepsilon_1 < 0$ and $\varepsilon_2 > 0$; see Melvin and Warne (1973, Lemma 2). Proposition 1 reveals that the *CES* assumption is unnecessarily strong.

4 THE RYBCZYNSKI THEOREM

Differentiating (7.2) and (7.3), and recalling that factor rewards are everywhere the same, we find that

$$\begin{aligned} \lambda_{11}\hat{x}_1 + \lambda_{12}\hat{x}_2 &= \hat{v}_1 + \beta_1 (\hat{w}_1 - \hat{w}_2) \\ \lambda_{21}\hat{x}_1 + \lambda_{22}\hat{x}_2 &= \hat{v}_2 - \beta_2 (\hat{w}_1 - \hat{w}_2) \end{aligned} \tag{7.9}$$

and

$$\begin{aligned} \lambda_{11}\hat{x}_1^* + \lambda_{12}\hat{x}_2^* &= \hat{v}_1^* + \beta_1 (\hat{w}_1 - \hat{w}_2) \\ \lambda_{21}\hat{x}_1^* + \lambda_{22}\hat{x}_2^* &= \hat{v}_2^* - \beta_2 (\hat{w}_1 - \hat{w}_2) \end{aligned} \tag{7.10}$$

where λ_{ji} is the proportion of the jth factor endowment employed by the ith industry,

$$\beta_1 \equiv \frac{\lambda_{11}\theta_{21}\sigma_1}{1 - \theta_{\pi 1}} + \frac{\lambda_{12}\theta_{22}\sigma_2}{1 - \theta_{\pi 2}}$$

$$\beta_2 \equiv \frac{\lambda_{21}\theta_{11}\sigma_1}{1 - \theta_{\pi 1}} + \frac{\lambda_{22}\theta_{12}\sigma_2}{1 - \theta_{\pi 2}}$$

and

$$\sigma_i \equiv (\hat{a}_{2i} - \hat{a}_{1i})/(\hat{w}_1 - \hat{w}_2)$$

is the elasticity of factor substitution in the ith industry. From (7.9) and (7.10), by subtraction,

$$\lambda_{11}(\hat{x}_1 - \hat{x}_1^*) + \lambda_{12}(\hat{x}_2 - \hat{x}_2^*) = \hat{v}_1 - \hat{v}_1^*$$

$$\lambda_{21}(\hat{x}_1 - \hat{x}_1^*) + \lambda_{22}(\hat{x}_2 - \hat{x}_2^*) = \hat{v}_2 - \hat{v}_2^*$$

Thus we arrive at a modified Rybczynski proposition.

Proposition 2: $\hat{x}_1 - \hat{x}_1^* \gtrless \hat{v}_1 - \hat{v}_1^* \gtrless \hat{v}_2 - \hat{v}_2^* \gtrless \hat{x}_2 - \hat{x}_2^*$

$$\text{if and only if } |\lambda| \equiv \begin{vmatrix} \lambda_{11} & \lambda_{12} \\ \lambda_{21} & \lambda_{22} \end{vmatrix} \gtrless 0$$

Of course, sign $|\lambda|$ = sign $|\Theta|$.

5 FINAL REMARK

We have shown that the Stolper–Samuelson and Rybczynski theorems, which form the central core of the modern theory of international trade, survive in only slightly modified form when technical information is taken to be private rather than public. In Sections 3 and 4 we adopted the extreme assumption that technical information is available to just one firm in each industry. However, it is easy to verify that the modified theorems are valid whatever the (fixed) number of firms in each industry. In particular, they are valid when there is just one firm in each industry in each country. What happens when in each industry there are several firms with firm-specific information is a topic worthy of further examination.

APPENDIX Sketch of the Proof of the Existence and Uniqueness of a Positive Equilibrium

World-wide, there is one producer in each industry. Otherwise, the assumptions are those of Melvin and Warne (1973). All undefined notation is from Sections 2 and 3.

From (7.2) and (7.3),

$$\sum a_{ji} (x_i + x_i^*) = v_j + v_j^* \tag{7.i}$$

so that, differentiating,

$$\Lambda_{11}(x_1 + x_1^*) + \Lambda_{12}(x_2 + x_2^*) = B_1(\hat{w}_1 - \hat{w}_2) \qquad (7.\text{ii})$$
$$\Lambda_{21}(x_1 + x_1^*) + \Lambda_{22}(x_2 + x_2^*) = B_2(\hat{w}_1 - \hat{w}_2)$$

where

$$\Lambda_{ji} \equiv a_{ji}(x_i + x_i^*)/(v_i + v_i^*)$$

and

$$B_1 \equiv \frac{\Lambda_{11}\theta_{21}\sigma_1}{1-\theta_{\pi 1}} + \frac{\Lambda_{12}\theta_{22}\sigma_2}{1-\theta_{\pi 2}}$$

$$B_2 \equiv \frac{\Lambda_{21}\theta_{11}\sigma_1}{1-\theta_{\pi 1}} + \frac{\Lambda_{22}\theta_{12}\sigma_2}{1-\theta_{\pi 2}}$$

From (7.ii),

$$(x_1 + x_1^*) - (x_2 + x_2^*) = (B_1 + B_2)(\hat{w}_1 - \hat{w}_2)/|\Lambda| \qquad (7.\text{iii})$$

where

$$|\Lambda| \equiv \begin{vmatrix} \Lambda_{11} & \Lambda_{12} \\ \Lambda_{21} & \Lambda_{22} \end{vmatrix}$$

On the other hand, the uniform homotheticity of preferences implies that

$$(d_1 + d_1^*) - (d_2 + d_2^*) \equiv \sigma_D \hat{p}^c \qquad (7.\text{iv})$$

where $\hat{p}^c$ is the commodity price ratio facing consumers and σ_D is a positive constant. Equations (7.iii) and (7.iv) yield

$$\sigma_D \hat{p}^c = \frac{B_1 + B_2}{|\Lambda|}(\hat{w}_1 - \hat{w}_2) \qquad (7.\text{v})$$

From (7.6) and (7.7), the relationship between the price ratio facing producers p^P and the ratio of factor rewards is described by

$$-\frac{A}{|\Theta|}\hat{p}^P = \hat{w}_1 - \hat{w}_2$$

where $|\Theta|$ is the determinant of Θ and

$$A \equiv (\theta_{11} + \theta_{21})\theta_{\pi 2}\varepsilon_2 - (\theta_{12} + \theta_{22})\theta_{\pi 1}\varepsilon_1 + (1 - \theta_{\pi 1})(1 - \theta_{\pi 2})$$

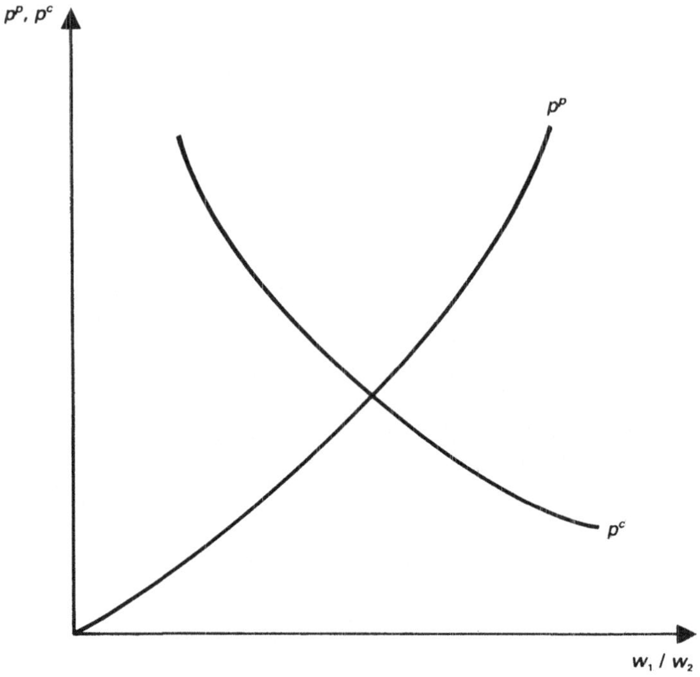

Figure 7.1

Since the utility function is *CES*, $\varepsilon_1 < 0$ and $\varepsilon_2 > 0$; hence $A > 0$.

Finally, a comparison of (7.5) and (7.6) reveals that there is a unique equilibrium and that the equilibrium is positive. Figure 7.1 illustrates for the case in which $|\Theta| > 0$.

Notes

1. In June 1951 I arrived in Montreal to take up my first real job, as assistant professor at McGill. Jack Weldon was already there, having just completed the first year of a similar appointment. During the ensuing summer there developed a friendship which was to last for the next thirty-five years. It is with the greatest pleasure that I respond to the invitation of his colleagues to contribute to a memorial volume.

   Jack Weldon was a first-rate creative theorist; recall that his article on Arrow's impossibility theorem (1952) was written very early and essentially alone. However he was also a probing critic with a magnificent eye for hidden assumptions and unexplored possibilities. The topic of my chapter with Shigemi Yabuuchi would have appealed to him. (M. C. K.)

2. Melvin and Warne (1973) have shown that there is a unique and positive solution if the utility function is of the CES type and if there is a single producer in each industry *in each country*. Their proof can be adapted to yield the same conclusion when, world-wide, there is a single producer in each industry. A sketch of such a proof may be found in the appendix.
3. The system (7.1)–(7.3) was studied by Helpman (1984). Helpman noted that the model implies the international equalisation of factor rewards and that if the ownership of firms is proportional to consumption then the pattern of trade accords with the Heckscher–Ohlin predictions. However he did not consider the Stolper–Samuelson and Rybczynski questions.

References

Batra, R. N. (1972) 'Monopoly Theory in General Equilibrium and the Two-Sector Model of Economic Growth', *Journal of Economic Theory*, 4, pp. 355–71.

Batra, R. N. (1973) *Studies in the Pure Theory of International Trade* (New York: St Martin's Press).

Helpman, E. (1984) 'Increasing Returns, Imperfect Markets, and Trade Theory', in R. W. Jones and P. B. Kenen (eds), *Handbook of International Economics*, vol. 1 (Amsterdam: North-Holland) pp. 325–65.

Melvin, J. R. and R. D. Warne (1973) 'Monopoly and the Theory of International Trade', *Journal of International Economics*, 3, pp. 117–34.

Weldon, J. C. (1952) 'Problem of Social Welfare Functions', *Canadian Journal of Economics and Political Science*, 18, pp. 452–63.

8 Metzler's Tariff Paradox and the Transfer Problem[1]

John S. Chipman

1 INTRODUCTION

It has been known since the time of Torrens (1848) and Mill (1848) that a country, if it can be considered as acting as a rational unit, can gain by imposition of a tariff (provided the foreign country does not retaliate), since a tariff will improve its terms of trade. If the improvement in the terms of trade is sufficiently great, it is possible that the domestic price of importables, which includes the tariff, will still be lower than formerly relative to the export price, in which case the tariff will not be protective. If, say, labour is the factor used relatively intensively in the import-competing industry and capital in the export industry, then by the Stolper–Samuelson theorem (cf. Stolper and Samuelson, 1941) the tariff will reduce real wages instead of raising them. This is the paradox studied by Metzler (1949a, 1949b).

The condition obtained by Metzler (1949a, 1949b) for this result, assuming the initial tariff rate to be zero, is that the sum of the tariff-imposing country's marginal propensity to consume the importable and the foreign country's elasticity of demand for imports be less than unity.[2] By decomposing the foreign country's elasticity of demand for imports into an income term and a substitution elasticity, an equivalent necessary and sufficient condition is easily obtained: that the sum of two terms be negative, one of which is the foreign country's (intrinsically positive) compensated trade elasticity of demand for its exportable, and the other of which is the difference between the home and foreign countries' marginal propensities to consume this same good. Thus, Metzler's paradox can occur only if the tariff-imposing country's marginal propensity to consume its importable is less than the foreign country's. But this is Samuelson's condition for a transfer to the tariff-imposing country to improve its terms of trade – the so-called 'orthodox' presumption (cf. Samuelson, 1952).

The result can be given a very simple interpretation in terms of the transfer problem, given the usual assumption that the government distributes tariff or tax revenues to consumers and that preferences in each country can be aggregated. Suppose the imposition of the tariff is carried out in two stages: in Stage 1, the home country imposes the tariff and remits the proceeds to the foreign country; in Stage 2, the foreign country transfers them back to the home country. (A precise analysis of this decomposition is presented at the end of Section 3.) Stage 1 is equivalent to the imposition by the foreign country of an export tax (analogously to a 'voluntary export restraint'); by Lerner's symmetry theorem (Lerner, 1936; see also Bhagwati and Johnson, 1961), this improves its terms of trade and worsens that of the home country. The tariff rate now being fixed, the transfer of tariff revenues back to the home country affects its internal price ratio of imports to exports in the same proportion as the external price ratio; for the Metzler paradox to occur, the transfer must therefore improve its terms of trade – by enough to compensate for the previous deterioration in Stage 1. A sufficient condition to rule out the Metzler 'paradox' is therefore that the transfer should have what Samuelson (1952) called the 'anti-orthodox' (paradoxical?) effect of worsening or leaving unchanged the receiving country's terms of trade. I leave it to others to decide whether this proposition should itself be termed 'paradoxical'.

An easy by-product of the result is that the so-called Marshall–Lerner stability condition (which is assumed to hold) is a consequence of the 'anti-orthodox' presumption.

Finally it is shown that, provided the two countries' export goods are non-inferior in terms of their respective inhabitants' preferences, a tariff levied by country 1 is superior (in the sense of 'potential welfare') from the point of view of country 1 to an equal export tax levied by country 2 – regardless of whether a transfer from country 2 to country 1 improves or worsens country 1's terms of trade. A similar method could be used to demonstrate the superiority of an import quota to a 'voluntary export restraint'.

2 ANALYTIC FORMULATION

Let there be two countries, each producing two commodities with the aid of two factors of production. Country 1 is initially exporting commodity 1 to and importing commodity 2 from country 2. Let consumption, production, trade (net import), and the price of commodity j in country k be denoted x_j^k, y_j^k, $z_j^k = x_j^k - y_j^k$, and p_j^k respectively, and let l_i^k be the endowment of factor i in country k. These are related by $z_j^1 + z_j^2 = 0$ $(j = 1, 2)$, $p_1^1 = p_1^2 = T_2 p_2^2$ where $T_2 \geqslant 1$ is the tariff factor and $T_2 - 1$ the ad valorem tariff rate (cf. Jones, 1969). Let country k's national-product function and Rybczynski function for commodity j be denoted

$$\Pi^k(p_1^k, p_2^k, l_1^k, l_2^k), \quad \hat{y}_j^k(p_1^k, p_2^k, l_1^k, l_2^k) \tag{8.1}$$

respectively, where $\hat{y}_j^k = \partial\Pi^k/\partial p_j^k$ (cf. Samuelson, 1953; Chipman, 1972, 1974).

Assuming consumer demand to be aggregable in each country, let the aggregate demand function for commodity j in country k be denoted

$$x_j^k = h_j^k(p_1^k, p_2^k, Y^k) \quad (j, k = 1, 2) \tag{8.2}$$

where Y^k is disposable national income in country k. These functions are homogeneous of degree 0 and are assumed to satisfy the budget-balance condition

$$\sum_{j=1}^{2} p_j^k h_j^k(p_1^k, p_2^k, Y^k) = Y^k \tag{8.3}$$

Country k's trade-demand function for commodity j is defined by

$$\begin{aligned} z_j^k &= \hat{h}_j^k(p_1^k, p_2^k, D^k; l_1^k, l_2^k) \qquad (8.4)\\ &= h_j^k(p_1^k, p_2^k, \Pi^k(p_1^k, p_2^k, l_1^k, l_2^k) + D^k) - \hat{y}_j^k(p_1^k, p_2^k, l_1^k, l_2^k) \end{aligned}$$

(cf. Chipman, 1979), where D^k is the deficit in country k's balance of payments on current account, when reckoned in its internal prices. These functions are homogeneous of degree 0 and satisfy the balance-of-payments condition

$$\sum_{j=1}^{2} p_j^k \hat{h}_j^k(p_1^k, p_2^k, D^k) = D^k \tag{8.5}$$

The Slutsky substitution terms of the trade-demand functions are defined by and equal to

$$\hat{s}_{ij}^k(p_1^k, p_2^k, D^k; l_1^k, l_2^k) = \frac{\partial \hat{h}_i^k}{\partial p_j^k} + \frac{\partial \hat{h}_i^k}{\partial D^k}\hat{h}_j^k = s_{ij}^k - t_{ij}^k < 0 \tag{8.6}$$

where $s_{ij}^k = \partial h_i^k / \partial p_j^k + (\partial h_i^k / \partial Y^k)\, h_j^k$ and $t_{ij}^k = \partial \hat{y}_i^k / \partial p_j$ respectively the Slutsky substitution terms for the demand function (8.2) and the transformation terms corresponding to the Rybczynski function (8.1). I shall denote the Slutsky–Hicks substitution elasticities of the trade-demand functions by

$$\hat{\sigma}_{ij}^k = \frac{p_j^k \, \hat{s}_{ij}^k}{z_i^k} \tag{8.7}$$

Since by convention country k exports commodity k, we have $\hat{\sigma}_{kk}^k > 0$ and $\hat{\sigma}_{jj}^k < 0$ for $j \neq k$.

Country k's marginal propensity to consume commodity j is defined as

$$m_j^k = p_j^k \frac{\partial h_j^k}{\partial Y^k} \quad (j, k = 1, 2) \tag{8.8}$$

Let ϱ denote the proportion of the tariff proceeds that accrue to country 1, and $1 - \varrho$ the proportion that accrue to country 2, where $0 \leqslant \varrho \leqslant 1$. Then the two countries' excess-demand (offer) functions for commodity j, expressed as functions of country 1's internal prices, are defined by (implicitly for $j = 2$)

$$\begin{aligned} \bar{z}_j^1(p_1^1, p_2^1, T_2, \varrho; l_1^1, l_2^1) &= \hat{h}_j^1\left(p_1^1, p_2^1, \varrho\left(1 - \frac{1}{T_2}\right) p_2^1 \bar{z}_2^1(p_1^1, p_2^1, T_2, \varrho; l_1^1, l_2^1)\right) \\ \bar{z}_j^2(p_1^1, p_2^1, T_2, \varrho; l_1^2, l_2^2) &= \hat{h}_j^2\left(p_1^1, \frac{p_2^1}{T_2}, -(1-\varrho)\left(1 - \frac{1}{T_2}\right) p_2^1 \bar{z}_2^2(p_1^1, p_2^1, T_2, \varrho; l_1^2, l_2^2)\right) \end{aligned} \tag{8.9}$$

provided (as I shall assume)

$$T_2 - \varrho(T_2 - 1)m_2^1 > 0,\ 1 + (1 - \varrho)(T_2 - 1)m_2^2 > 0 \tag{8.10}$$

– sufficient conditions for which are that $m_1^1 \geqslant 0$ and $m_2^2 \geqslant 0$, i.e., each country's export good is non-inferior. In terms of country 2's internal prices, we may likewise define the functions

$$\hat{z}_j^k(p_1^2, p_2^2, T_2, \varrho; l_1^k, l_2^k) = \bar{z}_j^k(p_1^2, T_2 p_2^2, T_2, \varrho; l_1^k, l_2^k) \quad (j = 1, 2) \tag{8.11}$$

When valued in terms of country 1's internal prices, country 1's current-account deficit (and country 2's current-account surplus) is equal to

$$D^1 = p_1^1 \tilde{z}_1^1 + p_1^2 \tilde{z}_2^1 = \varrho \left(1 - \frac{1}{T_2} \right) p_2^1 \tilde{z}_2^1 \gtreqless 0 \tag{8.12}$$

When valued in terms of country 2's internal prices, country 2's current-account deficit (and country 1's current-account surplus) is equal to

$$D^2 = p_1^2 \hat{z}_2^1 + p_2^2 \hat{z}_2^2 = -(1 - \varrho)\,(T_2 - 1)\, p_2^2 \hat{z}_2^2 \gtreqless 0 \tag{8.13}$$

Let us introduce the fictitious world accounting prices

$$\begin{aligned} p_1 = p_1^1 = p_1^2;\ p_2 &= \left[\frac{\varrho}{T_2} + 1 - \varrho \right] p_2^1 \\ &= [\varrho + (1 - \varrho)\, T_2]\, p_2^2 \end{aligned} \tag{8.14}$$

The bracketed factors are weighted averages of unity and the tariff factor or its reciprocal, the weights being the proportions of the tariff or tax proceeds accruing to the respective countries. Using these accounting prices as arguments we may define the corresponding offer functions

$$z_j^k(p_1, p_2, T_2, \varrho;\, l_1^k, l_2^k) = \tilde{z}_j^k \left(p_1^2, \frac{p_2}{\frac{\varrho}{T_2} + 1 - \varrho}, T_2, \varrho;\, l_1^k, l_2^k\right) \tag{8.15}$$

for $j, k = 1, 2$. We see that these are homogeneous of degree 0 in p_1, p_2 (as are the $\tilde{z}_j^k$ in and the p_1^1, p_2^1 and the $\hat{z}_j^k$ in the p_1^2, p_2^2) and satisfy the balanced-trade condition $\Sigma_{j=1}^2\, p_j z_j^k = 0$. Using these facts we derive the identities

$$\eta^k = -\frac{p_j}{z_j^k}\frac{\partial z_j^k}{\partial p_j} = \frac{p_k}{z_j^k}\frac{\partial z_j^k}{\partial p_k} = \frac{p_k}{z_k^k}\frac{\partial z_k^k}{\partial p_k} + 1 \quad (j \neq k,\ k = 1, 2) \tag{8.16}$$

where the first equality defines country k's Marshallian elasticity of demand for imports. Clearly also,

$$\frac{p_j}{z_j^k}\frac{\partial z_j^k}{\partial p_j} = \frac{p_j^1}{\tilde{z}_j^k}\frac{\partial \tilde{z}_j^k}{\partial p_j^1} = \frac{p_j^2}{\hat{z}_j^k}\frac{\partial \hat{z}_j^k}{\partial p_j^2} \quad (j, k = 1, 2) \tag{8.17}$$

Thus we find, making use of (8.17), (8.16), and (8.2)–(8.9), that the respective countries' elasticities of demand for imports are given by

$$\eta^1 = \frac{[\varrho + (1 - \varrho)T_2]m_2^1 - T_2\,\hat{\sigma}_{22}^1}{T_2 - \varrho(T_2 - 1)m_2^1}$$

$$\eta^2 = \frac{1 - m_2^2 + \hat{\sigma}_{22}^2}{1 + (1 - \varrho)\,(T_2 - 1)m_2^2} \tag{8.18}$$

3 THE MAIN RESULT

World equilibrium prices are determined by setting $\bar{z}_1^2 + \bar{z}_2^2 = 0$ in (8.9), since the corresponding condition $\bar{z}_1^1 + \bar{z}_2^1 = 0$ follows from the balance-of-payments condition (8.12). Commodity 1 will be taken as numeraire, and its price fixed at $p_1^1 = \bar{p}_1^1\ (= \bar{p}_1^2)$. The function

$$p_2^1 = \bar{p}_2^1(T_2, \varrho; p_1^1, l_1^1, l_2^1, l_1^2, l_2^2) \tag{8.19}$$

is defined implicitly by

$$\bar{z}_2^1(\bar{p}_1^1, \bar{p}_2^1, T_2, \varrho; l_1^1, l_2^1) + \bar{z}_2^2(\bar{p}_1^1, \bar{p}_2^1, T_2, \varrho; l_1^2, l_2^2) = 0 \tag{8.20}$$

Thus,

$$\frac{\partial \bar{p}_2^1}{\partial T_2} = -\frac{\dfrac{\partial \bar{z}_2^1}{\partial T_2} + \dfrac{\partial \bar{z}_2^2}{\partial T_2}}{\dfrac{\partial \bar{z}_2^1}{\partial p_2^1} + \dfrac{\partial \bar{z}_2^2}{\partial p_2^1}} \quad \text{and} \quad \frac{\partial \bar{p}_2^1}{\partial \varrho} = -\frac{\dfrac{\partial \bar{z}_2^1}{\partial \varrho} + \dfrac{\partial \bar{z}_2^2}{\partial \varrho}}{\dfrac{\partial \bar{z}_2^1}{\partial p_2^1} + \dfrac{\partial \bar{z}_2^2}{\partial p_2^1}} \tag{8.21}$$

From (8.16) and (8.17) we have

$$-\frac{p_2^1}{\bar{z}_2^1}\left[\frac{\partial \bar{z}_2^1}{\partial p_2^1} + \frac{\partial \bar{z}_2^2}{\partial p_2^2}\right] = -\frac{p_2^1}{\bar{z}_2^1}\,\frac{\partial \bar{z}_2^1}{\partial p_2^1} + \frac{p_2^1}{\bar{z}_2^2}\,\frac{\partial \bar{z}_2^2}{\partial p_2^1}$$

$$= \eta^1 + \eta^2 - 1 \tag{8.22}$$

The condition $\eta^1 + \eta^2 - 1 > 0$ is the well-known 'Marshall–Lerner' condition for dynamic stability, and it will be assumed to hold.

Denoting

$$m_2^{1\prime} = \frac{m_2^1}{T_2 - \varrho(T_2 - 1)\, m_2^1},\ m_2^{2\prime} = \frac{m_2^2}{1 + (1 - \varrho)\,(T_2 - 1)\, m_2^2} \tag{8.23}$$

and

$$\hat{\sigma}_{22}^{2\,\prime} = \frac{\hat{\sigma}_{22}^{1\,\prime}}{T_2 - \varrho(T_2 - 1)\, m_2^1},\ \hat{\sigma}_{22}^{2\,\prime} = \frac{\hat{\sigma}_{22}^{2\,\prime}}{1 + (1 - \varrho)\,(T_2 - 1)\, m_2^2} \tag{8.24}$$

we obtain from (8.9) the elasticities

$$\frac{T_2}{\bar{z}_2^1}\,\frac{\partial \bar{z}_2^1}{\partial T_2} = \varrho m_2^{1\prime},\ \frac{T_2}{\bar{z}_2^2}\,\frac{\partial \bar{z}_2^2}{\partial T_2} = \varrho m_2^{2\prime} - \hat{\sigma}_{22}^2 \tag{8.25}$$

and

$$\frac{1}{\bar{z}_2^1}\,\frac{\partial \bar{z}_2^1}{\partial \varrho} = (T_2 - 1) m_2^{1\prime},\ \frac{1}{\bar{z}_2^{2\prime}}\,\frac{\partial \bar{z}_2^2}{\partial \varrho} = (T_2 - 1)\, m_2^{2\prime} \tag{8.26}$$

Accordingly, from (8.21) we obtain, using (8.18),

$$\frac{T_2}{\bar{p}_2^1}\,\frac{\partial \bar{p}_2^1}{\partial T_2} = \frac{\varrho m_2^{1\prime} + (1 - \varrho) T_2\, m_2^{2\prime} + \eta^2 - 1}{\eta^1 + \eta^2 - 1} \tag{8.27a}$$

$$= \frac{\varrho\,(m_2^{1\prime} - m_2^{2\prime}) + \hat{\sigma}_{22}^{2\,\prime}}{\eta^1 + \eta^2 - 1} \tag{8.27b}$$

and

$$\frac{1}{\bar{p}_2^1}\,\frac{\partial \bar{p}_2^1}{\partial \varrho} = \frac{(T_2 - 1)\,(m_2^{1\prime} - m_2^{2\prime})}{\eta^1 + \eta^2 - 1} \tag{8.28}$$

The expression in (8.27a) furnishes a generalisation of Metzler's criterion for his paradox to occur, namely that the sum of a weighted average of the two countries' tariff-adjusted marginal propensities to consume country 1's importable (commodity 2), and country 2's elasticity of demand for imports of commodity 1, be less than unity. It reduces to Metzler's (1949a) criterion when $\varrho = T_2 = 1$. The expression in (8.27b), combined with (8.28), provides an alternative criterion in terms of the transfer problem. A transfer of the tariff revenues back to country 1, according to (8.28), lowers the domestic price of country 1's importable (commodity 2) if and only if $m_2^{1\prime} < m_2^{2\prime}$; this is a generalisation of Samuelson's condition for the 'orthodox presumption' to hold.

We may now derive the decomposition described in the Introduction to this chapter. Suppose country 1's tariff factor T_2 to be increased from 1 to T_2^1. Dropping the arguments following the semicolon in (8.19) and denoting $\tau_2 = \log T_2$ and $\bar{\pi}_2^1(\tau_2, \varrho) = \log \bar{p}_2^1(e^{\tau_2}, \varrho)$, and regarding the functions $m_2^{k\prime}$, $\hat{\sigma}_{22}^{k\prime}$, η^k as composed with (8.19) and depending upon τ_2 and ϱ, we have from (8.27) and the definition of a partial derivative,

$$\lim_{\tau_2^1 \to 0} \frac{\bar{\pi}_2^1(\tau_2^1, 1) - \bar{\pi}_2^1(0, 1)}{\tau_2^1} = \left.\frac{\partial \bar{\pi}_2^1}{\partial \tau_2}\right|_{(\tau_2, \varrho) = (0, 1)} = \left.\frac{m_2^{1\prime} - m_2^{2\prime} + \hat{\sigma}_2^{22\prime}}{\eta^1 + \eta^2 - 1}\right|_{(\tau_2, \varrho) = (0, 1)} \tag{8.29}$$

This is the elasticity of country 1's import price with respect to the tariff factor when country 1 keeps the revenues, evaluated at a unit tariff factor (zero tariff rate).

Now, regarding $\bar{\pi}_2^1$ as the potential function of a line integral, its increment along the path $(0, 1) \to (\tau_2^1, 1)$ (i.e., the path $(\tau_2, 1)$, $0 \leqslant \tau_2 \leqslant \tau_2^1$) must be the same as its increment along the polygonal path $(0, 1) \to (0, 0) \to (\tau_2^1, 0) \to (\tau_2^1, 1)$ (see Figure 8.1). The expression on the left in (8.29) may therefore be decomposed into the sum of three expressions:

The first expression gives the increment along the segment $(0, \varrho)$, $1 \geqslant \varrho \geqslant 0$:

$$\lim_{\tau_2^1 \to 0} \frac{\bar{\pi}_2^1(0, 0) - \bar{\pi}_2^1(0, 1)}{\tau_2^1} = \lim_{\tau_2^1 \to 0} \frac{1}{\tau_2^1} \int_1^0 \left.\frac{\partial \bar{\pi}_2^1}{\partial \varrho}\right|_{\tau_2 = 0} d\varrho = 0 \tag{8.30a}$$

The last equality follows from (8.28), since $T_2 = 1$; this corresponds to the trivial result that if the tariff rate is zero, reallocation of the non-existent revenues from country 1 to country 2 can have no effect.

The second expression gives the increment along the segment $(\tau_2, 0)$, $0 \leqslant \tau_2 \leqslant \tau_2^1$:

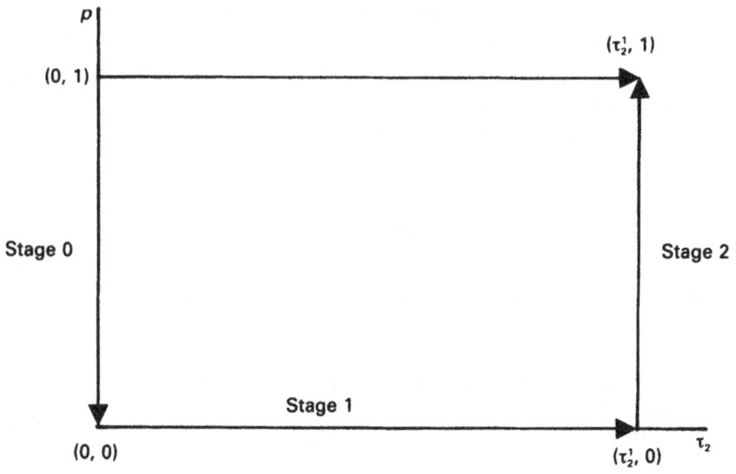

Figure 8.1 Decomposition of tariff into foreign export tax and remission of foreign tax revenues

$$\lim_{\tau_2^1 \to 0} \frac{\bar{\pi}_2^1(\tau_2^1, 0) - \bar{\pi}_2^1(0, 0)}{\tau_2^1} = \left.\frac{\partial \bar{\pi}_2^1}{\partial \tau_2}\right|_{(\tau_2, \varrho) = (0, 0)}$$

$$= \left.\frac{\hat{\sigma}_{22}^{2\,\prime}}{\eta^1 + \eta^2 - 1}\right|_{(\tau_2\,\varrho) = (0, 0)} \tag{8.30b}$$

The last equality is from (8.27); this gives the elasticity of country 1's import price with respect to the tariff factor when country 2 collects all the revenues, evaluated at a unit tariff factor (zero tariff rate).

The third expression gives the increment along the segment (τ_2^1, ϱ), $0 \leqslant \varrho \leqslant 1$:

$$\lim_{\tau_2^1 \to 0} \frac{\bar{\pi}_2^1(\tau_2^1, 1) - \bar{\pi}_2^1(\tau_2^1, 0)}{\tau_2^1} = \lim_{\tau_2^1 \to 0} \frac{1}{\tau_2^1} \int_1^0 \left.\frac{\partial \bar{\pi}_2^1}{\partial \varrho}\right|_{\tau_2 = \tau_2^1} d\varrho \tag{8.30c}$$

$$= \lim_{\tau_2^1 \to 0} \frac{1}{\tau_2^1} \left.\frac{\partial \bar{\pi}_2^1}{\partial \varrho}\right|_{(\tau_2, \varrho) = (\tau_2^1, \varrho^*(\tau_2^1))} \qquad (0 \leqslant \varrho^*(\tau_2^1) \leqslant 1)$$

$$= \lim_{\tau_2^1 \to 0} \frac{e^{\tau_2^1} - 1}{\tau_2^1} \left.\frac{m_2^{1\prime} - m_2^{2\prime}}{\eta^1 + \eta^2 - 1}\right|_{(\tau_2\,\varrho) = (\tau_2^1, \varrho^*(\tau_2^1))}$$

$$= \left.\frac{m_2^{1\prime} - m_2^{2\prime}}{\eta^1 + \eta^2 - 1}\right|_{(\tau_2,\, \varrho) = (0,\, \varrho^*(0))}$$

The second equality is by the mean-value theorem of the integral calculus, the third is from (8.28), and the fourth follows by l'Hospital's rule. This gives the transfer effect.

It should be noted (and is obvious from (8.9)) that when evaluated at $\tau_2 = 0$ (i.e., $T_2 = 1$), the expressions obtained in (8.30b) and (8.30c) are independent of ϱ; thus, (8.29) is the sum of (8.30b) and (8.30c), which correspond to Stages 1 and 2 of the Introduction.

Finally we note from (8.18) that

$$\eta^1 + \eta^2 - 1 = [\varrho + (1 - \varrho)T_2]\,(m_2^{1\prime} - m_2^{2\prime}) - T_2\, \hat{\sigma}_{22}^{1\prime} + \hat{\sigma}_{22}^{2\prime} \quad (8.31)$$

Since $\hat{\sigma}_{22}^{1\prime} < 0$ and $\hat{\sigma}_{22}^{2\prime} > 0$, a sufficient condition for stability is $m_2^{1\prime} \geqslant m_2^{2\prime}$ – which is Samuelson's condition for the 'anti-orthodox' presumption to hold.

4 SUPERIORITY OF A DOMESTIC IMPORT TARIFF TO A FOREIGN EXPORT TAX

A simple by-product of the above analysis is the demonstration that an import tariff levied by country 1 is superior from country 1's point of view to an export tax levied by country 2. In view of the basic decomposition described in the previous section, this amounts to showing that in Stage 2, the transfer of tariff proceeds from country 2 to country 1 improves the latter's welfare. The result is true provided each country's export good is non-inferior – an assumption that is not needed in the classical transfer problem (Mundell, 1960, p. 80). A similar analysis could be used (under the same assumptions) to establish the superiority of an import quota to a 'voluntary export restraint'.

Country k's trade-demand function (8.4) is, from the Slutsky symmetry and non-negative-definiteness conditions applied to the trade-Slutsky terms $\hat{\sigma}_{ij}^k$, generated by an indirect trade-utility function

$$\hat{V}^k\,(p_1^k, p_2^k, D^k; l^k) \quad (8.32)$$

This may be used as a measure of country k's potential welfare in the sense that a rise in this index means that, for some lump-sum redistribution of income (assumed costless), all individuals may be made better off.

The world-equilibrium volume of country 1's imports is given by the function

$$\bar{z}_2^1(T_2, \varrho; p_1^1, l^1, l^2) = \tilde{z}_2^1(p_1^1, \bar{p}_2^1(T_2, \varrho; p_1^1, l^1, l^2), T_2, \varrho; l^1) \qquad (8.33)$$

where the function $\bar{p}_2^1$ is defined by (8.19). Likewise, from (8.12), the world-equilibrium level of country 1's current-account deficit, valued in country 1's internal prices, is given by

$$\bar{D}^1(T_2, \varrho; p_1^1, l^1, l^2) = \varrho\left(1 - \frac{1}{T_2}\right)\bar{p}_2^1(T_2, \varrho; p_1^1, l^1, l^2)\,\bar{z}_2^1(T_2, \varrho; p_1^1, l^1, l^2) \qquad (8.34)$$

Substituting (8.34) and (8.19) in (8.32) (for $k = 1$), we define country 1's indirect potential-welfare function

$$W^1(T_2, \varrho; p_1^1, l^1, l^2) = \hat{V}^1\left[p_1^1, \bar{p}_2^1(T_2, \varrho; p_1^1, l^1, l^2), \bar{D}^1(T_2, \varrho; p_1^1, l^1, l^2)\right] \qquad (8.35)$$

We are to find the sign of $\partial W^1/\partial\varrho$ for $T_2 > 1$.

Differentiating (8.35) with respect to ϱ, and using the Antonelli–Allen–Roy partial differential equation

$$\frac{\partial \hat{V}^1}{\partial p_2^1} = -\hat{h}_2^1\frac{\partial \hat{V}^1}{\partial D^1} \qquad (8.36)$$

we obtain

$$\frac{\partial W^1}{\partial \varrho} = \frac{\partial \hat{V}^1}{\partial p_2^1}\left[\frac{\partial \bar{p}_2^1}{\partial \varrho} - \frac{1}{z_2^1}\,\frac{\partial \bar{D}^1}{\partial \varrho}\right] \qquad (8.37)$$

The expression for $\partial\bar{p}_2^1 / \partial\varrho$ is given by (8.28). From (8.34) and (8.33) we find that using (8.28), (8.26), and the definition (8.15),

$$\frac{\partial \bar{D}^1}{\partial \varrho} = \left(1 - \frac{1}{T_2}\right) p_2^1 z_2^1 \left[1 + \varrho\,(T_2 - 1)\,\frac{m_2^{1\prime}\,\eta^2 + m_2^{2\prime}\,(\eta^1 - 1)}{\eta^1 + \eta^2 - 1}\right] \qquad (8.38)$$

(Note that the second term in the bracketed expression could be negative if $\eta^1 < 1$, $\varrho > 0$, T_2 is sufficiently large.)

Substituting (8.38) in (8.37) we obtain, using (8.28), (8.31), (8.23), (8.24), and (8.17),

$$\frac{\partial W^1}{\partial \varrho} = \frac{\partial \hat{V}^1}{\partial p_2^1} \frac{p_2^1 (T_2 - 1)}{\eta^1 + \eta^2 - 1}$$

$$\frac{\hat{\sigma}_{22}^1 [1 + (T_2 - 1)m_2^2] - \hat{\sigma}_{22}^2}{[T_2 - \varrho (T_2 - 1)m_2^1] [1 + (1 - \varrho) (T_2 - 1)m_2^2]} \tag{8.39}$$

Since $\hat{\sigma}_{22}^{1\prime} < 0$ and $\hat{\sigma}_{22}^{2\prime} > 0$, from (8.10) the third factor on the right is negative. Assuming preferences to be insatiable, (8.32) satisfies $\partial \hat{V}^1 / \partial D^1 > 0$ hence (8.36) implies $\partial \hat{V}^1 / \partial p_2^1 < 0$. Assuming stability to hold, $\eta^1 + \eta^2 - 1 > 0$. It follows that $\partial W^1 / \partial \varrho > 0$ provided $T_2 > 1$. If the proceeds are initially collected by country 2 and subsequently all transferred back to country 1, the latter's gain is measured by

$$W^1 (T_2, 1; p_1^1, l^1, l^2) - W^1 (T_2, 0; p_1^1, l^1, l^2)$$

$$= \int_0^1 \frac{\partial W^1 (T_2, \varrho; p_1^1, l^1, l^2)}{\partial \varrho} \, d\varrho > 0 \tag{8.40}$$

This is positive because the integrand is positive.

Notes

1. I wish to thank the Stiftung Volkswagenwerk, Hannover, the Riksbankens Jubileumsfond, Stockholm, and the National Science Foundation (Grant SES-8607652) for research support.
2. A similar condition, that the proportion of the tax revenues spent on the home country's exportables exceed the foreign elasticity of demand for imports, had already been considered by Lerner (1936, pp. 310–11) as a condition under which the home country would benefit from a tariff even if the foreign country collected the revenues – or in other words, the home country would benefit from an export tax imposed by the foreign country. This is because the foreign export tax in that case would worsen the foreign country's (hence improve the home country's) terms of trade. For this reason Johnson (1960, pp. 223–4) distinguished the 'Lerner case' in which a tariff worsens a country's terms of trade from the 'Metzler case' in which a tariff raises the domestic price ratio of exports to imports. For convenience we may refer to the 'Lerner paradox' and 'Metzler paradox' to distinguish these two cases. See also the discussion in Kemp (1969, p. 96). It should be noted further that Lerner (1936) dealt with a model in which the government has (in general) different preferences from the

consumer, while Metzler instead assumed that the government distributes tariff revenues to consumers (hence in effect has the same preferences as consumers). The Metzler convention is employed here.

References

Bhagwati, Jagdish and Harry G. Johnson (1961) 'A Generalized Theory of the Effects of Tariffs on the Terms of Trade', *Oxford Economic Papers*, N.S., 12 (October) pp. 225–53.

Chipman, John S. (1972) 'The Theory of Exploitative Trade and Investment Policies: A Reformulation and Synthesis', in Luis Eugenio Di Marco (ed.), *International Economics and Development* (New York: Academic Press) pp. 209–44.

Chipman, John S. (1974) 'The Transfer Problem Once Again', in George Horwich and Paul A. Samuelson (eds), *Trade, Stability, and Macroeconomics* (New York: Academic Press) pp. 19–78.

Chipman, John S. (1979) 'The Theory and Application of Trade Utility Functions', in Jerry R. Green and Jose Alexandre Scheinkman (eds), *General Equilibrium, Growth, and Trade* (New York: Academic Press) pp. 277–96.

Johnson, Harry G. (1960) 'Income Distribution, The Offer Curve and the Effects of Tariffs', *Manchester School of Economic and Social Studies*, 28 (September) pp. 214–42.

Jones, Ronald W. (1969) 'Trariffs and Trade in General Equilibrium', *American Economic Review*, 59 (June) pp. 418–24.

Kemp, Murray C. (1969) *The Pure Theory of International Trade and Investment*, (Englewood Cliffs, N.J.: Prentice-Hall).

Lerner, Abba P. (1936) 'The Symmetry Between Import and Export Taxes', *Economica*, N.S., 3 (August) pp. 306–13.

Metzler, Lloyd A. (1949a) 'Tariffs, the Terms of Trade, and the Distribution of National Income', *Journal of Political Economy*, 57 (February) pp. 1–29.

Metzler, Lloyd A. (1949b) 'Tariffs, International Demand, and Domestic Prices', *Journal of Political Economy*, 57 (August) pp. 345–51.

Mill, John Stuart (1848) *Principles of Political Economy*, 2 vols (London: John W. Parker).

Mundell, Robert A. (1960) 'The Pure Theory of International Trade', *American Economic Review*, 50 (March) pp. 67–110.

Samuelson, Paul A. (1952) 'The Transfer Problem and Transport Costs: The Terms of Trade When Impediments are Absent', *Economic Journal*, 62 (June) pp. 278–304.

Samuelson, Paul A. (1953) 'Prices of Factors and Goods in General Equilibrium', *Review of Economic Studies*, 21 (no. 1) pp. 1–20.

Stolper, Wolfgang and Paul A. Samuelson (1941) 'Protection and Real Wages', *Review of Economic Studies*, 9 (November) pp. 58–73.

Torrens, Robert (1848) *The Budget. On Commercial and Colonial Policy* (London: Smith, Elder & Co.).

9 On Models of the Wheat Boom in Canadian Economic History

John H. Dales

> It is a theoretically interesting fact that the rent on an opportunity which maximizes the return to its owner and brings about the socially correct investment in it is . . . exactly the amount by which the product of the whole competitive system would be reduced if the opportunity were held out of use or destroyed, and the investment which would be combined with it were put to the next best possible use. (F. H. Knight in 1924).[1]

I

Mention of Canadian economic history almost always elicits the knowing response of 'Ah, yes, the Innis staple theory', or its variant, 'the Toronto staple theory'. More than a decade ago Hugh Aitken pointed out that this 'theory' had nothing to do with any testable proposition in economics, and the point bears repeating. Innis's magnificent works on the cod fishery and the fur trade stand with Eileen Power's lectures on *The Wool Trade in English Medieval History* and L. C. Gray's *History of Agriculture in the Southern United States to 1860* as classics in the histories of staple economies. These authors' interest was not only, nor even mainly, in economic growth, but rather in the relationship between the economics of the staple product and the development of institutional structures, especially political, legal, and financial institutions. The hallmark of Innis's work in particular was his fascination with the unintended *by-products* of economic life. To the extent that there is any 'theory' embedded in these classic studies of staple products it is a theory of institutional development, not of economic growth. Yet today, the hackneyed 'staple theory', as used in the Canadian context, seems to imply, if it means anything at all, a theory of Canadian economic growth, or, even worse, a Canadian theory of economic growth. I wish for it only oblivion.

This chapter is about two 'attacks' on the staple theory, in both cases interpreted as a theory of Canadian economic growth, and in both cases centred around the 'Wheat Boom' in the prairie provinces during the first decade of this century. Section II deals with a famous article published twenty years ago by E. J. Chambers and D. F. Gordon entitled 'Primary Products and Economic Growth: An Empirical Measurement'. Section III considers an article that seems to be much less well known, C. Southey's 'The Staples Thesis, Common Property, and Homesteading', published in 1978. In Section IV, I outline some personal views about the Wheat Boom, and the relevance of common property theory (or what may be called the theory of a zero price) to Canadian public policy.

II

Chambers and Gordon (hereafter 'C.–G.') set their stage with the statement that 'Canadian economists and economic historians, in particular, have long held that their country's experience is strong evidence of the positive effects of "staple" exports . . . . on economic development.' They then note 'that the staple theory of Canadian development is somewhat ambiguous' because Canadian writers 'did not distinguish mere population growth . . . from growth in the sense of increases in per capita income', but conclude that 'it is reasonable to think that they believed that successful staple exports were crucial to growth in both senses' (pp. 315–6). The authors then set themselves the problem of measuring the impact of the Wheat Boom on the growth of per capita income in Canada. Fair enough. I would myself think that economic historians, and not only Canadian writers, have thought of growth more in terms of total magnitudes – population and GNP – than in per capita terms; and I bridle a bit at the adjective 'mere' since I think that it is of some interest to try to account for different rates of growth in the total magnitudes among countries. But the authors have stated their problem clearly, and it is obviously one worth investigating – quite apart from the mumbo-jumbo of the staple theory.

C.–G. address their problem by way of a carefully specified, two-sector, general equilibrium model. It is a very *special* model in that the wage in the economy is determined solely in the 'gadget' sector, composed of manufacturing industries that use only labour in their production, and are subject to constant costs; the gadget sector serves as a sort of reserve army of labour for the 'wheat' sector, disgorging or absorbing labour at a constant wage as the demand for labour in wheat expands or contracts. The wheat boom is then interpreted as a productivity increase in the wheat sector, and a consequent increase in the demand for labour in Western wheat production. At the new equilibrium, the increase in GNP (and GNP per person, since the population remains unchanged) is shown to be equal to the increase in Western wheat rents during the decade. This increase is calculated empirically, and turns out to be less than one-twelfth of the increase in income per person during the decade (and less than 2 per cent of that income at the end of the decade). The authors interpret these figures to be so small as to constitute a refutation of the 'staple theory' as they defined it. I do *not* find C.–G.'s estimate of wheat's impact on per capita income to be surprisingly low; indeed, as will appear, I am convinced that it is a very generous upper-bound estimate. Before discussing the estimate, however, I must first comment on the model itself. It was the model that drew critical fire when it was first published; indeed, it set off something of a controversy[2] that for a while enlivened the rather stagnant field of Canadian economic history. In retrospect I find the controversy (in which I had some slight part) very puzzling, because it now seems to me that the model is a meaningless distraction that is irrelevant to both the authors' empirical work and their interpretation of it.

The ordinates in C.–G,'s diagrammatic version of the model are labelled 'MVP', which stands for the marginal value product of labour, which in turn equals the real wage. But the calibration must be taken to be real wages in Canada *relative to the rest of the world*. This is so because C.–G.'s 'gadget boom', their assumed increase in the productivity of labour in the gadget sector (i.e. the non-wheat sector), is shown to raise the demand curve for labour in gadgets, and therefore to raise the real wage, which in turn leads to immigration. Were Canadian gadget productivity to increase only as much as gadget productivity in the rest of the world, neither result would occur; the MVP of labour in gadgets would not rise (the increased physical productivity being offset by the resulting fall in the price of gadgets);[3] and since real wages in Canada would not rise relative to real wages abroad there would be no incentive for immigration. The model as it stands, therefore, not only shows that the productivity of labour in Canadian wheat rose relative to the rest of the world (which is what led to the wheat boom), but also shows that productivity in Canadian gadgets increased relative to the rest of the world (an assumption for which the authors provide no justification).

Awkwardness increases when the model and the empirical work are considered together. The wheat boom is calculated to have accounted for something more than one percentage point of a 23 per cent increase in per capita income in Canada over the decade, the other twenty-two percentage points being accounted for by the gadget boom. According to the model, these figures are all relative to the rest of the world. We seem to be left with the possibilities of accepting the model and believing that the increase in per capita income in the rest of the world was zero, or of raising the estimate of the increase in per capita income in Canada by whatever increase there was in the rest of the world, or of accepting the C.–G. estimate of wheat's contribution to per capita income and ignoring their model.

I very much favour the last choice, not only because the wheat estimate can be supported by very simple economic reasoning (outlined in the next paragraph), but also because of the inherent inadequacies of the model itself. The C.–G. model is a model of the Canadian economy under the '*ceteris-paribus*-like' assumption that the rest of the world remains unchanged during the exercise; and no model of an economy as 'open' as Canada's, and that claims to be a general equilibrium model, can afford such an assumption. Although Canadian prices are assumed to be set by world prices, the absence of any explicit link to international trade in the model suggests its emptiness. On reflection it seems to have been the authors' ingenious invention of the gadget industry, with its infinitely elastic demand curve for labour, that played them false. One of its purposes seems to have been to deny the wheat boom any influence on the heavy immigration to Canada during the period. But its major, though probably unintended, effect was to cut Canada off from the rest of the world, thereby simplifying the model to the point of sterility.

Had Chambers and Gordon chanced to remember Frank Knight's 'interesting fact' that introduces this chapter they could, of course, have proceeded directly to their empirical work. But very simple reasoning would also have allowed them to justify their calculations without the gadgetry of their model. Let me first propose an analogy. W. E. G. Salter (1960), in his trenchant little book on productivity, pointed out that a productivity gain in a single industry in a competitive economy cannot be captured by the factors in that industry, save for any rents or quasi-rents that accrue to owners of any 'specific' factors in the industry. Under the normal assumption of perfectly elastic supply curves of labour and capital to the industry, factor *supplies* in the industry might increase greatly yet have no effect on factor *prices*. The productivity gain is widely diffused throughout the economy by a fall in the price of the product experiencing the gain. An analogous process and outcome should surely be expected when a productivity gain occurs in one country in the world economy. Despite the thicket of obstructions to international trade and factor movements, the principle holds; the wheat boom should have been expected to have a major effect on the immigration of labour and capital to Canada, and a very minor effect on factor prices in Canada. Its effect on per capita income in Canada would be confined to the increase in rent on the 'specific' factor, divided by the increased population, while the remaining benefit would be diffused throughout the world by the effect of the new Canadian supplies on world wheat prices. Productivity improvement anywhere benefits everyone everywhere.[4] I believe that this process represents the sort of implicit model of 'booms' in natural resource industries that Canadian economic historians have long had in mind, and that lay behind Innis's well-known dictum that rapid growth in Canada often reflects 'the application of mature technology to virgin natural resources'. Should one wish to put these considerations in 'model' form it would only be necessary to assume a perfectly elastic supply of labour and capital to Canada.[5] The model would then grind out C.–G.'s observation that the wheat boom, which increased GNP in Canada by 'over a fifth' nevertheless increased GNP per person by only a little over a hundredth (p. 316).

When Chambers and Gordon published their article the only available national income statistics for Canada for the first decade of this century were those produced by O. J. Firestone. They showed an approximate twenty-three percentage point increase in per capita income in Canada over the decade, which was three or four percentage points higher than the comparable figure for the United States.[6] However, the C.–G. model, as we have seen, implied that the 23 per cent Canadian increase was *relative to* the rest of the world (which, in Canada, usually means the United States). Something was wrong. It seems clear that the model was at fault, that C.–G.'s assumption of a large (over 20 per cent) increase in gadget productivity in Canada relative to the rest of the world was an inadvertence. However, new, and much more reliable, national accounts for Canada since 1870 have recently been published by Professor M. C. Urquhart, and surprisingly (at least to me) they go a long way to validating the literal interpretation of the C.–G. model. Urquhart calculates the first decade's growth in Canadian income per person to have been 37 per cent (rather than Firestone's 23 per cent) or seventeen-and-a-half percentage points higher than the corresponding United States – not far from the twenty-three percentage points higher implied by the C.–G. model!

What can explain this very rapid rise in per capita income in Canada relative to the United States? I do not think anyone believes that a huge increase in labour productivity in Canadian manufacturing relative to manufacturing abroad – the suggestion based on a very narrow interpretation of the C.–G. 'gadget' sector – is the answer. However, the gadget sector in C.–G.'s two-sector model must be interpreted as the 'non-wheat' sector, and there *are* a few reasons for thinking that developments in the non-wheat economy tended to raise the standard of living in Canada faster than in the United States during the Wheat Boom years. New technologies made possible the exploitation of exceptionally large mineral, forest, and hydroelectric resources in Canada during these years (Dales, 1966, pp. 85–7), though increases in these resource rents were probably no more significant, quantitatively, than the increase in wheat rents. More important, the surge in measured income per person in Canada during the decade reflected in part, perhaps in large part, both considerable improvement in the international terms of trade, which Urquhart (1986, p. 33) reckons at 12 per cent, and a high ratio of labour force to population that is characteristic of periods of heavy immigration. For the rest, the great Canadian prosperity of the first decade of this century consisted largely of an enormous construction boom in railways and Western towns. Urquhart describes it accurately as 'a classic investment boom, a major part of it related directly or indirectly to the settlement of the West' (1986, p. 35). But while investment booms are likely to add to output per person, especially when financed in large part by imports of capital, they are also likely to be associated with inflation and pressure on real wages – another statistical approximation to what Innis once referred to as 'that fighting phrase, the standard of living'. I leave the matter there, apart from noting that wheat's percentage contribution to income per person in Canada would, on the basis of Urquhart's figures, be reduced to only a little more than half of the C.–G. estimate; and that I would find such a result only mildly surprising.

III

C. Southey, in an article published in the *Canadian Journal of Economics* in 1978, upstages Chambers and Gordon by arguing that most staple industries in Canada, and specifically wheat, have contributed *nothing* to Canadian per capita income. Southey uses a model that is basically similar to the C.–G. model (though it is more elaborate, and includes international trade effects); it consists of a staple sector, a manufacturing sector that exhibits constant costs, and a migration function that depends on real wages. But Southey points out that the cod fishery, his first example of a staple, was an 'open access' or 'common property' resource; and common property resources of course yield no rent, since variable resources exploiting the 'opportunity' (to use Knight's word) are employed up to the point where their *average* value product equals their opportunity cost. So the only factor income in the model is the wage bill.

Southey then proclaims an apparently surprising implication of his model that I shall discuss briefly, though I find it unsurprising, and though it has nothing to do with what I consider to be the major contribution of his article. An increase in the price of fish which one would normally expect to lead to an expansion of the fishery, an increase in welfare, and immigration, in the Southey model leads to a decrease in real wages and emigration. The reason is that any inflow of labour to the fishery (probably from 'gadgets') will drive down average physical product of fishing effort until the average value product, even at the higher price of fish, equals the (unchanged) money wage in gadgets. Southey interprets this outcome as a reduction in real wages, since the unchanged money wage buys less fish than before (but of course the same number of gadgets). The real wage, therefore, falls, triggering emigration. But this is too clever by half. The only mystery about the analysis concerns the reason for the increase in the price of fish in the first place. If it reflected some decrease in productivity (perhaps from resource depletion), the world would be unqualifiedly worse off; the labour force, however, would either increase or decrease according to whether the percentage fall in fish consumption was less than or greater than the percentage fall in the average physical product of fishing. If, on the other hand, tastes had changed, so that both the price *and* consumption of fish rose at unchanged incomes and productivity, the labour force in the primary sector would increase, and *measured* output in real income per capita would fall; but 'welfare' per person would surely have increased. Finally, whether the measured decrease in real income per person is an accurate or a perverse measure of the change in welfare, Southey's conclusion that it will lead to emigration seems unwarranted. On the supposition that tastes are similar in all countries, the rise in the price of fish will have led to a fall in measured output per person in *all* countries. Even if 'average' tastes differ among national populations, there would be no point in an individual's emigrating from Canada unless he expected *his* taste for fish to diminish as a result of his move.

Southey breaks new ground when he leaves his general equilibrium exercise, and turns to a partial equilibrium analysis of wheat. He argues that Dominion Lands policy, the Canadian name for homestead legislation, in fact turned Western agricultural land into an open access resource, which therefore yielded zero rent. (Why, one wonders, did Canadian economic historians stand still for *this* heresy, after jumping up and down all over Chambers and Gordon?)

Southey's argument is that everyone had a non-exclusive right to apply for a homestead entry (initially for 160 acres of land), and that the value of this giveaway would inevitably be competed down to zero by the would-be homesteaders themselves. Dissipation of the rent would take the form of an *uneconomically early* start of farming; fearing that delay might mean that someone else would get the prize, everyone would leave for the West early, accept early losses, and in the process reduce the value of the prize (or bid up the cost of winning it) until nothing was left.[7]

The detailed argument is built on the reasonable assumption that, from the perspective of 1900, the value of wheat land would be expected to grow over time, if only because population was growing in Western Europe, the main prospective market for wheat. The optimum time to begin farming, Southey shows, would be the year when the expected annual rent had grown to a figure just sufficient to cover the annualised cost of establishing the farm (including the value of forgone earnings during the set-up period). Under homesteading rules, however, entrants will, for fear of losing out to others, accept negative income (rent less the annualised set-up costs) for a number of years and move West sooner – actually as soon as the rent becomes zero (or when the present value of all future rents equals the capitalised value of losses during the early years). Indeed it is not hard to imagine some homesteaders being willing to take up land even earlier than that, and to absorb negative rents that will not be fully offset during their lifetime, the balance to be achieved by positive rents that accrue to their children.

The logic of the argument seems unassailable, and it would be interesting to give it some empirical content.[8] Of course the equating of the present values of future negative and positive rents would not be thought of in those terms, and any attempt by homesteaders to calculate their 'break-even' year could have been no more than guesswork. We all make guesses; but since optimists and the uninformed, who tend to be notoriously poor gamblers, may be especially attracted to free lunches, governmental giveaways often have a dark side. We know that there was a good deal of misery associated with homesteading, some of which no doubt resulted from unwise gambles taken by those with inadequate knowledge of farming on the western plains. As Adam Smith knew, the necessity of paying a market price for an asset promotes 'prudence' in the purchaser; the 'failure rate' of settlers on purchased land must surely have been much lower than on homesteads where Chester Martin (1938, p. 431) calculated that over 40 per cent of homestead entrants failed to prove up their entry and get title to the land.

IV

I agree with Chambers and Gordon that Canadian economic historians have given the Wheat Boom far too much prominence in both classrooms and textbooks: 'The period 1900–1915,' they write 'is impressed upon every Canadian student as a golden age in the economic growth of Canada, inextricably linked with wheat exports from the prairies' (p. 316, n3).[9] Elsewhere in their essay Chambers and Gordon observe that during the decade of the wheat boom 'agricultural production in Ontario increased absolutely as much as in Saskatchewan, while Quebec and Ontario increases were together fully 79 per cent of that in the entire prairie region' (p. 322n). Points well taken; gadgets and Eastern agriculture, as well as Western wheat, figured prominently in the great Canadian boom 1900–1910.

The analysis of public policy has always been an important part of both economic theory and economic history, and Southey's article, in my opinion, constitutes a damning indictment of the Canadian homestead and railway land grant policies (which were relatively on a far grander scale than their American models).[10] What is much more important, Southey's analysis should forcefully draw our attention to the economics of a zero price (otherwise known as the economics of non-exclusive rights, or common property resources). Though this theory has a long history, its modern version, and its relevance for Canadian economic history, can be attributed to Scott Gordon's well-known article on the fishery (Gordon, 1954). The theory has been greatly expanded during recent years, notably by S. Cheung (1974), to show the wasteful, and usually self-defeating, effects of all sorts of governmental price controls, subsidies, grants, and give-aways. Yet the theory seems to have little currency in Canada, where both the historical and contemporary economies have been riddled with such policies (see Dales, 1983).

The sequence of public policies in Western Canada reads like a comedy of errors. Having bought the land, the government of Canada then gave most of it away; later compensated the Western provinces for having given it away; compensated Western farmers for farming so far inland by forcing railways to give them special rates on export grain; and most recently has compensated the railways for having been forced to subsidise the farmers. This bizarre history that began with, and was in part spawned by, 'free homesteads', makes it easy to believe that, whatever the Wheat Boom's impact on national income, its contribution to income per person was probably zero at best.[11] Ill-considered policy dissipated rent and, unless Knight was wrong, kept the Canadian standard of living at what it would have been had prairie lands 'been held out of use or destroyed . . . .'.

Notes

1. F. H. Knight, 'Some Fallacies in the Interpretation of Social Cost', *Quarterly Journal of Economics*, 1924, pp. 582–606, p. 591n. Knight credited this point to Professor Allyn Young's 'chapter on Rent in Ely's Outline of Economics (pp. 409, 410 in the fourth edition)'.
2. The items in the controversy are listed in Southey's 'References' (Southey, 1978, p. 558) under the names of Bertram, Chambers and Gordon (1966), Dales *et al.*, Grant, and Lewis. An important article, 'Some Further Reflections on the Staple Thesis', was presented by Chambers and Gordon to the Conference on Quantitative Economic History, held at the University of Western Ontario in March 1978. This paper has not been published so far as I know, which is too bad since besides refuting many of the criticisms levelled at the original article it contains further useful empirical work.
3. This deduction assumes that a given percentage increase in labour productivity in gadgets results in an equal percentage fall in the price of gadgets, the normal assumption in a competitive economy; and that the combined income and price elasticity of demand for gadgets equals unity, an

assumption of convenience. (Labour would move into or out of the gadget sector depending on whether this elasticity were greater or less than unity.)

4. In the penultimate section of their essay, comprised of a group of loosely worded *obiter dicter*, C.–G. support the then popular theory that 'investment in human capital' was a key factor in economic growth. After noting that 'for the world as a whole technological advance has been a necessary condition for much of whatever economic growth has taken place' (p. 327), which I take to mean that such advance has led to per capita growth everywhere, they go on to argue that a small country's 'rate of growth, nevertheless, may vary significantly with its ability to apply . . . [technological advance] occurring elsewhere' (p. 328). Growth here seems to apply more to GNP than to GNP per capita, and even to imply that countries that don't apply advances 'occurring elsewhere' are not likely to benefit very much from them.
5. C.–G. later allow an immigration of 200 000 rent-seekers to take advantage of the Canadian homestead legislation, but the minimising of the wheat boom's effect on immigration was perhaps the hardest part of the model for Canadian economic historians to swallow. The authors tell us (p. 323, n17) that they originally considered a completely elastic supply curve of immigrants to Canada, but abandoned this specification when they 'realized that it was incompatible with a gadget-type industry and stability (a horizontal supply curve and a horizontal demand curve for labour)'. This comment makes little sense to me: although the gadget *sector* is kept in stable equilibrium by the rising supply curve of labour to it, any subset of gadget *industries* is bound to be in neutral equilibrium since the supply curve of labour to it will be horizontal at the existing wage for the same reason that the supply curve of labour to wheat is horizontal.
6. See the figures presented in Dales, 1966, p. 136.
7. Southey points out, pp. 553–4, that his analysis is analogous to earlier analyses of prospecting for minerals. It is interesting, too, to note the very close analogy of homesteading to the allocation of taxi medallions in Toronto. By fulfilling certain eligibility requirements, including an apprenticeship driving for someone else, and waiting for some years, a person can get a 'free' medallion, currently worth about $80 000; or, like the would-be wheat farmer, the would-be medallion owner can simply buy the desired property on the open market.
8. Southey's full analysis includes the consideration that 'in so far as the railways acquired land in the form of land grants, as a reward for initiating and building railways, then these activities – [the development and sale of farms] – were simply homesteading on a grand scale!' (p. 557). His model predicts that farming would begin on homestead land before it began on railways land (p. 557n), a prediction that is in keeping with the fact that the CPR delayed choosing its full land entitlement until it was eventually forced by law to choose the remainder of its grant. I might also note that Innis would not have been astonished by the general import of Southey's analysis; in his lectures he argued that the Prairie Farm Rehabilitation Act of 1935 was an implicit recognition by the Federal government that their policies had led to the West's being opened much too precipitately.

9. It may be noted that Innis bears little, if any, responsibility for this emphasis; to judge by his published work, his main interest in wheat seems to have been in the struggle by A. J. McPhail, the head of the wheat pools' Central Selling Agency, to hold in check the proponents of a populist – and meaningless – demand for the 'orderly marketing' of wheat.
10. In Canada, of the approximately 150 million acres of Western lands alienated from the Crown by 1960, Martin's estimates indicate that some 38 per cent went to homesteaders and 25 per cent to railways. The comparable percentages for the United States were 28 per cent and 10 per cent of a total of one billion acres. (See Urquhart and Buckley, 1965, pp. 308–9 and Series K6–8 and 15–17; also US Department of Commerce, *Historical Statistics of the United States* (Washington, 1961) p. 231.)
11. Provincial ownership of natural resources has led to all too many examples of policies that sacrifice 'intensive' for 'extensive' growth. In Ontario, for example, the law that requires the Hydro Electric Power Commission to sell electricity at cost (i.e., to equate average revenue with average cost) exactly replicates the common property equilibrium, and thus has destroyed virtually all rent from the province's magnificent water powers.

References

Aitken, H. G. J. (1977) 'Myth and Measurement; The Innis Tradition in Economic History', *Journal of Canadian Studies* (Winter) pp. 96–105.

Chambers, E. J. and D.F. Gordon (1966) 'Primary Products and Economic Growth', *Journal of Political Economy* (August) pp. 315–30.

Cheung, S. (1974) 'A Theory of Price Control', *Journal of Law and Economics* (April) pp. 53–71.

Dales, J. H. (1966) *The Protective Tariff in Canada's Development* (Toronto: University of Toronto Press).

Dales, J. H. (1983) 'Distortions and Dissipations', *Canadian Public Policy* (June) pp. 257–63.

Gordon, H. S. (1954) 'The Economic Theory of a Common Property Resource: The Fishery', *Journal of Political Economy* (April) pp. 124–42.

Innis, H. A. (ed.) (1940) *The Diary of Alexander James McPhail* (Toronto: University of Toronto Press).

Martin, C. (1938) *'Dominion Lands' Policy* (Toronto: Macmillan of Canada).

Salter, W. E. G. (1960) *Productivity and Technical Change* (Cambridge: Cambridge University Press).

Southey, C. (1978) 'The Staples Thesis, Common Property, and Homesteading', *Canadian Journal of Economics* (August) pp. 547–59.

Urquhart, M. C. (1986) 'New Estimates of Gross National Product, Canada,

1870–1926', in Stanley L. Engerman and Robert E. Gallman, *Long-Term Factors in American Economic Growth* (National Bureau of Economic Research, Studies in Income and Wealth, vol. 51: Chicago and London).
Urquhart, M. C. and K. A. H. Buckley (eds) (1965) *Historical Statistics of Canada* (Cambridge: Cambridge University Press.)

10 Can We Avoid Another Great Depression?[1]

Clarence Lyle Barber

As the Great depression has receded in time, fears of its recurrence, which were widespread in 1945, have gradually ebbed as memories have faded, a new generation has arrived upon the economic scene and the world has experienced an extended period of sustained growth. Still, as the stock market crash of October 1987 reminded us all, fears of another severe depression linger. This chapter examines the basis for these concerns. In particular, it outlines the changes in structure, in economic institutions and in attitudes to economic policy that might be expected to affect the world economy's vulnerability to severe and protracted declines. In approaching the topic, this chapter first examines what we mean by the Great Depression and summarises briefly what economists believe to have been its origin.

The Great Depression of the 1930s derived its label from the fact that it was virtually worldwide in its impact, unprecedented in its severity and very long-lasting. Even by the end of the decade recovery was incomplete. Indeed, it can be argued that had it not been for the outbreak of The Second World War and the large defence expenditures that followed, depressed economic activity might well have continued in many parts of the world more or less indefinitely. In retrospect, one of the depression's most striking characteristics was the speed with which it developed. In just three years, from 1929 to 1932, real output had fallen by 28 per cent in the United States, 25 per cent in Canada and 20 per cent in both Germany and Austria. In this same three-year period, in the United States, wholesale prices fell 32 per cent, with prices of farm products falling 54 per cent and prices of crude materials by 44 per cent. These large declines in basic commodity prices were undoubtedly a prime factor in causing declines in real income in many less developed countries, thus spreading the effects of the depression throughout the world. They may also have been an important contributing cause of many of the bank failures that plagued the US economy in the early 1930s. Another characteristic of the Great Depression was the severe decline in capital spending which occurred. Measured from the peak to trough year, real capital spending fell 108 per cent in Germany, 84 per cent in the United States, 80 per cent in Canada, 65 per cent in Hungary, 59 per cent in Austria, 37 per cent in Italy and 33 per cent in Sweden and Czechoslovakia.

The incidence of the Great Depression was very uneven. Most severely affected were Canada and the United States, each with a decline in real national product from peak to trough of about 30 per cent and Germany and Austria with declines of 23 per cent. In contrast, Japan experienced little if any decline in real output and a number of European countries experienced declines of 10 per cent or less. The latter include, in terms of percent and in order of increasing severity of the decline, Denmark (−4.5), the United Kingdom (−5.5), Switzerland (−5.8), Norway (−8.0) and Italy (−8.8). France, Netherlands and Sweden each experienced declines of about 12 per cent.

The data strongly suggest that Germany and the United States are the two countries whose economies were primarily responsible for the severity of the depression. Germany suffered a 23 per cent decline even though surrounded by countries whose output fell 10 to 12 per cent or less. Germany is also the only country for which there is clear evidence of imports declining in advance of exports. Between 1929 and 1931 Germany's exports fell only 12 per cent. In the same period, her imports fell 50 per cent. In the United States, on the other hand, exports and imports appear to have declined at about the same rate and to the same extent (see Barber, 1978).

Recovery from the trough of the depression was also uneven. By 1939, a decade after the decline began in most countries, output in France and Austria was still from 10 to 14 per cent below its 1929 level, and in Canada, the Netherlands, Switzerland and the United States it had increased only from 1 to 5 per cent. In contrast, output over the decade was up 59 per cent in Japan, 51 per cent in Germany, 34 per cent in Finland, 28 per cent in Norway and Sweden and 21 per cent in the United Kingdom. Russia appears to have been little affected by the depression and her real national product rose over the decade by 80 per cent. Apart from Germany, Japan and Russia, almost all countries were still operating well below their potential in 1939. In the United States, for example, the unemployment rate was 17 per cent and real national product has been estimated to have been at about 80 per cent of potential. Unemployment rates of from 18 to 20 per cent still prevailed in Belgium, Denmark, the Netherlands and Norway.

The uneven impact of the depression on different countries must have reflected, in part, the uneven decline in different prices, in particular the much greater decline in primary product prices as compared with the prices of finished goods. This disparity of price change produced large changes in income distribution both within and among countries. In Canada, for example, net farm income which had averaged 15.5 per cent of total income from 1926 to 1928 fell to just 4.3 per cent in the mid-1930s. Throughout the world the output of most farm or plantation type products showed few effects from the depression as farmers, with most of their costs fixed, continued to produce despite very low prices. The effects of this disparity in price change showed up in much worse terms of trade for countries whose economies were heavily dependent on the output of primary products and much better terms of trade for many industrial countries. Thus, terms of trade for the United Kingdom improved 24 per cent between 1929 and 1933 and some observers have argued that this played a significant part in Britain's recovery. In contrast, the terms of trade between primary products and manufactures fell 27 per cent between 1929 and 1932 (Lewis, 1952, p. 118).

Despite the large fall in wages and prices that occurred in many countries during the early 1930s there appears to be no clear instance where the classical mechanism of wage price flexibility worked to restore full employment. The only countries that managed to maintain or restore full employment during the 1930s were (1) Russia, operating under an entirely different economic system, (2) Germany, which used a large increase in government expenditures combined in the later stages of recovery with wage and price controls and far-reaching foreign exchange controls, and (3) Japan, which used a large depreciation of the yen along with vigorous monetary and fiscal measures (see James, 1986, and Nakamura, 1987).

Economists still disagree as to the causes of the Great Depression. One recent re-examination of this question has emphasised a difference between those who would attribute the major decline of the early 1930s to a weakness in autonomous spending forces and those who would stress excessively restrictive monetary policy in the United States in the late 1920s followed by weak and inept monetary policy in the early 1930s (Brunner, 1981). My own analysis has stressed the effects of declining rates of population growth both in the United States and throughout the developed world (Barber, 1978). The stresses resulting from the reparations imposed on Germany after The First World War have been cited as an important aggravating factor (Haberler, 1976). Any attempt to evaluate these different viewpoints is beyond the scope of this chapter.

What economic policies were pursued as the world's economy moved from a relatively high level of operation in 1929 to the trough of the depression in 1932 or 1933? And how did these policies change during the recovery period? In 1929 almost all governments were strongly committed to *laissez-faire* views. Apart from regular cyclical fluctuations the world's economy had operated at a satisfactory level with relatively little government interference except in times of war for 150 years or more. The prescribed monetary policy was to follow the 'rules of the game' laid down for the gold standard (Drummond, 1987). Government expenditures were still modest as a percent of income especially for central governments in federal countries and it was expected that budgets would be kept in balance. More active policy measures were taken on the international trade and payments side. At various times, governments raised tariffs, depreciated their exchange rates and adopted foreign exchange controls. Let us consider in turn monetary policy, fiscal policy and international trade and exchange policies.

Countries following the gold standard 'rules of the game' were expected to subordinate their monetary policy to the requirements of these rules. According to these rules, inflows of gold should result in expansionary monetary policies, lower interest rates and rising prices. Outflows of gold should lead to monetary contraction with rising interest rates and falling prices. This set of rules may have given satisfactory results in the nineteenth century when Britain dominated much of the world, prices and wages were flexible and capital outflows from the centre rose and fell in response to changes in interest rates. But by the late 1920s, the system had begun to break down. Wages and prices no longer responded readily to changes in monetary policy, so that exchange rates which were out of line with the underlying cost structure could produce prolonged stagnation as in Britain after her return to pre-war parity for the pound in 1925. Increasingly countries receiving gold, such as France and the United States in the late 1920s, were sterilising the inflow, thus throwing the burden of adjustment on the countries losing gold. In addition, many countries had begun to hold their central bank reserves not in the form of gold but as bank deposits in gold standard countries. This gold exchange standard made the centre countries such as Britain more subject to the strains caused by the withdrawal of funds in periods of economic difficulty. The concept of a monetary policy primarily oriented to supporting the domestic economy was just beginning to be recognised.

The dominance of gold-standard beliefs and policies meant that no country gave its domestic economy strong monetary support during the first two years of the depression. Even the United States, one of the countries least exposed to the effects of foreign trade, allowed its banking system to move almost to the verge of collapse with little more than token support from the central bank (Friedman and Schwartz, 1963, ch. 7). The change in the stock of money in percentage terms from 1929 to 1932 for selected countries was as follows: Germany (−40), the United States (−21), Italy (−15), Canada (−10), Australia (−6), Britain (+2), Sweden (+3) and France (+13).

As the depression deepened nominal interest rates declined, but with prices continuing to fall real rates of interest remained high. In the United States in 1932 the real yield on prime commercial paper was about 12.8 per cent and on high grade corporate bonds about 15 per cent. In the depths of the depression, many firms and individuals were unable to borrow on any terms at all. In these circumstances, the yield on safe government securities offers little guide to the cost of credit to would-be private borrowers in the country as a whole. The financial crisis that developed in Germany, Austria and central and eastern Europe in the summer of 1931, a product of the restrictive monetary policies being pursued at that time, may have aborted an incipient recovery of which there were signs in the spring of that year (James, 1986).

In the mid to late 1930s, as recovery was getting under way in many countries, there was a substantial easing of monetary conditions, particularly in the United States. With the widespread depreciation of currencies the price of gold rose, and this along with the lower level of wages and prices induced a substantial increase in gold production. Fears arising from Hitler's rise to power led to a substantial flow of gold out of Europe and into the United States. As a result of these factors, the US gold stock rose from less than \$4 billion in 1929 to some \$17.6 billion by the end of 1939. Total cash reserves of member banks in the federal Reserve System increased from \$2.4 billion in 1929 to \$11.5 billion by 1939. Yet some 44 per cent of these reserves were being held as excess reserves at that time. With interest rates at record low levels, the banks were reluctant to buy longer-term securities for fear of a subsequent decline in bond prices. Since the yield on treasury bills was virtually zero they simply held excess reserves. Despite these extremely low rates of interest, the economy remained depressed. It was this experience that led many economists to conclude that the use of monetary policy as a tool to stimulate recovery was like pushing on a string.

Let us turn now to a brief review of the fiscal policies followed during the 1930s. As the depression deepened, all countries found their budgets moving into a deficit position as their revenues declined and expenditures were incurred to support the rising level of unemployed. In federal countries this initial impact was much greater for provincial (state) and local governments. Quite often these governments increased their capital spending to provide added employment. But as the depression deepened almost all governments reduced their expenditures and raised tax rates, thus reinforcing the decline in income. Even in Britain, one of the countries least affected by the decline, the Labour government followed a policy of trying to keep the budget balanced (Richardson, 1983). And this policy was continued until major rearmament expenditures began at the end of the decade. In some countries very substantial tax increases were implemented. In the United States in the latter part of 1931, President Hoover recommended a tax increase designed to provide an amount equal to one-third of existing revenue. This increase was implemented in mid-1932, almost at the depth of the depression (Stein, 1969). Congress did not question the need for the tax increase which Hoover justified on the need to balance the budget. Yet total government revenue in the United States had already increased from 11 per cent of GNP in 1929 to 15.5 per cent in 1932, with most of this increase occurring at the state and local level. In Canada, major tax increases were implemented at the federal level between 1930 and 1935 (Perry, 1955, vol. I, part VI). By the late 1930s, revenue at all levels of government had increased by almost 50 per cent relative to GNP. Severe tax increases and cuts in government spending were implemented also in Germany (Haberler, 1976, and James, 1986). The rise in tax rates in Canada, the United States and elsewhere must have created a significant barrier to recovery. By increasing the size of the marginal propensity to tax and save, the multiplier effects of any revival in capital spending would be reduced by these higher tax rates.

In the face of continued high levels of unemployment throughout the 1930s, belief in the virtue of a balanced budget was weakened and support for an active fiscal policy gathered strength. The theoretical analysis provided in Keynes's *General Theory* undoubtedly played a key role in changing the views of economists on this question. But with the exception of Germany and Japan, prior to the outbreak of The Second World War no other country had made a major commitment to fiscal expansion. In Canada, the federal budget was back in surplus (on a national accounts basis) by 1937 even though unemployment as a per cent of the non-farm labour force was still 18 per cent and there were large amounts of concealed unemployment in agriculture. In the United States, President Roosevelt had been gradually convinced of the merits of fiscal expansion but the deficit in the federal budget for 1939 was still some $1.4 billion lower than it had been in 1936. In the later 1930s, Sweden, perhaps reflecting the views of her own economists, undertook moderate monetary and fiscal expansion (Jonung, 1981). As a result, by 1939 its real output was up 28.5 per cent over its 1929 level.

During the decline from 1929 to 1932, many countries imposed higher tariffs and many currencies were depreciated. The United States imposed a major tariff increase under the Smoot-Hawley Act which went into effect in June 1930. In Canada, the newly elected Conservative government introduced tariff increases in 1930 and 1931 on the order of 50 per cent (Perry, 1955). In this period also Britain abandoned her traditional free trade policy and imposed high tariffs. The result of this widespread resort to increased protection in a period of declining income was a reduction of about 25 per cent in the volume of world trade (League of Nations, 1938).

Among the earliest countries to depreciate their currencies were primary producers like Australia, Argentina and Brazil. They were followed a year or more later by Britain, Norway, Sweden, the United States and others. A group of countries known as the 'gold bloc' retained their gold standard parities until the mid-1930s but they, too, were eventually forced to allow their currencies to depreciate. While these currency depreciations have often been categorised as beggar-my-neighbour policies, a recent study has questioned this view. (Eichengreen and Sachs, 1985). These authors argue that the initial depreciation benefits the country undertaking it and when pursued by a group of countries may lead to higher levels of output, particularly when followed by more expansive monetary and fiscal policies. Unlike tariffs, these depreciations could lead to an increased volume of trade and need not reduce the efficiency of world output.

Let us now consider in what ways the world economy has changed since 1929 and whether these changes make a major depression more or less likely. Changes have occurred both in the structure of the economy and in the attitudes of the public and key market participants. Some of the principal changes are as follows.

Perhaps most important is the much larger role played by government today. Towards the end of the 1980s total government outlays in industrial countries averaged about 45 per cent of GDP. In 1929 this ratio was about 10 per cent in the United States, 16 per cent in Canada and 17 per cent in the United Kingdom. In federal countries, even more important has been the increased role of central governments. In Canada, central government expenditures increased from 5.9 per cent of GNP in 1929 to 23.0 per cent in 1987. In the United States this increase was from 2.6 to 23.7 per cent. Not only are governments much larger today but much more of their revenues are obtained from direct taxes on personal and corporate income. In Canada, direct tax revenues increased from 13 per cent of total revenues in 1929 to 52 per cent in 1987. In the United States, with social insurance contributions included, the corresponding increase has been from 35 per cent in 1929 to 70 per cent in 1987. This increased role of direct taxes has undoubtedly given government budgets a greater degree of built-in flexibility. The increased role of unemployment insurance and the deduction of direct tax revenues at the source must have had a similar effect. The increase in the relative size of government budgets and their greater stabilising properties may well have been the main reason for the much greater stability in real output that has prevailed throughout the developed world since 1945 (see Baily, 1978).

There have also been important changes in industrial structure since 1929. Almost everywhere, the share of agriculture in employment and output has declined whereas the share of the service sector has risen. Today's agriculture has also become more commercial using many off-farm inputs and thus will be less likely to maintain the stable output that existed in the 1930s in the event of a major decline. The service sector may contribute to the economy's stability in some degree since its output is not affected by inventory fluctuations. Because a larger proportion of today's expenditures are of a discretionary type the economy as a whole may be more vulnerable to declines in consumer spending.

Another change has been a decline in the flexibility of wages and prices. Evidence for the United States shows that over the period since 1945 wages and prices have become less and less responsive to mild recessions (Cagan, 1979). Even farm prices are less flexible than they were in the past because of the greater prevalence of farm price support programmes. Many economists believe that the reduced flexibility of wages and prices has contributed to a long-term trend towards higher prices.

A major difference between today and 1929 lies in the area of policy. Economists now understand much more about the effects of government economic policies than they did in 1929. In addition, changes in public attitudes allow more scope in the policies that can be implemented. Let us consider in turn monetary, fiscal and exchange rate policy. The disappearance of the gold standard and the limitations it imposed upon the implementation of monetary policy has greatly increased the likelihood that any major downturn will be met by a prompt and substantial easing in monetary policy. An easier monetary policy may still be limited by fear of the policy's effects on inflation and the exchange rate. However, if a number of major countries move towards an easier monetary policy at the same time, the effects on the exchange rate caused by capital outflows would be minimised. And if the decline in economic activity is serious, the probability of inflation will be much reduced. The widespread insurance of bank deposits in the United States and elsewhere has eliminated the runs on banks which had such a disruptive effect on the monetary situation in the past.

In contrast to the balanced budget views of 1929, fiscal policy, the deliberate use of government expenditures and tax levels to affect the economy, is now an accepted tool. However, there is less confidence as to what can be achieved than was true a decade or more ago. Examination of the sharp economic downturn that occurred in 1981–2 suggests that governments in the OECD group of countries were reluctant to take active fiscal measures to hasten recovery from the recession but they did readily accept the much larger deficits which appeared as the economy declined. This reluctance reflected concerns about the still high rate of inflation despite rising levels of unemployment. The data given in Table 10.1 show the combined budgets of all governments moving into a larger deficit position from 1980 to 1983 by an amount corresponding almost exactly to the change estimated as due to built-in budget stabilisers. Again, in the recovery years from 1984 to 1987, the decline in deficits can be largely attributed to the effects of built-in stabilisers. The issues raised by continued budget deficits of substantial size over an extended period are discussed further below. However, there can be little doubt that, with the much larger size of today's government budgets, if any

Table 10.1 Cumulative changes in general government financial balances, OECD countries, 1980 to 1987

Budgetary changes	*1980–83*	*1984–87*
	per cent of GNP/GDP	
Change in actual balance	–2.6	+1.5
Built-in stabilisers	–2.6	+1.3
Change in structural balance	–0.1	+0.1

Note: The sum of rows 2 and 3 differ from row 1 only by the amount of rounding errors.
Source: *Economic Outlook*, OECD, Paris, December 1986 and December 1984.

attempt had been made to move quickly towards a balanced budget the effects on the world economy might have been devastating. It was the willingness to accept larger deficits which avoided the onset of a serious depression at that time.

However, the overall balances shown in Table 10.1 conceal quite diverse behaviour on the part of different countries. On the one hand, in the United States a very active fiscal policy was pursued in the 1980s by the Reagan administration. A major tax cut combined with a large increase in defence spending raised the federal deficit to 5.6 per cent of GNP for 1983 and the effects of this policy were felt not only in the United States but also throughout the developed world. Although the policy was rationalised on now discredited supply-side arguments, it amounted in fact to a major use of an active Keynesian-type fiscal policy. In contrast, some countries pursued quite restrictive fiscal policies. Using the International Monetary Fund's measure, fiscal impulses, we find that for all levels of government, over the eight years 1980 to 1987 a contractionary fiscal impulse was exerted equal to 4.9 per cent of G.D.P. in Japan, 4.1 per cent in the United Kingdom and 2.9 per cent in West Germany. In this same period, an expansionary fiscal impulse was exerted equal to 3.7 per cent of GDP in Canada and 2.0 per cent in the United States (IMF, 1988, p. 76). In view of the large size of the United States economy, it is evident that the 1981–2 recession would have been significantly more severe if the United States had followed the essentially passive or contractionary fiscal policies of other developed countries.

Exchange rate policies also are now free from the restrictions imposed by the gold standard. At the present time there are a number of blocks of countries whose currencies float relative to one another. Active policy consists largely of the use of monetary policy to support or stabilise exchange rates and the co-ordination of the mix of monetary and fiscal policies by major countries in an attempt to avoid unduly wide fluctuations in exchange rates and the development of large imbalances in the current accounts of different countries. These policies are monitored and to some degree influenced by international organisations such as the International Monetary Fund, the GATT and the OECD. Recent years have witnessed much wider swings in exchange rates and larger current account imbalances than was true in the past. However, the effect of these swings on the world's ability to avoid a serious depression is not easy to evaluate.

The many international organisations that exist today also monitor and influence international trade policies. As a result, the existence of GATT, the IMF, the OECD and other organisations make changes in tariffs and other protective measures more subject to negotiation and agreement than was true in the 1920s. Any measure that would have effects equivalent to those of the Smoot-Hawley tariff which came into effect in 1930 now seems much less likely. Thus, the protectionist bill passed by the US Congress in 1988 was less extreme than many observers had predicted. Despite an increased use of non-tariff barriers in recent years, the volume of world trade in the 1980s continued to grow at a rate about 20 per cent faster than real output. The very large reduction in tariff levels that has occurred since 1945 has made the world economy much more interdependent than it was in 1929. Along with this change must have come a reduced ability of many countries to manage their own macro-economies. The potential adverse effects of this may well have been offset by the increased consultation that now occurs through organisations such as the IMF, the OECD, the EEC and other similar groups.

Over the decade of the 1980s many developed countries have been recording substantial government deficits. For the seven major developed countries, central government deficits over the decade 1979 to 1988 averaged 4.1 per cent of GNP. When significant deficits continue through an entire decade a substantial growth occurs in debt levels and in the share of interest payments in government budgets. This has led many observers to argue that governments, faced with much larger debt levels, may feel they have little room for increasing expenditures and/or cutting taxes in the event of a serious downturn in the world economy. In fact, between 1980 and 1985, central government debt to GNP ratios for all industrial countries increased from 32.1 per cent to 44.7 per cent, and interest expenditures as a per cent of GDP increased from 2.4 to 3.6 per cent. To provide some perspective it should be noted that over the decade of the 1930s the average annual federal deficit was just 2.0 per cent of GNP in Canada and 2.5 per cent in the United States. Moreover, federal interest expenditures in Canada relative to GNP only increased from 2.1 per cent in 1930 to 2.4 per cent in 1939. In the United States the corresponding rise was from 0.5 per cent in 1930 to 0.7 per cent in 1939. Over the course of the Great Depression lower interest rates offset much of the effects of the growth in debt levels. Let us then consider the seriousness of these recently rising debt levels. Do they jeopardise government's ability to offset the effects of a serious downturn in the economy?

The years since 1960 divide into two distinct periods: rapid growth in real output from 1960 to 1973 and much slower growth since that date. Real output in the OECD group of countries grew at an average rate of 5.0 per cent per annum from 1960 to 1973 and 2.5 per cent from 1974 to 1987. Much of this decline reflects a much slower rate of productivity growth. Since 1973, output per man hour in the developed group of countries has been increasing at only about one-half the rate that prevailed in the earlier period and total factor productivity at less than one-quarter of its earlier rate. Along with this slower rate of total output growth has come a marked reduction in the level of capital formation. Over the period 1960 to 1973, real gross fixed capital formation in the OECD group of countries grew at an average rate of 6.0 per cent. Since that date, from 1973 to 1986, its average annual growth rate has fallen to 1.6 per cent. This decline in the growth of real fixed capital spending appears to have been the direct result of the sharp decline in the rate of output growth, although cause and effect can run both ways. It is what a simple accelerator model would lead one to expect.

Along with the above changes has come an increase in the size of government deficits. In the period leading up to 1973, government budgets were usually in balance and when adjusted for the effects of inflation often showed a surplus. Since 1973, unadjusted budgets have invariably shown substantial deficits. However, when adjustment is made for the distorting effect that higher rates of inflation have had on nominal interest rates and debt interest payments, these deficits become much smaller or change back into surpluses. Since the 1982 downturn, even inflation-adjusted deficits have become

Table 10.2 Deficits and debts of central governments, industrial countries, 1972 to 1988

	Reported deficits	*Inflation adjusted deficits**	*Ratio of debt to GDP*
	(per cent of GDP)		*(per cent)*
1972–74	−1.78	+0.65	28.7
1975–77	−4.29	−1.48	31.0
1978–80	−3.32	−0.45	32.7
1981–83	−4.59	−1.98	36.5
1984–86	−4.90	−3.13	43.7
1987–88	−3.80	−2.60	

* An adjustment for inflation was calculated using the implicit price of GNP and the net debt of central governments. For more detail on methods of adjusting for inflation see Jump and Wilson, 1986.
Source: Compiled from data given in *Government Finance Statistics Yearbook*, vol. XI, 1987, International Monetary Fund.

significantly larger. Thus, if we average the data given in Table 10.2, we find that over the period 1972 to 1980 the inflation adjusted deficit was just 0.5 per cent of gross domestic product. For the period following from 1981 to 1988 this ratio rises to 2.6 per cent.

In exploring the relation between government sector balances and the balance between private sector capital spending and saving, it is useful to consider the following macro-economic relation. A basic textbook macro-economic equation tells us that:

$$S + M + T^n = I + X + G \tag{10.1}$$

where S denotes gross private sector savings, M imports of goods and services, T^n government revenues net of income transfers, I gross private capital spending, X exports of goods and services and G government spending on goods and services. The private sector is here defined to include capital spending and retained earnings of government-owned business enterprises. When rearranged this equation becomes:

$$(S - I) + (M - X) = (G - T^n) \tag{10.2}$$

This equation can also be written in functional form as follows:

$$(S(y) - I(r)) + (M(y) - X) = (G - T^n(y)) \tag{10.3}$$

where y designates income and r the rate of interest. A more complete equation would show both exports and imports as a function also of some measure of the exchange rate adjusted for any relative change in price levels between the country concerned and the rest of the world. For the world as a whole, the foreign sector balance disappears and there is a direct relation between the two remaining sectoral balances.

Equation (10.3) underlines the fact that the balance in any one sector is dependent on the interaction of the three different sectors. A substantial rise in the government deficit could reflect, in the main, the effects of a major tax cut and an increase in government spending such as occurred in the United States in the early 1980s, or it could result primarily from the decline in income induced by a fall in private capital spending at a time when the private savings function remained relatively constant as seems to have been true for Canada between 1981 and 1983. The former is sometimes called an active deficit and the latter a passive deficit. In a more comprehensive analysis, some form of equation (10.3) would be combined with an equation for the demand and supply of money and an equation representing equilibrium in the balance of payments.

Unfortunately, in recent years the role of private sector capital spending and saving has received little attention from economists, so much so that data for this sector are not readily available for most countries. Yet developments in the private sector may often be the key to an understanding of developments in the government and foreign sectors. Consider, for example, the changes which have occurred in each of these sectors over the period from 1982 to 1987 in three major countries, the United States, Japan and West Germany (see Table 10.3).

Because of its lower savings rate the United States may have found it easier to stimulate a revival from the 1981–2 recession than was true in Canada and a number of other countries. However, the combination of strong fiscal action with tough monetary policy and the slower recovery of much of the rest of the world produced an almost 60 per cent increase in the US real effective exchange rate between the end of 1980 and early 1985. Because of this rise in the value of the US dollar a significant part of the increased spending in the United States during this period was diverted to foreign goods. As a result the United States foreign balance moved into a large deficit position on current account. This meant that the large United States government deficits were to some degree offsetting private

Table 10.3 Sectoral balances, United States, Japan and West Germany, 1982 and 1987 compared

	1982	*1987* (*billion $ US*)	*Net changes 1982 to 1987*
United States			
Foreign sector	–1	–161	–160
Private sector	110	–48	–158
Govt. sector	–111	–105	6
Japan			
Foreign sector	7	87	80
Private sector	48	97	49
Govt. sector	–41	–10	31
West Germany			
Foreign sector	5	45	40
Private sector	28	64	36
Govt. sector	–23	–19	4

Source: Data for the United States are from the US National Accounts. Data for Japan and West Germany are from the IMF's *World Economic Outlook*, October 1988. Since no data for the private sector are easily available for these two countries, data were derived from the totals for the other two sectors. The government sector includes all levels of government. The foreign sector for Japan and West Germany are the current account in their balance of payments. Because of statistical discrepancies amounting to $8.1 billion in 1987 and $.1 billion in 1982, the totals for the United States do not balance.

sector surpluses in other countries, especially in Japan and West Germany. This appreciation of the United States dollar has now been fully reversed but the current account deficit has only recently begun to decline.

Some numerical dimensions of these changes are shown by the data in Table 10.3. Thus, in the United States, although the foreign sector balance deteriorated by $160 billion between 1982 and 1987 the government sector balance remained almost unchanged. In contrast, the private sector balance moved from a surplus of savings over investment amounting to $110 billion in 1982 to an excess of investment spending over saving of $48 billion in 1987. The net change for this sector was almost as large as that for the foreign sector. On the other hand, in both Japan and West Germany there were large improvements in their foreign sector balances and substantial increases in their private sector surpluses of savings over domestic investment. While no attempt is made here to explain this divergent

Table 10.4 Government, foreign and private sectoral balances, OECD countries, 1960 to 1988

	Government ($T'-G$)	Foreign Sector ($X-M$)	Private Sector ($S-I$)
		(per cent of gross domestic product)	
1960–67	–0.2	0.3	+0.5
1968–73	–0.2	0.4	+0.6
1974–79	-2.3	–0.1	+2.2
1980–86	-3.6	–0.4	+3.2
1981	-2.8	–0.3	+2.5
1982	–4.2	–0.3	+3.9
1983	–4.6	–0.2	+4.4
1984	-3.8	–0.6	+3.2
1985	-3.6	–0.6	+3.0
1986	-3.6	–0.2	+3.4
1987[e]	-2.5	–0.4	+2.1
1988[e]	-2.4	–0.4	+2.0

[e] estimated. Private sector balance, calculated residually, includes statistical discrepancy. The data in this table are not adjusted for inflation. Such an adjustment would reduce the absolute size of the numbers for the government and private sectors by a significant amount, particularly in the higher inflation years of the 1970s and early 1980s. There would also be some effects on the foreign sector magnitudes.
Sources: *Historical Statistics, 1960–1986*, OECD, Paris, 1988, tables 6.15 and 6.7; and *Economic Outlook*, 43, June 1988.

behaviour pattern, it does seem clear that any economic analysis that neglects developments in the private sector balance may miss an important part of the story. In this context, it is useful to note the view expressed by Keynes in his *General Theory* that 'there has been a chronic tendency throughout human history for the propensity to save to be stronger than the inducement to invest. The weakness of the inducement to invest has been at all times the key to the economic problem' (Keynes, 1936, pp. 347–8). According to this view, one would expect the appearance of chronic government deficits in recent years to reflect the decline in private capital spending relative to private saving. There are some reasons for believing this to be true.

What has transpired over the past few decades is shown clearly by the data given in Table 10.4. Thus, the excess of gross private saving over gross private capital spending ($S–I$) which was negligible in the 1960s averaged 2.2 per cent of GDP in the period 1974–9 and 3.2 per cent from 1980 to 1986. Since the foreign sector balance for the OECD area as a whole has been small throughout the period covered, the private sector surplus of saving in excess of capital spending corresponds closely to the government sector deficit. In this table the government sector includes all levels of government not just the central government as in Table 10.2. The negative balance in the government sector and the positive balance in the private sector both increased significantly during the 1981–2 downturn, remained relatively high during the mid-1980s and have declined moderately since then.

When private sector surpluses are being balanced by government sector deficits, the willingness of the private sector to save is in a sense being aborted; it fails to result in an increase in the stock of capital, because of a deficiency in private capital spending. Some economists believe that the economic system automatically generates sufficient capital spending to balance the amounts people wish to save – in effect, that Say's Law is operative. They argue that government deficits, by causing high interest rates, crowd out the capital spending needed to balance private sector savings. However, the evidence suggests that in some periods it may be the lack of capital spending that has 'crowded in' the government deficits. Consider the period 1980 to 1983, a period during which, as the data in Table 10.1 show, government budgets for the OECD group of countries as a whole experienced no structural change yet budget deficits rose sharply as income levels grew much more slowly or declined and unemployment levels rose sharply. For this same three-year period International Monetary Fund data show that real gross fixed investment in all industrial countries declined by 6.7 per cent (IMF, 1988, p. 61). These data are consistent with the view that it was this sharp decline in capital spending that caused real incomes to fall, thus inducing the increase in government deficits and, in the face of an unchanged level of private saving, produced the large private sector surpluses. Over the four years 1983 to 1986 it can be estimated that the excess of private sector savings over capital spending amounted, for the OECD as a whole, to some $1230 billion. Governments, by acquiescing in the rise of their deficits in the face of declining or slowly growing incomes, in effect, validated the aspirations of private savers to this extent. In so doing they prevented a much larger decline in income. As a result, during this period private savers acquired government securities in the above amount instead of claims to or claims secured by real privately owned capital assets.

In view of the high level of private savings in the developed world as a whole there is a certain irony in the fact that real interest rates, which rose sharply in the early 1980s in the face of severe monetary restraint, have declined only moderately since then. The United States with its relatively low level of private sector saving has been an exception here. Its private sector deficit over this period has been more than offset by the large private sector surpluses in the rest of the developed world. But the United States policy mix which features a very loose fiscal policy combined with a comparatively tight monetary policy has contributed to the maintenance of high real interest rates throughout the world. This US policy seems to have induced many other countries to pursue restrictive monetary policies despite their much more restrained fiscal policies.

What conclusions can be drawn from this analysis? It can be argued that the world has already avoided a major depression. The 1981–2 downturn, if it had occurred in an economy similar to the one that existed in 1929, could easily have become much more severe. But the much larger size of the government sector in all countries and the increased stabilising power of government budgets quickly checked the decline. As a result, on an annual basis, world output did not fall at all and output in the industrial countries declined by only 0.3 per cent. This rapid check to the decline required governments to accept much larger deficits. Using inflation-adjusted data it can be estimated that the deficits of all governments in industrial countries increased from an average of about 1 per cent of GDP during the years 1979 to 1981 to around 3.2 per cent for the years 1982 to 1985. There has been some decline in deficits since 1985 but for 1988, on an inflation-adjusted basis, the above average may still be about 1.5 per cent of GDP.

Continued government deficits even after six years of growth in real output reflects the existence of private savings rates in a number of major countries well in excess of private capital spending levels. In the meantime, these government deficits have been adding to the amount of relatively safe financial assets in the hands of the private sector and this must have added substantially to that sector's financial strength. This, in turn, may have helped to stimulate the recent strengthening of capital spending in a number of countries.

Although a severe decline of the 1929 type may not be at all probable, the now long continued excess of private savings over private capital spending suggests that all is not well in the capitalist enterprise world. Instead of a sharp severe decline of the 1929 type, the world may be witnessing a slow drift towards higher unemployment rates. Such a development is already evident in Western Europe, the area where the slowdown in capital spending is most pronounced. Above all the situation calls for a concerted attack on the high level of real rates of interest that exist throughout the world. Not only would such a decline induce some increase in capital spending but it would also help alleviate the heavy debt burden of third world countries. There is also a need to examine seriously whether private sector savings rates are too high throughout much of the developed world – perhaps as a result of the generous tax shelters for savings many governments have provided? As Keynes so clearly recognised, continued growth and prosperity in our enterprise economies is dependent on a level of capital spending adequate to offset the amounts private savers are prepared to provide. And capital spending, in turn, is heavily dependent on adequate rates of economic growth. However, as long as governments are prepared to run substantial deficits, as they have been in the 1980s, the world can avoid another Great Depression.

Note

1. My last professional contact with Jack Weldon occurred during the second round of hearings of the Macdonald Commission. These took the form of debates with an invited panel of prominent citizens. Jack appeared in Montreal and raised the question of why we now look back on the 1960s as a Golden Era, even though our living standards are higher today. Was it the result of the lower level of unemployment at that time and the feeling that jobs were easy to obtain? Or was it the steady growth in real incomes and the lower level of inflation? Or was it some combination of all these factors together with the smaller degree of uncertainty that existed then? The question was characteristic of Jack. It showed his ability to cut through conventional views and get to the heart of what determines economic welfare. His presence on the Canadian economic scene will be sorely missed.

References

Baily, M. N. (1978) 'Stabilization Policy and Private Economic Behavior', *Brookings Papers on Economic Activity*, 1, p. 14.

Barber, C. L. (1978) 'On the Origins of the Great Depression', *Southern Economic Journal*, 44, pp. 432–56.

Brunner, K. (ed.) (1981) *The Great Depression Revisited* (London: Martin Nijhoff).

Cagan, P. (1979) *Persistent Inflation: Historical and Policy Essays* (New York: Columbia University Press).

Drummond, I. M. (1987) *The Gold Standard and the International Monetary System, 1900–39* (London: Macmillan).

Eichengreen, B. and J. Sachs (1985) 'Exchange Rates and Economic Recovery in the 1930's', *Journal of Economic History*, 45, pp. 925–46.

Friedman, M. and A. Schwartz (1963) *A Monetary History of the United States* (Princeton: Princeton University Press).

Haberler, G. (1976) *The World Economy, Money, and the Great Depression, 1919–1939* (Washington: American Enterprise Institute).

International Monetary Fund (1988) *World Economic Outlook, October, 1988* (Washington: The Fund).

James, H. (1986) *The German Slump: Politics and Economics, 1924–1936* (Oxford: The Clarendon Press).

Jonung, L. (1981) 'The Depression in Sweden and the United States: A Comparison of Causes and Policies', in K. Brunner (ed.), *The Great Depression Revisited* (London: Martin Nijhoff).

Jump, G. V. and T. A. Wilson (1986) 'Savings in Canada: Retrospective and Prospective', in J. Sargent (Research Coordinator), *Economic Growth: Prospects and Determinants* (Toronto: University of Toronto Press).

Keynes, J. M. (1936) *The General Theory of Employment, Interest and Money* (London: Macmillan).

League of Nations (1938) *Review of World Trade, 1937* (Geneva).

Lewis, W. A. (1952) 'World Production, Prices and Trade, 1870–1960', *The Manchester School of Economic and Social Studies*, 20.

Nakamura, T. (1987) 'The Japanese Economy in the Inter-War Period, A Brief Summary', in R. Dore and R. Sinha (eds), *Japan and World Depression (Then and Now) Essays in Memory of E. F. Penrose* (Macmillan: London).

Perry, J. H. (1955) *Taxes, Tariffs and Subsidies* (Toronto: University of Toronto Press).

Richardson, H. W. (1983) 'Fiscal Policy in the 1930's', in *The Managed Economy*, C. Feinstein (ed.) (Oxford: The University Press) pp. 68–92.

Stein, H. (1969) *The Fiscal Revolution in America* (Chicago: University of Chicago Press).

11 The Rise of Unemployment since the 1950s

David Schwartzman[1]

Demographic explanations of the rise in unemployment in the United States since the 1950s have had little success (Summers, 1986). Greater female labour force participation has had no noticeable effect, and there are now relatively fewer unemployment-prone teenagers than in 1965. Surprisingly, unemployment has gone up despite a higher general level of education.

This chapter looks at skill and unemployment. Despite the prosperity of recent years, a high rate of unemployment has persisted – so much so that economists have revised the 'natural' rate upward. However, it is misleading to treat the unemployment rate as an aggregate. Occupational unemployment rates vary greatly. Few managers, professionals, and technical workers have suffered unemployment in the prosperity of the 1980s: the unemployment has been concentrated among unskilled operatives and labourers. The unskilled continue to suffer too high a rate of unemployment for it to be dismissed as due to friction or lack of mobility. By contrast, unemployment among the skilled is low enough to be so explained. Indeed, the unemployed in this group are so few as to set off inflation alarms.

Since the high rate of unemployment is limited to the unskilled, this chapter applies a microeconomic analysis. The conclusion is that this unemployment is due to the high rate of investment that has led to the introduction of techniques utilising fewer unskilled workers. The immediate effect of the investment to raise output and thus employment masked the later adverse effects on the employment of the unskilled. Once the new capital goods were in place, less unskilled labour hours were required to produce a given level of output. The change in techniques has been induced by the increase in the cost of unskilled labour relative to both interest rates and the prices of capital goods. This increase in relative cost has been due in part to inflation to which full-employment fiscal and monetary policies have contributed. Thus these public policies have had the perverse effect of increasing the unemployment rate of the unskilled. At the same time the policies increased the demand for skilled labour whose jobs have not been threatened by the investment. Market pressures from the policy-induced rates of investment have been among the factors contributing to inflation. The combination of inflation and unemployment seen in the 1970s and the persistence of unemployment, together with what has come to be called moderate inflation in the 1980s, can be traced at least in part to fiscal and monetary policies intended to promote employment.

1 THE TREND OF UNEMPLOYMENT

The BLS (Bureau of Labor Statistics) has reported unemployment rates by occupations since 1958, but a change in the occupational classification in 1983 has deprived us of a continuous series covering later years. Table 11.1 compares the occupational unemployment rates in 1987 with those of the most closely comparable occupation classes for the also prosperous year of 1979. The total unemployment rate of 5.8 per cent in 1979 was less than in 1978 when it was 6.1 per cent and in 1980 when it was 7.1 per cent. Although the total unemployment rate in 1987 of 6.2 per cent was the lowest since 1980, it was above the rate in 1979. In both years the unemployment rate varied inversely with the level of skill among occupations. In 1987 the highest rate – among handlers, equipment cleaners, helpers and labourers – was higher than the rate in 1979 for the most closely comparable group, non-farm labourers, which in this earlier year also suffered the highest unemployment. In both years unemployment in the other unskilled groups – machine operators, service and farm workers – was high. The negative correlation between average weekly earnings of males by occupations and unemployment rates in 1979 – the correlation coefficient was −.90 – further demonstrates the inverse relationship between skill and unemployment.

We also observe that the rise in the unemployment rate varied inversely with the skill level. Table 11.2 shows rising trends in unemployment rates by occupations between 1958 and 1982. It should be noted that unemployment was high both at the beginning and at the end of the period covered, so the perception of rising trends is not due to the high rates in the recession year 1982. Table

Table 11.1 Unemployment rates by occupation in 1987 and 1979

1987 Occupation	*Unemployment rate* %	*1979* Occupation	*Unemployment rate* %
Total	6.2	Total	5.8
Professional	2.0	Professional & technical	2.4
Technicians & related	3.2		
Managerial	2.4	Managerial	2.3
Sales	3.4	Sales	3.9
Administrative support	4.5	Clerical	4.6
Precision production	6.0	Craft	4.5
Machine operators	8.0	Operatives ex. transport	8.4
Handlers, equipment cleaners, helpers, labourers	13.9	Non-farm labourers	10.8
Service	7.5	Service	7.1
Farm workers	7.0	Farm workers	3.8

Sources: Bureau of Labor Statistics, *Employment and Earnings*, January 1988, p. 170; *Statistical Abstract of the United States 1980*.

11.3 shows that the trend rates of growth in unemployment varied inversely with skill among occupations. Non-farm labourers do not lead, because their unemployment rate was high at the beginning of the period. Operatives, comprising most manufacturing workers, suffered the highest rate of growth. Service workers, who are largely unskilled, also show a high rate of growth of unemployment. Confirming the negative relationship between skill and the rise in unemployment, the correlation coefficient between earnings in 1979 and the trend rates of unemployment shown in Table 11.3 is −.74.

Table 11.2 Unemployment rates by occupational groups, 1958–82

Year	*Total* %	*Prof. & tech.* %	*Managers* %	*Sales* %	*Clerical* %	*Craft* %	*Operatives* %	*Labourers* %	*Service* %	*Farm* %
1958	6.8	2.0	1.7	4.1	4.4	6.8	11.0	15.1	6.9	3.2
1959	5.5	1.7	1.3	3.8	3.7	5.3	7.6	12.6	6.1	2.6
1960	5.5	1.7	1.4	3.8	3.8	5.3	8.0	12.6	5.8	1.7
1961	6.7	2.0	1.8	4.9	4.6	6.3	9.6	14.7	7.2	2.8
1962	5.5	1.7	1.5	4.3	4.0	5.1	7.5	12.5	6.2	2.3
1963	5.7	1.8	1.5	4.3	4.0	4.8	7.5	12.4	6.1	3.1
1964	5.2	1.7	1.4	3.5	3.7	4.1	6.6	10.8	6.0	3.1
1965	4.5	1.5	1.1	3.4	3.3	3.6	5.5	8.6	5.3	2.6
1966	3.8	1.3	1.0	2.8	2.9	2.8	4.4	7.4	4.8	2.2
1967	3.8	1.3	.9	3.2	3.1	2.5	5.0	7.6	4.5	2.3
1968	3.6	1.2	1.0	2.8	3.0	2.4	4.5	7.2	4.4	2.1
1969	3.5	1.3	.9	2.9	3.0	2.2	4.4	7.5	4.2	1.9
1970	4.9	2.0	1.3	3.9	4.1	3.8	7.1	9.5	5.3	2.6
1971	5.9	2.9	1.6	4.3	4.8	4.8	8.3	10.8	6.3	2.6
1972	5.6	2.4	1.8	4.3	4.7	4.3	7.0	10.3	6.3	2.7
1973	4.9	2.2	1.4	3.7	4.2	3.7	5.7	8.5	5.8	2.6
1974	5.6	2.3	1.9	4.2	4.6	4.4	7.5	10.1	6.3	2.6
1975	8.5	3.2	3.0	5.8	6.6	8.3	13.2	15.6	8.6	3.6
1976	7.7	3.2	3.1	5.4	6.4	6.9	10.1	13.7	8.8	4.5
1977	7.1	3.0	2.8	5.3	5.9	5.7	8.9	12.1	8.2	4.7
1978	6.1	2.6	2.1	4.1	4.9	4.7	7.5	10.8	7.5	3.9
1979	5.8	2.4	2.1	3.9	4.7	4.5	7.8	10.9	7.2	3.9
1980	7.1	2.5	2.4	4.4	5.3	6.6	11.4	14.6	7.9	4.6
1981	7.6	2.8	2.7	4.6	5.7	7.5	11.4	14.7	8.9	5.3
1982	9.8	3.3	3.5	5.6	7.0	10.2	16.2	18.5	10.6	6.5

Source: Bureau of Labor Statistics.

Table 11.3 Trend rates of unemployment rates by occupation 1958–82

Occupation	*Trend rate*
Total	.103
Professionals & technicians	.064
Managers & administrators	.015
Sales workers	.049
Clerical workers	.106
Craftworkers	.094
Operatives	.168
Non-farm labourers	.084
Service workers	.132
Farm workers	.115

Note: Calculated from trend equations fitted to data in Table 11.2.

2 THE DEMAND FOR LABOUR

The analysis of the demand for labour will be based on the following equation:

$$e_t = f(w_t, y_t, k_t) \tag{11.1}$$

where e = employment
w = wage rate
y = output
k = net capital stock
and t = year

The wage rate and output are usually included in employment models. Net capital stock also is included in equation (11.1), since for any given output, an increase in net capital stock will reduce the demand for labour.

Now, k_t will be the cumulative total of previous additions to stock:

$$k_t = \sum_{i=t-j+1}^{i=t} (k_i - k_{i-1}) \tag{11.2}$$

where j = the life of capital equipment and k_i is net of depreciation at t and valued at prices also at t. The additions to capital stock in any period will be a function of the ratio of the real interest rate to the real wage rate, the ratio of the real price of capital goods to the real wage rate, current output, and the current capital stock:

$$(k_i - k_{i-1}) = g\ (r_{i-1} / w_{i-1}, p^k_{i-1} / w_{i-1}, y_{i-1}, k_{i-1}) \qquad (11.3)$$

In contrast to the usual macroeconomic argument, the wage rate is introduced explicitly, and the rate of interest is treated as one component of a relative price, not as simply the price of capital. The model also includes the ratio of the price of capital goods to the wage rate. Equation (11.3) conforms to the usual analysis by introducing current output. We also add the capital stock. If for any reason the stock of capital is higher than desired, the investment in the current period will be lower. Thus, if public policy succeeds in encouraging investment in one period, the level will be lower in subsequent periods. The variables are expressed in real terms.

The model emphasises the effect of changes in r_i / w_i and p^k_i / w_i on $(k_i - k_{i-1})$ and on k_t, and through these variables on e_t. The discussion of the effect of r_i / w_i and of p^k_i / w_i on e_t will feature changes in k_t / e_t. Even with a given technology, it is possible to have plants that use different combinations of labour and capital. Thus an increase in k_t makes it possible for any given level of output to be produced with less labour. Whether the total demand for labour is reduced or not as a consequence of the change in the capital/labour ratio depends on how much output changes.

We will examine decade average rates of growth of the capital/labour ratio. A positive growth rate of this ratio, even in the absence of technical change, means that capital is being substituted for labour. If the total output grows faster than capital, then the growth of the capital/labour ratio need not entail a smaller total demand for labour. However, if capital grows faster than both output and employment, then total employment will decline (Salter, 1966, pp. 40–1). Further, a large reduction in the cost of capital relative to the cost of labour will induce labour-saving technical changes that adversely affect employment.

The discussion of the increase in the relative cost of labour will assume constant labour quality. This assumption commits no egregious error, since wages have risen more than the quality of labour. Moreover, the assumption is close to true for unskilled labour, this chapter's focus. The gain in quality, which usually is measured by educational attainment, has been concentrated in the more skilled occupational groups and has also resulted in more newcomers to the labour force entering skilled occupations. Unskilled workers late in the postwar period had little more schooling than their predecessors. Moreover, the important qualities for unskilled occupations – dexterity, speed, strength and endurance – gained little or nothing from more years of schooling.

To remove remaining doubts alternative estimates of the growth of wages are provided, which assume that the quality of unskilled labour has grown at the same rate as the quality of the labour force as a whole. I also assess the effect of adjusting for quality on the estimates of employment growth.

Economists agree that wages rise with productivity. By contrast, the interest rate may be constant with respect to productivity. If it is constant, then as the relative cost of labour rises with productivity unemployment may do so as well. As we will see, the ratio of the real rate of interest to real wages rose between the first two and the second two decades of the century. During and since the Second World War the ratio fell. The effect of productivity growth on relative factor prices was delayed until the Second World War and postwar periods.

Inflation also raised the relative cost of labour. Postwar stimulative monetary and fiscal policies designed to raise employment held nominal interest rates low to induce investment. The policies achieved the same goal unintentionally as well, by raising the rate of inflation and thus reducing the real rate of interest. Employment was generated immediately in the construction and other capital goods industries. However, over a long period, the policies reduced the employment of unskilled labour in industries using the new capital goods. Total employment rose immediately, but in subsequent periods the capital/labour ratio was higher than it otherwise would have been and employment was lower.

3 WAGES, INTEREST RATES, AND THE COST OF CAPITAL GOODS 1900–87

This review of the history of wages and the interest rate will measure nominal wages by the average hourly earnings of production workers in manufacturing. Most of these workers are operatives and labourers, but the data also cover such skilled factory workers as foremen and mechanics. By including skilled workers, the data understate the

Table 11.4 Index numbers of real annual earnings of year-round full-time workers in manufacturing by sex and occupation, 1939, 1960, 1969 and 1980 (1939 = 100)

	1939	*1960*	*1969*	*1980*
Males				
Professional & technical	100	134	154	179
Managers & props.[1]	100	132	155	166
Clerical workers	100	138	173	163
Sales workers	100	163	203	208
Craft workers	100	154	177	178
Operatives	100	161	184	187
Service workers[2]	100	165	190	200
Labourers[1]	100	161	191	198
Females				
Professional & technical	100	141	172	177
Managers & props.[1]	100	141	160	157
Clerical workers	100	137	152	152
Sales workers	100	134	150	194
Craft workers	100	NA	169	174
Operatives	100	165	186	189
Service workers[2]	100	164	182	195
Labourers[1]	100	NA	171	196

[1] excludes those on farms.
[2] excludes those in private households.
Note: Current-dollar earnings deflated by GNP implicit price deflator.
Source: Decennial Censuses of Population.

rise in earnings of unskilled workers. As Table 11.4 shows, the earnings of operatives, labourers and service workers employed full-time and year round, increased more than those of other occupations, except sales workers over the period 1960–80.

Average hourly earnings also are a deficient index of the cost of unskilled workers, because they exclude fringe benefits, which have risen relatively. Over the period 1950 to 1987 the deflated average hourly compensation of all manufacturing employees rose 21 per cent more than deflated average hourly earnings of manufacturing production workers.[2] The difference in rates of growth is 0.65 per cent per year. Since this chapter's thesis is that the rise in the relative cost of unskilled labour induced substitution, the cautious approach is to understate the rise by relying on the measure excluding fringe ben-

Table 11.5 Average annual rates of growth of average hourly earnings in current and constant dollars, of total factor productivity and of the GNP deflator, by decades 1900–87

	Average annual rate of increase			
	Productivity	*Wages*		*GNP*
		Current	*Constant*	*Deflator*
	%	%	%	%
1900–10	0.9	3.2	1.0	2.3
1910–20	1.3	10.3	2.4	7.9
1920–30	1.6	0.0	5.1	–5.1
1930–40	2.3	1.8	3.0	–1.2
1940–50	2.3	7.8	1.7	6.1
1950–60	1.9	4.5	1.9	2.6
1960–70	1.7	4.0	0.9	3.1
1970–80	0.4	7.7	0.6	7.1
1980–87	1.0	4.4	–0.1	4.5

Sources: Average hourly earnings in manufacturing from *Economic Report of the President 1988*, p. 298; and *Historical Statistics*, vol. 1, pp. 169–70, Series D–104. GNP deflator from *Economic Report of the President 1988*, p. 252. Extended by Series for bituminous coal mining wages, p. 170, Series D-814. Total factor productivity growth between 1900 and 1950 in private domestic economy based on *Historical Statistics*, vol. 2, p. 948, Series W–6, and for 1950–87 based on data supplied by Bureau of Labor Statistics.

efits. Another justification for this choice is that unskilled workers did not gain fringe benefits proportionally as large as those obtained by managerial, professional and other skilled workers.

In each decade before the Second World War nominal wages rose more than prices, as measured by the GNP implicit deflator and the wholesale price index (Table 11.5). In the 1920s nominal wages remained at the same level as in the preceding decade while prices fell, resulting in a large increase in real wages. In the 1930s real wages again rose despite the high level of unemployment. Nominal wages rose while prices fell. In these two decades the growth of real wages substantially exceeded the growth of productivity in the private domestic economy.

Over the war and postwar period, nominal wages went up faster than prices, except in the 1980s, when nominal wages only kept up with inflation. However, the gains in constant-dollar wages were smaller throughout the war and postwar period than in any of the prewar decades since 1910. As we will see, the fall in the real rate of interest was chiefly responsible for the rise in the relative cost of unskilled labour. The fall in the prices of capital goods relative to the wage level also contributed.

We turn to the rate of interest. In Table 11.6 Moody's Aaa bond rate, an index of long-term corporate bond rates, measures the nominal rate of interest. The estimate of the real rate of interest for any year is the nominal rate minus the change in the GNP implicit price deflator for that year.

The decade average nominal interest rate did not rise between 1900 and 1939, despite large changes in the inflation rate. Between the first and second decades the inflation rate rose 3.9 percentage points, but the nominal interest rate went up only 0.6 percentage points, resulting in a negative average real interest rate in the second decade. After 1921 the 1920s saw price stability, but the average nominal interest rate was the same as in the preceding decade. Thus the average real interest rate was as high as 5.1 per cent. The depressed 1930s saw the average real interest rate rise to as much as 5.6 per cent. The nominal interest rate fell by less than 1 percentage point while prices fell by 1.7 per cent. This average real interest rate was not exceeded before the 1980s. During the 1940s and 50s the nominal interest rate was lower than in any previous decade, despite continuing inflation. The 1940s saw a negative real interest rate. In the 1950s, the nominal interest rate did not rise sufficiently in the face of moderate inflation to bring the real interest rate back up to the prewar level. The inflation rate continued at the same level in the 1960s, and the nominal interest rate rose sharply. Nevertheless, the real rate remained substantially below the levels of the 1920s and 30s. Between the 1960s and 70s, the inflation rate rose more than the nominal interest rate; the real rate of interest fell further. In the 1980s the real rate of interest reached its peak.

Owing to the remarkable rigidity of the nominal interest rate in the face of both inflation and deflation, over nearly all of the postwar period the real interest rate was much lower than in the 1920s and 30s. A sharp drop in the rate of inflation in the 1920s did not push down the nominal interest rate, and although it fell in the 1930s, the fall in the rate of inflation was greater. Moreover, increases in the nominal rate lagged far behind the postwar climb of the rate of inflation until the 1980s.

A linear regression analysis of the average real interest rate against the rate of inflation, as shown in columns 3 and 2 in Table 11.6

Table 11.6 Average nominal and real interest rates, average annual rate of price increase and indexes of real interest rate (1929 = 100) by decades, 1900–87

	Nominal interest rate	*Annual price increase*	*Real interest rate*	
			rate	*Index (1929=100)*
	(1) %	*(2)* %	*(3)* %	*(4)*
1900–09	4.2	2.5	1.7	28
1910–19	4.8	6.4	−1.6	−25
1920–29	4.8*	−0.2*	5.1*	82*
1930–39	3.9	−1.7	5.6	91
1940–49	2.7	5.7	−3.0	−49
1950–59	3.3	2.5	0.8	12
1960–69	5.0	2.6	2.4	38
1970–79	8.2	6.6	1.7	27
1980–87	11.8	5.2	6.6	104

* Estimates for 1920–29 based on years 1922–29. Estimates for decade as a whole, including 1920 and 1921, are (1) 5.1, (2) −2.7, (3) 7.8, (4) 126.

Sources and Notes: Nominal interest rate: Moody's Aaa bond rate 1919–87 from *Economic Report of the President*, various years, and *Historical Statistics*, vol. 2, series X477, p. 1003, and unadjusted index of yields of American railroad bonds, ibid, series X476, p. 1003. Annual price increase: GNP implicit price deflator from *Economic Report of the President*, various years, and *Historical Statistics*, vol. 1, series E1, p. 197 for 1919–85. Extended by Wholesale Price Index for all commodities, *Historical Statistics*, vol. 1, series E23, p. 199. Real interest rate computed for each year by subtracting price increase for that year from the nominal interest rate. Decade averages of annual real interest rates then computed.

suggests that the nominal rate lagged behind the inflation rate even over intervals of as long as a decade. The results of the analysis are as follows:

$$RI = 4.14 - .60\dot{p} \quad (t = -1.76) \qquad (11.4)$$

$$\bar{R}^2 = .21$$

where RI = real interest rate, and $\dot{p}$ = rate of price increase. The corresponding regression analysis of the nominal interest rate reveals

Table 11.7 Indexes of real wages and interest rates and of the wage/interest rate ratio by decades 1900–87 (1929 = 100)

	Indexes		
	Wages	*Interest Rate*	*Wage/ Interest Rate*
1900–09	50	28	179
1910–19	52	–25	(1)
1920–29	89	84*	106
1930–39	113	91	124
1940–49	156	–49	(1)
1950–59	180	12	1500
1960–69	206	38	542
1970–79	221	27	819
1980–87	222	104	213

(1) Not shown because average real interest rate negative in this period.
* Estimate based on years 1922–9.
Sources: See Tables 11.5 and 11.6.

no relationship. The coefficient of determination is .02. Other studies have also found that inflation reduces the real interest rate.[3]

We come now to the crucial ratio of real wages to the real interest rate. Over the whole of the pre-Second World War period the ratio fell (Table 11.7). The increase did not come before the 1940s and the 1950s, but the increase in these two decades was enormous. Defining a unit of capital as the quantity purchased for $1 in 1929 and a unit of labour as the quantity purchased for the same amount in the same year, in the 1950s a unit of labour cost 15.0 times as much as a unit of capital. In the 1960s the cost of a unit of labour still was as much as 5.4 times as large as a unit of capital, and in the 1970s it rose again to 8.2 times. The sharp rise in the real interest rate in the 1980s still left the cost of a unit of labour as high as 2.1 times the cost of a unit of capital. Choosing 1929 as the base is arbitrary, but consider the alternatives. The war years, with their negative real interest rates, would be a bad choice. The Great Depression with its high real interest rates is equally bad. Replacing 1929 with the period 1922–9 would not alter the conclusion.

We still have the prices of investment goods to consider. Real wages also rose more than these prices deflated for general price changes (Table 11.8). Applying the same method of comparing

Table 11.8 Indexes of average real wages, average real prices of investment goods and of the wage/real prices of investment goods ratio, by decades, 1929–87 (1929 = 100)

	Indexes		
	Investment goods prices	*Wages*	*Wages/ investment goods prices*
1930–39	107	113	106
1940–49	119	156	131
1950–59	123	180	146
1960–69	122	206	169
1970–79	122	221	181
1980–87	115	222	193

Notes: Index of real prices of investment goods based on GNP implicit price deflator for gross private domestic non-residential investment deflated by GNP implicit price deflator for all goods and services. Index of real wages based on average hourly earnings in manufacturing deflated by GNP implicit price deflator for all goods and services.
Sources: GNP implicit price deflator and GNP implicit price deflator for gross private domestic fixed non-residential investment from *Economic Report of the President 1988*, p. 252. See Table 11.5 for sources for average hourly earnings.

relative prices as before, the price of a unit of labour in the 1950s was 1.5 times the price of a unit of capital goods in 1929, in the 1960s it was 1.7 times, in the 1970s 1.8 times, and in 1980–7 1.9 times. The largest increases in relative wages occurred between the 1930s and the 1950s.

We have not taken account of the possible gain in the quality of unskilled labour. Our measure of wages therefore may overstate the increase in the cost of such labour. Table 11.9 shows an index of wages adjusted to reflect quality improvement. The notes to the table describe the method of adjustment, which relies on Edward Denison's (1985, p. 107) estimate of the improvement of the quality of labour in the economy as a whole.

If my argument that unskilled workers gained little if any improvement in skill is correct, then the quality-adjusted wage index in Table 11.9 understates the increase in the cost of unskilled labour, and the adjusted index of the wage/interest rate ratio understates the rise in its relative cost. Nevertheless, this adjusted index shows a much higher relative cost of unskilled labour in the postwar period than in 1929. The fall in the real interest rate after the 1930s was so great that

Table 11.9 Indexes of real wages, the wage/interest rate ratio, and the wage/investment goods prices ratio adjusted for labour quality (1929 = 100)

	Wages	*Indexes* *Wage/ interest rate*	*Wage/ investment goods prices*
1930–39	110	121	103
1940–49	145	(1)	122
1950–59	159	1324	129
1960–69	173	455	142
1970–79	177	654	145
1980–87	170	163	147

Notes: The Wages column is based on the wages index in Tables 11.7 and 11.8 adjusted for change in quality of labour by assuming a rate of improvement of 0.5 per cent per year between 1929 and 1987. Edward Denison, *Trends in American Economic Growth 1929–1982* (Washington, D.C.: Brookings Institution, 1985) p. 107, estimated that the combination of the change in the age–sex composition and gains in years of schooling improved the quality of the labour force at the average annual rate of 0.53 per cent between 1929 and 1982.
(1) Not shown because average real interest rate in this period was negative.

no conceivable gain in the quality of labour could offset its effect on the relative cost of labour. The adjustment reduces the index of the wage/investment goods prices ratio in the postwar period. But the gain in wages during the Second World War and in the first two postwar decades were much larger than the gains in labour quality. The adjusted estimate of the increase in the cost of labour relative to investment goods remains substantial through the 1960s. Thus in the last three decades the adjusted estimate of the cost of labour was over 40 per cent higher than in 1929. Moreover, a correctly adjusted index would show a larger rise in the relative cost of unskilled labour.

4 THE GROWTH OF CAPITAL AND OF LABOUR HOURS

This part, which discusses the growth of capital and of labour as a whole, shows that the capital/labour ratio in the private domestic economy as a whole, in manufacturing, and in private, non-farm, non-manufacturing industries grew. No attempt is made to estimate the growth of the capital/labour ratio induced by factor price changes. This would be a difficult task, since factor employment changes lagged far behind the price changes. While new plants reflect price changes immediately, existing plants are long-lived. In any year the new plant and equipment constitutes a small fraction of the total stock, and displaced labour represents a small percentage of total employment. Moreover, the labour required to produce the new plant and equipment adds to employment prior to installation. Any attempt to observe the effect of factor prices on employment in annual data will fail.

The focus is on unskilled labour, but in this part the measure of the quantity of labour refers to all labour, not to unskilled labour only. The observations suggest that capital has been substituted for labour as a whole. Part 5 of this chapter, which discusses employment by occupation, shows that between 1950 and 1987 the relative employment of unskilled workers declined. Capital has been substituted for unskilled labour more than for skilled labour.

(a) Private Domestic Economy

In the private domestic economy, capital growth rates in the decades following 1960 were much higher than in the prewar decades. As we have seen, the wage/interest rate ratio rose sharply during the 1940s and 50s. The capital stock grew more rapidly in the 1950s than in the 1920s, but in the 1960s and 70s the growth rate was much higher than it had been in any prior decade. Even in the 1980s, when the wage/interest rate ratio was lower than at any time after the Second World War, the capital stock continued to grow at a higher rate than in any of the prewar decades. The decade capital growth rates of the postwar period do not vary with the average wage/interest rate ratios. It took some time for the capital stock to respond to the high relative cost of labour in the 1950s. The lag in the growth of capital can be seen also in the 1980s, when the growth continued at nearly as high a level as in the preceding decade despite the sharp drop in the wage/interest rate ratio.

As a consequence, the capital/labour ratio grew very rapidly in the postwar period (Table 11.10). The ratio grew so much that in 1987 it was 2.1 times as large as in 1950. It was too large to be attributable to an improvement in the quality of labour. If we add 0.5 percentage points per year to the rate of growth of labour to adjust for quality, as in Table 11.9, the rate of growth of the adjusted capital/labour ratio would remain high. We also see that capital productivity declined in

Table 11.10 Private domestic economy: average annual rates of growth of output, labour hours, capital, capital per labour hour, and capital productivity by decades, 1900–87

	Output %	*Labour hours* %	*Capital* %	*Capital/ labour* %	*Output/ capital* %
1900–10	3.9	2.4	3.2	0.8	0.7
1910–20	2.9	0.9	2.5	1.6	0.4
1920–30	2.6	0.4	2.2	1.8	0.4
1930–40	1.9	−0.5	−0.6	−0.2	2.6
1940–50	4.8	1.4	2.5	1.1	2.4
1950–60	3.0	0.3	2.7	2.5	0.3
1960–70	3.7	1.0	3.8	2.8	−0.1
1970–80	2.8	1.7	3.7	2.0	−0.9
1980–87	3.2	1.6	3.3	1.7	−0.1

Sources: Estimates for 1900–50 based on J. W. Kendrick, *Productivity Trends* (Princeton, N.J.: Princeton University Press, 1961) (National Bureau of Economic Research), pp. 334–5. 1950–87: Based on BLS News Release, 30 September 1988, p. 12.

the postwar period, in contrast to the prewar period. These observations are consistent with the hypothesis that capital was substituted for and displaced labour after the war as a result of the rise in the cost of labour relative to that of capital goods.

The objection may be made that the capital growth rate increased with the growth rate of total output, as well as with the relative cost of unskilled labour. To the extent that capital grows with output, it will displace labour independently of changes in relative factor prices. In the prewar as well as the postwar decades, the growth rate of capital far exceeded the growth rate of labour hours. The only exception was the decade of the Great Depression. What is argued here is that the steep postwar rise in the relative cost of labour accelerated the displacement.

Another objection is that the labour demand elasticity is low with respect to wages and the wage/interest rate ratio. However, studies based on annual data may have shown a low elasticity, because capital–labour substitution is a long-run process. Moreover, even a low elasticity will produce some change in employment when the labour/capital cost ratio rises as much as it did between 1929 and the 1950s. Further, this objection is weaker in relation to sectors of the economy and occupational groups.

Table 11.11 Manufacturing: average annual rates of growth of output, labour hours, capital, capital per labour hour, and capital productivity by decades, 1900–87

	Output %	*Labour hours* %	*Capital* %	*Capital/ labour* %	*Output/ Capital* %
1900–10	4.9	3.4	6.2	2.8	−1.3
1910–20	3.8	2.0	5.4	3.4	−1.5
1920–30	2.6	−2.3	0.7	3.1	1.9
1930–40	3.3	0.6	−1.6	−2.1	4.8
1940–50	5.3	3.6	3.5	−0.2	1.8
1950–60	2.7	0.8	3.4	2.6	−0.7
1960–70	4.0	1.4	4.4	3.0	−0.4
1970–80	2.7	0.4	3.6	3.1	−0.9
1980–87	3.3	−0.4	1.7	2.1	1.6

Sources: 1900–50: J. W. Kendrick, *Productivity Trends* (Princeton, N.J.: Princeton University Press, 1961) (National Bureau of Economic Research), p. 465, Table D-2. 1950–87: Based on BLS News Release, 30 September 1988, p. 13.

(b) Manufacturing

Manufacturing industries have responded to the rise in the cost of labour relative to capital goods in the postwar period. After the Second World War capital growth rates in manufacturing were not higher than in the first two decades of the century, but they did exceed the growth rates of the 1920s and 1930s (Table 11.11). Moreover, in the postwar period the capital/labour ratio grew faster in this sector than in the whole private domestic economy. In 1987 the ratio in manufacturing was 2.8 times as large as in 1950. The growth in the capital/labour ratio was too large to be accounted for by the improvement in the quality of labour, assuming that the improvement was at the same rate as Denison estimated for the economy as a whole. Finally, capital productivity fell between 1950 and 1980, indicating capital–labour substitution over this period.

We can observe, as others have, that the decline in this sector's share of private employment has not been due to a decline in its share of output. The fall in manufacturing's share of private gross domestic product at current prices from 32 to 22 per cent between 1950 and 1986[4] is fully explained by the fall in relative prices. Manufacturing's share measured in constant 1982 dollars was 25 per cent in both

Table 11.12 Private non-farm non-manufacturing industries: average annual rates of growth of output, labour hours, capital, capital per labour hour, and capital productivity by decades, 1950–87

	Output %	*Labour hours* %	*Capital* %	*Capital/ labour* %	*Output/ capital* %
1950–60	3.3	1.2	2.6	1.5	0.7
1960–70	3.8	1.6	3.8	2.2	0.0
1970–80	2.9	2.5	4.0	1.5	−1.1
1980–87	3.1	2.6	3.9	1.3	−0.8

Source: Based on data supplied by the Bureau of Labor Statistics.

years.[5] However, over the same period employment in manufacturing fell from 39 per cent of total private employment to 23 per cent.[6] The number of labour hours employed in this sector grew only 25 per cent between 1950 and 1986, while private labour hours as a whole grew 46 per cent.[7] It was not the decline in the share of total output that reduced manufacturing's share of total employment, and at least part of the explanation appears to be the greater growth in capital stock.

(c) Private Non-farm Non-manufacturing Industries

In the postwar period, capital grew at a more rapid rate than labour hours in private non-farm non-manufacturing industries (Table 11.12). We also see that capital productivity declined. Clearly, as in manufacturing, capital was substituted for labour in the postwar period in this sector.

5 EMPLOYMENT BY OCCUPATIONS

The elasticity of substitution of capital for labour appears to vary inversely with skill. Hamermesh and Grant (1979) reach the conclusion that it does, in their review of the relevant literature. Indeed, they suggest that the more highly skilled workers are complementary with physical capital and are jointly substitutable with physical capital for less-skilled labour. Not surprisingly, the rise in the relative price of labour reduced the employment of unskilled workers more than the employment of skilled workers.

Table 11.13 Average annual rates of growth of employment by occupations by decades 1950–80

	1950–60 %	*1960–70* %	*1970–80* %	*1950–80* %
Total	1.0	1.8	2.3	1.7
Professional and technical	4.0	4.0	3.6	3.9
Managers and administrators	3.3	1.6	3.0	2.6
Salesworkers	0.5	1.4	2.6	1.5
Clerical workers	3.1	3.4	3.0	3.2
Craft and kindred workers	0.4	1.7	2.3	1.5
Operatives, incl. transport	0.2	1.5	0.1	0.6
Non-farm labourers	−0.6	0.5	2.0	0.6
Service workers	2.9	1.9	3.1	2.6
Farm workers	−2.8	−5.0	−1.3	−3.1

Sources: Based on *Statistical Abstract of the United States 1982–83*, p. 386, table 648; and *Historical Statistics*, Part 1, pp. 140–5, Series D 233–682.

Table 11.13 reports estimates of the average annual rates of growth of employment by occupations by decades between 1950 and 1980 and over that entire period for the economy as a whole. The lack of continuity in the classification beyond 1982 prevents us from showing growth rates for the same occupational groups between 1980 and 1987. Table 11.14 shows growth rates for broader occupational groups for this later period. For the moment we restrict our attention to 1950–80. In the private domestic economy the average annual rate of growth of capital stock between 1950 and 1980 was 3.4 per cent.[8] This rate of growth far exceeds the rate of growth of employment in the whole economy (1.7 per cent) shown in Table 11.11. More to the point, the rates of growth of employment in the unskilled occupations, operatives, including transport operatives (0.6 per cent) and non-farm labourers (0.6 per cent) were very low – much lower than the rate of growth of total employment. We ignore the large fall in the employment of farm workers, which resulted from improved methods of agricultural production. Greater demand for services required growth in the number of service workers (2.6 per cent), among which were many unskilled workers. The increase in the demand for hospital, restaurant, and other services employing unskilled workers more than offset the effect of the rise in the cost of unskilled labour in this sector. Moreover, the classification of service workers is broad and includes many skilled as well as unskilled

Table 11.14 Average annual rates of growth of employment by occupation, 1980–87

	%
Total	1.8
White-collar workers	3.0
Craft and kindred workers	1.0
Operatives and non-farm labourers	−1.1
Service workers	2.2

Sources: Based on Bureau of Labor Statistics, *Employment and Earnings*, January 1988, p. 179; and *Statistical Abstract of the United States 1982–83*, p. 386, table 648.

workers. We should also observe that the number of professional, technical, and managerial workers grew much more than total employment. This observation is consistent with the suggestion by Hamermesh and Grant mentioned earlier that skill and capital are complementary.

We turn to the period 1980–87 and Table 11.14. In this period the growth rate of capital in the economy as a whole was 3.3 per cent, while the growth rate of total employment was 1.8 per cent. The number of white-collar workers continued to grow rapidly (3.0 per cent). The number of craft and service workers grew at a more moderate rate. What is remarkable is that the number of operatives and non-farm labourers declined (−1.1 per cent). Not only is this the first decade in which the employment of unskilled non-farm workers fell, but the rate of fall was large. However, we cannot attribute all of the reduction in the employment of unskilled workers to the substitution of capital. The growth of imports accelerated in the 1980s, and the domestic manufacturing industries which employed relatively large numbers of unskilled workers were particularly vulnerable to import competition.

The objection may be made that with the rise in the general level of education fewer unskilled workers were coming into the labour force. It was not capital investment and the resultant fall in demand that caused employment of unskilled workers to decline. It was a matter of supply, not of demand. Whatever may have happened to the number of unskilled workers coming into the labour force, supply cannot be the end of the story, since the unemployment rate rose. If supply did fall off, it did not do so rapidly enough to offset the effect of capital substitution on unemployment.

6 MONETARY POLICY, INFLATION, AND THE REAL INTEREST RATE

The rise in velocity in the 1950s caused a modest rate of inflation, which resulted in a very low real interest rate. In the subsequent years, the Fed expanded the money supply at a rapid rate, which raised the inflation rate to new heights and kept the real interest rate at a low level.

We can see in Table 11.15 that in the 1950s the Fed's conservative monetary policy did not prevent inflation. The 3.3 per cent rate of growth of the supply of money, as measured by M2, was approximately equal to the real GNP growth rate. But the growth rate of income velocity was 2.8 per cent. As a result, prices rose at the average rate of 2.5 per cent as measured by the GNP implicit deflator, which is shown in the lower part of the table under 'Average over 1950–59'. The entry beside 'GNP deflator' in the upper part of the table is the average annual rate of growth between 1950 and 1960. Of course, the sum of this growth rate and the growth rate of real GNP necessarily equals the sum of the growth rates of M2 and of velocity. We note that the average real rate of interest was only 0.8 per cent.

In the next decade, the money supply growth rate of 7.0 per cent was much higher than the 3.7 per cent growth rate of real GNP. Prices rose at the rate of only 2.6 per cent, because velocity fell at a rate of 2.0 per cent. The nominal interest rate rose between the 1950s and the 1960s from 3.3 per cent to 5.0 per cent. Since the average inflation rate (calculated as an average of the rates each year) remained approximately the same, the real interest rate rose about as much as the nominal rate. The resulting average real interest rate of 2.4 per cent was much higher than in the 1950s. However, it still was much lower than in the prewar period.

The growth in the money supply accelerated in the 1970s, and velocity also increased sharply, resulting in a 6.6 per cent average inflation rate. The rise in the nominal interest rate to 8.2 per cent did not match the increase in the inflation rate, and the real interest rate fell to 1.7 per cent.

Table 11.15 Average annual rates of growth of M2, velocity, real GNP, GNP deflator 1950–60, 1960–70, 1970–80, 1980–87, and average Aaa bond and real interest rates

	Average annual rate of growth			
	1950–60 %	*1960–70* %	*1970–80* %	*1980–87* %
M2	3.3	7.0	9.5	8.2
Velocity	2.8	−2.0	3.6	−1.1
Real GNP	3.2	3.7	2.8	2.6
GNP deflator	2.9	1.3	10.3	4.5
	Average over			
	1950–59 %	*1960–69* %	*1970–79* %	*1980–87* %
Aaa bond rate	3.3	5.0	8.2	11.8
GNP deflator	2.5	2.6	6.6	5.2
Real interest rate	0.8	2.4	1.7	6.6

Note: The average annual rates of growth in the upper panel are the rates computed on the basis of the two terminal years for each period. Those in the lower panel are averages of the growth rates computed each year on the previous year's base.

Sources: M2: 1950–60, Milton Friedman and Anna J. Schwartz, *A Monetary History of the United States, 1867–1960* (Princeton University Press, 1963) Table A-1, pp. 719–22, col. (8). Other years: *Economic Report of the President*, various years. Velocity: GNP/M2. Real GNP: *Economic Report of the President*, various years. Aaa bond rate: *Economic Report of the President*, various years. Real interest rate: Aaa bond rate – GNP deflator. GNP deflator: *Economic Report of the President*, various years.

In the 1980s M2 continued to rise much more rapidly than real GNP, but velocity fell moderately. The average inflation rate remained at the high level of 5.2 per cent. However, the nominal interest rate rose sharply, and the real interest rate reached the historically high level of 6.6 per cent.

The immediately stimulative effect of monetary policy in the 1960s evidently delayed the long-run substitution effect of the high investment rate of the 1950s and of that decade on employment. The rapid expansion of total output prevented unemployment from rising sharply. However, the continuing high level of investment reduced employment in the 1970s and 1980s.

If the estimate of equation (11.4) is correct, a restrictionist monetary policy cutting the inflation rate by 2 percentage points would have raised the real interest rate by approximately 1.2 percentage points. Such an increase might have been sufficient to prevent the rise in the unemployment rate. Since the relative price of labour would have been reduced only moderately, the effect on capital–labour substitution also would have been moderate. But the demand for unskilled labour would have had to grow only a little more rapidly to keep the rate of unemployment from exceeding the level of the 1950s.

7 CONCLUSION

Capital–labour substitution is not the whole story. Part of the increase in the unemployment of the unskilled was due to the substitution of low-wage foreign labour. However, this part of the rise in unemployment occurred late in the postwar period, and the trend began well before.

The growth of professional and managerial employment points to the substitution of skilled for unskilled labour. Since the growth of government support for education increased the supply of skilled labour, public policy encouraged the substitution of human as well as physical capital for unskilled labour.

Full-employment policies have sought to promote investment by expanding the money supply and through tax incentives. The resulting employment gains were for only short periods. Over the period as a whole the policies had the perverse effect of inducing the substitution of capital for unskilled labour. Public policy also raised the unemployment of the unskilled by inducing a greater supply of skilled labour.

The demand for unskilled labour would have fallen even without the perverse effects of public policy. Most of the rise in the relative price of unskilled labour was due to other causes. But the rise in the unemployment rate represented only a small part of the unskilled labour force. The effect of public policy may have been sufficient to produce the rise in the unemployment rate for this class of labour.

Notes

1. Professor, Department of Economics, Graduate Faculty, New School for Social Research. Subhash Gupta, Michael Kapsa, Yiorgos Kotsolakos and Persefoni Tsaliki provided statistical assistance. The chapter has benefited from comments by Nilufer Catagay, David Gordon, David Howell, Michel Juillard, Jacob Mincer, Edward Nell, Anwar Shaikh, Ross Thomson and the editors.
2. Based on *Economic Report of the President 1988*, p. 300, table B-46, p. 298, table B-44, and p. 252, table B-3.
3. On the basis of quarterly data, Carmichael and Stebbing (1983) conclude that the after-tax nominal interest rate does not vary with the rate of inflation; the after-tax real interest rate falls by the full inflation rate. Their measure of the real interest rate is also the nominal interest rate minus the rate of inflation in the current period.
4. Based on *Economic Report of the President 1988*, p. 260.
5. Based on ibid, p. 261.
6. Based on ibid, pp. 296–7.
7. Based on BLS News Release, 30 September 1988, pp. 10, 12.
8. Based on BLS News Release, 30 September 1988, p. 10.

References

Carmichael, J. and P. W. Stebbing (1983) 'Fisher's Paradox and the Theory of Interest', *American Economic Review*, 83, pp. 619–30.

Denison, E. S. (1985) *Trends in American Economic Growth, 1929–1982* (Washington, D. C.: Brookings Institution).

Hamermesh, D. S. and J. Grant (1979) 'Econometric Studies of Labor–labor Substitution and Their Implications for Policy', *Journal of Human Resources*, 14, pp. 518–41.

Salter, W. E. G. (1966) *Productivity and Technical Change* (Cambridge: Cambridge University Press).

Summers, L. H. (1986) 'Why is the Unemployment Rate So Very High Near Full Employment?', *Brookings Papers on Economic Activity*, 2, pp. 339–94.

12 Public Pensions: A Social Response or a Misuse of Individual Saving?

Louis Ascah and
Athanasios Asimakopulos

1 INTRODUCTION

What are public pensions? Should they be viewed and analysed as schemes of forced individual saving that provide income when retired, or as tax and transfer arrangements that are used to produce incomes for the elderly that are consistent with social goals? If these pensions are viewed as the outcomes of 'forced' individual savings, then judgements about the scope and usefulness of these programmes would revolve around the rates of return that these 'savings' appear to earn in this form, as compared to what they would have earned if they had been invested in alternative forms. Different criteria would be appropriate if public pensions are considered to be tax-and-transfer arrangements. It is the social adequacy of the results of the programmes over time, rather than a calculation of individual rates of return, that becomes relevant. To pass muster, of course, these plans should treat equally individuals who are equal in relevant characteristics (e.g. age, earnings, marital status, etc.).

Many of the recent proposals for radical changes in the United States social security programme (e.g. Ferrara, 1985; Boskin, Kotlikoff and Shoven, 1985) are largely based on the former view of public pensions, while Weldon (1976, 1986) advocates the latter approach. Weldon also raises fundamental questions about the ability of any government to determine the public pensions the working generation will ultimately receive. A government can determine fully only current pension taxes and payments, and thus the determination of the pension amounts received by its working generations will rest with future governments. Its pension laws cannot bind future governments, but these laws, and the example of its own treatment of the retired generations, give rise to political forces that are important elements in the pension decisions of future governments. With many aspects of future economic conditions that will be relevant to these decisions unknown – and with public pension programmes the 'future' covers a very long interval of time – all that a government can hope to do for its constituents is to ensure that the process to be used to calculate public pensions is not changed in a manner that is disadvantageous to them.

In the following we shall examine Weldon's analysis of public pensions, and proposals to reform the US Social Security system that are based on the 'individual saving' approach. It is useful to begin with a brief review of Samuelson's (1958) influential consumption-loan model. This model provides a rationale for social intervention to assist the retired, and recognises the need for a social welfare function in determining pension taxes and benefits, but it also introduces a 'saving' terminology that is found in the 'individual saving' approach.

2 THE EXACT CONSUMPTION-LOAN MODEL

The consumption-loan model provides a useful starting-point for the analysis of public pensions because it presents, in a very stark form, a situation that exists in modern industrial societies. A significant proportion of the elderly in these economies are unable through private arrangements to provide themselves with socially acceptable levels of income. In the consumption-loan model goods cannot be stored – workers produce goods for immediate consumption – and the only way that the retired can obtain the means to consume through private arrangements is to have lent goods during their working years to younger generations. Samuelson examines the scope for these private (or 'market') arrangements by dividing adult life into thirds – individuals work during the first two of these periods and are retired in the third – and by assuming that there are no ties between the working and retired generations that result in family transfers. With the loan of consumption goods as the only source for a private claim in this model, to be able to consume now the retired must have extended such loans to members of a younger generation, while they themselves were still working. These loans can only occur in the second adult period of an individual's life, with the loans being made to younger workers who must be encouraged to dissave. Consumption in the second adult period is limited by the obligation to repay these borrowings, and by the need to make loans that will provide consumption goods during retirement. The interest rates for these loans will depend on the preferences of the individuals for consumption in the different periods of their lives, on the size of each generation, and on their incomes. If it is assumed that a worker produces the same amount of goods in each of his two working periods, and that there is no time preference, then in this model the market for consumption loans would be in equilibrium at a *negative* rate of interest.[1]

Retirement consumption can thus be provided by the market, but only at a very high cost. There is scope for a social mechanism that provides this support without the wasteful distortion of consumption patterns. Samuelson uses the device of a cross-sectional family or clan with the same age distribution as the total population to examine a social arrangement for the provision of consumption goods during retirement. It is in this connection that Samuelson introduces a social welfare function to help determine the consumption levels for each generation, but the source of his function leads him into the trap of using 'saving' terminology for a tax-and-transfer scheme (cf. Asimakopulos, 1980b). He assumes that a clan 'will divide its available resources to maximize a welfare function differing only in scale from each man's utility function' (Samuelson, 1958, p. 472). This use of a representative individual's utility function leads naturally to the notation employed in examining the possibility for providing retirement income through private saving. The clan's withholding, and transfer to the retired, of part of the output produced by its working members is shown as 'workers' saving'. There is, however, no saving in this model. Total family output is consumed as it is produced, since it cannot keep, while each worker consumes all of the output over which he has command – that is, the amount remaining after the family has deducted from the output he produces the portion to be given to the retired.

Two additional elements transform Samuelson's promising beginning for the economic analysis of public pensions to an exercise that is of no more than scholastic interest. Attention is restricted to steady states in which the rate of growth of population is assumed to be known and constant forever; and the social welfare function is misspecified. In this way the distribution of output among generations in the current period is made to depend critically on the continuation of current trends in future periods reaching to infinity. A notional rate of interest on pension taxes, equal to the assumed rate of growth of population is used, in conjunction with the misspecified social welfare function, to calculate the optimum pension tax and payment. The resulting lifetime consumption pattern will only turn out to have been optimal if the population continues to grow at the same constant rate forever.[2] Only in this case – a case that in its dependence on infinity can never be shown to have been borne out by events even in the most favourable of circumstances – would all generations receive the notional rate of interest on their pension taxes. The misspecification of the social welfare function arises because no account is taken of the number of workers and retired persons when Samuelson uses the representative individual's utility function to construct this function. This individual's consumption in the working and retired periods of life are replaced by the per capita consumption of workers and the retired in order to obtain the social welfare function. With no adjustment for the relative numbers in the two generations, this procedure introduces a bias against members of the more populous group if the resulting social welfare function is used (as it is by Samuelson's clan) to distribute a given amount of goods among the different age groups. Any given amount of output would result in higher per capita consumption for the smaller group, and its consumption would thus tend to be favoured since relative sizes are ignored by Samuelson's social welfare function.[3]

In spite of its shortcomings, Samuelson's model[4] served as a starting-point for the analysis of public pensions by Asimakopulos and Weldon (1968), because it made clear the crucial role of a social welfare function in such an examination.

3 WELDON ON PUBLIC PENSIONS

Public pension plans are those programmes established by legislation that give rise to regular payments on the attainment of a certain age by all persons, or to the elderly whose incomes are considered too low, or to those who had been members of the labour force. The payments made to the last group could vary with relative earnings, so as to provide a degree of continuity with their pre-retirement revenues, up to some cut-off point. The purpose of these programmes is to ensure appropriate minimum levels of income for the elderly, with private arrangements such as employer pension plans and private saving being particularly significant as additional sources of revenue for those with higher pre-retirement incomes. The essential nature of public pensions is that they are intergenerational transfers, where the governments act to complement or to make up for the absence of transfers within family structures. The taxes and payments that give rise to these transfers can only be determined definitively at each point in time, and thus 'government pension plans are attempts not to determine the specific level of future income for any group but to redistribute present income and provide rules intended to influence, in a conditional way, how later governments redistribute income' (Asimakopulos and Weldon, 1968, p. 701).

The underlying theme in Weldon's approach to the analysis of public pensions is the recognition that they are social responses to a changing world in which, for a variety of reasons, private arrangements do not ensure adequate support for a substantial proportion of the elderly. Governments, with their power to tax, are in a position to transfer income between generations, and to ensure that public pensions are indexed to changes in price levels. Pensions provided by the private sector, and annuities purchased by individuals, do not have nearly the same degree of price protection. The growth of public pensions in Canada and the United States conforms to this theme. Bryden (1974) in a study of the policy-making process in Canada with regard to old age pensions argues that the widespread hardship among the aged made it necessary to introduce and improve public pension plans. Kotlikoff's (1987, p. 418) interpretation of the growth of unfunded Social Security in the United States is as follows: 'the government elected to redistribute to a generation that had suffered from the depression in the 1930s and had made significant contributions to the nation during World War II'.

Public pension plans, like all social programmes, can change over time as needs and circumstances change.[5] In levying taxes (which are sometimes labelled as 'contributions') to pay pensions to those who qualify for such payments currently, governments operate under laws that they and their predecessors have passed. These laws indicate not only the level of current pension taxes and payments, but they also contain general provisions for the calculation of future taxes and benefits. These provisions cannot be binding on future governments that must levy these taxes and pay these benefits, because each government is sovereign, subject to the constitutional provisions of the particular state. Continuity in public pension arrangements depends on a variety of factors: the political pressures of those who have been taxed under laws that stipulate procedures for calculating benefits; the self-interest of governments who want their successors to honour the pension laws they have passed; the pension promises that turn out not to be too onerous under future circumstances.

In order to describe the interplay of sequential sovereignty and continuity that is involved in pension arrangements, Weldon (1976) distinguishes between the State and governments. The State describes the governing institutions of a distinct geographical area that provide a historical continuity recognised by its inhabitants.[6] Associated with the State is a society that endures over time, even though its membership, the particular individuals that comprise that society, are changing with the passage of time. The term 'community' is used to describe this membership, with the term 'government' denoting the body that makes and enforces laws for this community. Communities, and their governments, are thus seen as changing continuously through births, aging, deaths, immigration and emigration, within the broad confines of an enduring State of society. The laws instituted by past governments continue to rule the lives of individuals in a State unless they are changed by current governments. The decision to accept pre-existing laws is seen as a positive action, a judgement that they are being considered as suitable for current conditions. Notwithstanding the strong forces for continuity in pension laws listed above, they may not be sufficient to prevent their less than full execution when economic conditions make past pensions promises overly generous in relation to the living standards of workers. The analytic examination of public pension plans must recognise that in the last resort the taxes paid and the pensions eventually received depend on the decisions of a sequence of transient governments. Each government can make a final decision only about the pension taxes paid and benefits received by members of its community. The quid pro quo that it offers to its workers is a process for the determination of their pensions that will have strong political support.

For analytical purposes, Weldon (1976, p. 564) associates a social welfare function with a community whose collective preferences are reflected in that function. Government is seen as an agent of the community, and it uses the function to decide on pension taxes and benefits. The variables in the social welfare function are the utilities of the individual members of the community, arranged in appropriate groups. With this one-to-one correspondence between governments and communities, the government at any point in time (e.g. the 'here and now') is concerned with the utilities of individuals alive in that period. But with most of these lives extending over future periods, the lifetime utilities depend on incomes that cannot be directly determined by the current government's taxes and transfers. To close the system for the determination of current pension taxes and benefits it is necessary to enter the values for the future pensions of those currently working, values that will be determined by future governments. Weldon sees this as being done by governments assuming that future pensions will be calculated in the same way as current pensions, and thus on the basis of current conditions values can be entered for these future pensions. Their actual values will depend on future circumstances, but the existence of rules that 'are perceived as rules that will be used to decide the present events of successor communities' (Weldon, 1986, p. 21) allows for a formal closing of the system. 'The special law or process government implements now and bequeaths to its successors proposed that those successors calculate their direct acts precisely as the present acts have been calculated' (Weldon, 1976, p. 571).

What is the role of public saving in a public pension plan? Some of these plans, for example the Quebec and Canada Pension Plans, and the United States Social Security under the current tax and benefit schedules, give rise to public saving as well as to pensions. There is no direct connection between the pensions to be paid and public savings made in connection with these programmes, because the payments of public pensions ultimately depend on a government's ability, and willingness, to tax workers for this purpose.[7] The provision of these savings, in so far as they are utilised in ways that improve the future economic situation of the country, will make it more likely that pension promises will be honoured. It also increases the moral claims to their pensions of those who contributed to public savings as well as to public pensions during their working lives. Weldon (1986, p. 23) came to believe that aggregate saving (private saving modified by public saving to produce a desired total) must thus be included in the social welfare function used to determine taxes and payments.[8] Public pensions to be paid in the future will be affected by the future governments' perceived budget constraints and their expenditure priorities. It may turn out that higher pension costs per worker are balanced to some extent by lower other government costs (for example, youth-related expenditures) per worker. The question of the intergenerational equity of public pension plans should not be treated in isolation from other intergenerational transfers. The *total legacy* (capital stock, ecology, natural resources, etc.) left to future generations must be considered. This means that there is no simple rule to determine the appropriate size for a public pension fund to help insure future pension payments.

With public pensions viewed as social responses to inadequate income from private sources, the focus is on social adequacy rather than individual equity.[9] The rate of return in pension income that any individual obtains from the pension taxes paid over a working life depends on many circumstances of that life, including family status, that are considered relevant in pension laws. In this aspect it is similar to other social arrangements that affect the economic opportunities and lives of individuals from the cradle to the grave. When public pensions are viewed as 'forced individual saving', as they tend to be in the writings turned to in the following sections, the focus is on individual equity and on the rates of return obtained on these 'savings'. There is a difference in the knowledge of future conditions assumed by these two approaches. The former emphasises the process that it is hoped will be used to determine pensions in future circumstances, whatever they might be. The latter tends to assume the existence of some known rate of return over long intervals of time.

4 FERRARA ON THE PRIVATISATION OF SOCIAL SECURITY

Ferrara (1985) presents a Social Security reform proposal that will change current pension taxes to individual saving in Individual Retirement Accounts (IRAs). The pensions to be received would be a function of the private sector rates of return on these savings that he expects to be very high.[10] Reference is made to the 6 per cent average real rate of return on stocks over a fifty-to-sixty-year period and to studies indicating that the before-tax real rate of return on private capital investment in the American economy is at least 12 per cent. Ferrara compares these returns with an (expected) real return through social security of around 1 per cent for the younger generation. To capture these returns for retirement income, Ferrara proposes that workers be allowed to contribute up to 20 per cent (initially, then rising to 100 per cent later) of their social security taxes to IRAs. They would receive a full credit (and not just a deduction) on their income tax for the amount of such contributions, with their future social security benefits being reduced proportionally.

There is a fundamental transition problem in switching from a pay-as-you-go pension plan to a fully-funded plan that Ferrara does not recognise. There must either be decreases in pensions paid to the present older generations, or increases in the contributions by workers that are sufficient to pay the promised pensions to the elderly and to build up the new funded plan. Thus just as the introduction of a pay-as-you-go pension plan greatly benefits members of the older generation who receive pensions without having paid much in pension taxes, the wind-up of such a plan (assuming that pension obligations 'accrued' to date are not repudiated) would adversely affect the working generations at that time, who pay full taxes but receive few benefits.[11]

Ferrara erroneously believes that the double payment problem faced by the working generations during the transition period can be avoided if the government borrows from its private sector to cover the revenue loss from the diversion of a portion of pension taxes to IRAs. But such a switch does not increase either total saving in the economy or the amount used for investment in the private sector. There is thus no increase in the economy's investment income that can be diverted to pay higher pensions without entailing a reduction in incomes elsewhere.

Ferrara's (1985, p. 181) pension reform proposal really boils down to a call for increased saving. The high rate of return on the private sector capital investment he envisages leads him to believe that reform might be attractive to the present working generations even if they are asked to increase their pension taxes in order to make these investments. He is not alone in calling for increased saving based on estimates of a high rate of return from investment in the private sector. Feldstein's (1974) paper on the 'optimal' financing of social security argued for a substantial increase in current pension taxes in order to increase real investment. With an estimate of the social rate of return (15 per cent) on such investment much higher than the assumed discount rate (6 per cent) – based on estimates of the decline in the marginal utility of income due to the steady growth of real wages and for the social discounting of future utility – the conclusion that higher saving for this purpose is desirable, comes as no surprise. But there is no particular reason (as has been pointed out by, e.g., Pechman, 1978, p. 38; Asimakopulos, 1980a, p. 27) why the argument for a drastic increase in saving should be attached to a public pension plan. The assumed high real rate of return on private investment may be a reason for building up a public savings fund to make these investments, but not a reason for changing a public pension plan.

Any estimate of real rates of return based on past experience – especially one that is designed to result in a massive increase in investment – must be handled with great caution (e.g. Pechman, 1978, p. 37; Munnell, 1987, p. 459). The long-term uncertainty of investment returns makes the results of a savings plan unknown in advance. Even if a high real rate of return could be earned, on average, over a long period of time, the volatility of returns could still leave a high degree of risk that would be unacceptable to those dependent on these returns for retirement incomes. Munnell (p. 488) points out the unstable nature of the return on common stocks used by Ferrara to obtain his estimates of a 6 per cent real return. Its standard deviation has been 21 per cent, so that in any given year there is a one-third chance that this return could be as high as 27 per cent or as low as −15 per cent. With such a scenario the elderly would almost certainly opt for a lower real rate of return on their pension taxes from a social security programme that also provides fully-indexed pensions that cannot be obtained in the market.

Public pension plans in general, and the Social Security system in the United States in particular, reflect the social welfare functions of their communities, and they provide for some redistribution within generations as well as between generations. They use formulas that provide higher benefits relative to contributions to workers with lower earnings.[12] This is in contrast to individual savings plans where benefits are strictly related to contributions. A scheme for voluntary opting-out of Social Security à la Ferrara would let higher income workers avoid the redistribution aspect of the plan as decided by the community. A concern with individual equity might sidetrack a programme that provides socially adequate pensions.

The next section examines social security reform proposals based on considerations of individual equity, which also try to allow for some redistribution between income groups in the same generation.

5 ACTUARIALLY DETERMINED SOCIAL SECURITY BENEFITS

Boskin (1986) and Boskin, Kotlikoff and Shoven (1985) (subsequently referred to as BKS) present proposals for fundamental Social Security reforms that directly link individual benefits to prior individual contributions in an actuarial fashion as in insurance and annuity purchases. These proposals are designed to reduce five problems that they judge to be associated with the current Social Security system, i.e. financial solvency, equity, efficiency, uncertainty and lack of information. All that these proposals would probably achieve is a change in the current distribution of benefits which favours single-earner family groups. Whether this is desirable is, of course, a value judgement.

BKS (p. 2)[13] are of the opinion that: 'The Social Security system is not equitable in that it offers very different rates of return to households in similar circumstances'. The spousal benefit which is equal to one-half of the worker's basic benefit is an important example of such differences. A married and a single worker, with the same histories of earnings, contribute equal amounts for unequal benefits. The unmarried worker also contributes to paying for survivors' insurance even though there would be no 'survivors' to receive these benefits. Boskin (p. 19) and BKS (p. 11) propose to eliminate these perceived inequities by applying the same guaranteed real rate of return on all credits to Social Security in a given year. Persons would 'purchase' only the types of insurance they require, and thus single workers would not see a portion of their credits used for survivor insurance etc.

The equity rule proposed is that the contributions by every worker in a given year would earn the same rate of return as the contributions of every other worker. However, this rule is then weakened by allowing for redistribution from those with higher incomes to those with lower incomes. Boskin (p. 141) proposes a two-tiered Social Security system where the first tier (called the annuity function) would be based on the strict equity rule, while the second tier (called the transfer function) funded from general revenues would supplement basic benefits for low-income workers and families. Even though rates of return may be identical when only the annuity function taxes and benefits are compared, it is quite clear that rates of return are not identical if all social security related taxes and transfers are compared. BKS (p. 6) suggest that progressivity in their system can be maintained by grossing up credited contributions for those with low incomes and grossing down credited contributions for those with high incomes. What this means is that the rate of return will not be the same on actual contributions. BKS (p. 29) also correctly point out that: 'Rates of return would differ by sex and race if unisex and unirace mortality probabilities are used in the actuarial calculations.'

Even with these exceptions to it, the proposed equity rule has a very narrow basis. Why should equity be defined as an equal (notional) rate of return on only a certain portion of taxes?[14] It is not only by contributing special taxes to a public pension plan that a pension is 'earned'. The 'saving' provided by the present generation of workers that can be used productively in order to reduce the relative burden of providing for them in the future, when they retire, is not limited to contributions to public pensions (which we have seen are in fact generally transfers and not saving). Taxes that are used for the education and training of younger persons, or to provide social overhead capital, or for research, can all be considered as forms of 'saving' that increase future incomes. Should these higher incomes not also be reflected in higher pensions? Further, does the logic of the BKS equity rule also imply that single workers should not pay taxes for schools since they do not need to purchase this good? Boskin himself (p. 127) in criticising proposals to fund Social Security with progressive general taxes rather than regressive payroll taxes suggests that a narrow view is not appropriate: 'every dollar of government revenue does not have to be raised from progressive tax sources even if it is considered desirable for the tax side of the budget to be progressive'.

BKS (pp. 15–16) propose that the rate of return to be used in calculating each year's purchase of annuities be determined by an independent Board of Actuaries to 'maintain balance in present value between tax receipts and benefit payments over the succeeding 75 years. Hence as demographic or economic projections change, the annual rate of return will be adjusted downward in the case of projected 75 year deficits and upward in the case of projected 75 year surpluses.'[15] This rate of return would be fixed and guaranteed by the government and 'annuities purchased in previous years based on previous rates of return will never be altered'. In their view, this guarantee would remove uncertainty about future benefits and restore belief in the programme. Boskin (pp. 142–3) is more careful regarding the fixity of the rate of return: 'There would be no ex post facto adjustment of rates of return to contributions made unless an absolutely unprecedented economic situation required it.'

As emphasised earlier, the future is fundamentally uncertain and pension promises are conditional. Changing pension promises from benefits related to future wages to supposedly guaranteed real annuities does not make them more secure. Predictions made over the long period relevant to pensions are likely to be wildly inappropriate (cf. Asimakopulos and Weldon, 1970, p. 228).

BKS (p. 4) argue that individuals currently make uninformed and probably inefficient decisions regarding private insurance coverage and saving because of inadequate information on, and uncertainty about, their social security benefits. They believe that the uncertainty will be eliminated by sending each participant an annual statement detailing taxes paid, credits received, and insurance benefits 'purchased' with the credits. This proposed elimination of uncertainty is illusory. Changing pension promises to 'fixed guaranteed annuities' does not make the promises less conditional or the future less unknown – it will only be in the future that the real values of these annuities will be known.[16]

Finally, there is the question of the financial solvency of the present system as contrasted with the reformed system. Boskin (p. 2) refers to a current 'crisis of unprecedented proportion' and suggests that the financial planning of millions of citizens may be perhaps completely undermined. He (p. 10) refers to the possibility of 'threatened insolvency' and to the danger that 'older and younger Americans will be pitted against each other in a battle over public funds', and he (p. 171) concludes the long-term financial problems will be solved under his proposal by adjustments in the rate of return. The 1983 amendments to Social Security appear to eliminate the gap between expected revenues and benefits over the next 75 years, but Boskin (p. 122) is sceptical about their ability to do this. He believes that this elimination is based on extremely optimistic assumptions about demographics, economics, and politics. He fears that the projected Social Security surpluses in the next few years will be dissipated by increases in benefits and reductions in Social Security taxes. The likely eventual result, according to Boskin (p. 150) is the re-emergence of a Social Security deficit in future years of over $1 trillion.

This problem of long-run balance between revenues and benefits, or 'solvency', exists with the Boskin (and BKS) reform proposals, as well as with the current system. Presumably he and his colleagues believe that it will be easier to keep a lid on benefits, and even to reduce them in order to achieve a long-run balance, with their 'actuarial' scheme, than with the present tax-transfer–temporary-fund approach. Given the same total benefits and taxes, a system with benefits actuarially related to contributions, with a rate of return chosen to insure long-run balance between benefits and taxes over the next 75 years, is no more financially solvent than a system which determines individual benefits in a different manner but which also has a projected long-run balance. If, as BKS (p. 19) state, their 'proposal involves no significant change in the time path of aggregate Social Security taxes or aggregate benefits' it is probably not any more 'solvent' than the current system. The tax and benefit structure over time, and the readiness of future generations to pay taxes to redeem pension promises, are the critical elements in the solvency of a public pension system. Boskin (pp. 140–1) is aware that the alteration of the relative benefits structure by his proposal will not change the cost to future generations of total benefits. If the only change is to provide everyone (subject to redistribution between income groups) with the same actuarial return on contributions, then the gap that he sees between the present values of expected benefits and taxes would be unaltered. With his belief that the future costs of the present system are too great, Boskin (p. 136) recommends a cut in benefits. 'There is no sound alternative to solving the funding problems of the Social Security system except to slow the growth of Social Security spending.' This is largely to be done at the expense of those 'who can provide for themselves [and who] should be prevented from relying on transfers from society at large' (p. 140).

The BKS proposal to adjust downward the annual rates of return in the case of projected deficits, when demographic and economic projections change, is just another method for decreasing future benefits. In fact, to the extent that governments attempted to maintain the fixed guaranteed rate of return on past taxes to the Social Security system, they would have less flexibility in dealing with adverse economic and demographic changes than under the present system which is not burdened by such a restriction.

6 CONCLUSION

Weldon's approach to public pensions presents them as social responses to serious deficiencies in private arrangements for the provision of retirement incomes. Current pensions are seen as being determined by the application of social welfare functions to the current economic circumstances of particular societies. In exchange for their pension taxes workers receive conditional promises of benefits in the form of rules for their determination. The actual amounts to be received can only be determined by future governments. These successor governments are independent as far as public pensions are concerned, but there are strong political pressures that tend to protect against unwarranted interference with the promises of earlier governments. The ability of future governments to pay pensions will depend in large part on the total legacy that they inherit from present generations, and not on the balance in any particular fund.

The Ferrara privatisation proposal that emphasises the saving aspect does not deal adequately with the transition problem that occurs when a switch is made from a pay-as-you-go plan to a fully-funded plan. The high rates of return held out for IRAs under this proposal are deceptive, because not enough attention is paid to their volatile and uncertain nature.

The Boskin, and Boskin, Kotlikoff and Shoven, proposals for actuarially determined Social Security benefits are much more carefully designed. However, the individual equity rule they propose is very narrow, and it does not allow enough scope for social judgements, and support, for families within a social security programme. The use of their equity rule would not change the degree of 'solvency' of Social Security. A public pension plan will always be subject to changes, since future governments will only pay whatever public pensions are politically and economically feasible. Pension promises that are very specific and, in the light of future economic conditions, are too generous may not be honoured in their entirety.[17]

Notes

1. Samuelson (1958, pp. 477–9) illustrates his analysis with a numerical example in which population is stationary and there is no time preference. The representative individual's utility function for consumption is represented by the sum of the logarithms of consumption in each of the three adult periods of his life. The equilibrium interest rate in this case is approximately equal to −67 per cent. A positive rate of population growth would tend to result in a higher rate of interest, but it would still be negative. A positive rate of time preference would also lead to a higher rate of interest.
2. Lerner (1959) made clear the 'chain letter' characteristics of this arrangement. In his response to Lerner, Samuelson (1959) admits that his 'idealization of an infinite past and future is central to my discussion and it divorces matters not only from realism but also from some of the more simple forms of intuitive reasoning' (pp. 519–20).
3. This position is argued in Asimakopulos (1967).
4. Samuelson's basic framework – the restriction to steady states and the designation of pension taxes as savings – has been used in a situation

where goods keep and there is a real rate of return on investment to obtain the so-called social insurance paradox (Aaron, 1966). This is a misnomer since that article focuses on investment alternatives for the individual's contributions and does not refer to social welfare functions and transfers, which are essential elements in any known scheme of social insurance. The paradox concerns the condition (namely, the sum of the rates of growth of real-wage rates and of the labour force is greater than the real rate of interest) under which a representative individual would be better off if a pay-as-you-go pension system prevailed rather than one in which pension taxes had been invested and accumulated at the economy's real rate of interest. The assumption of constant rates of growth to infinity and known real rates of return on investment, which are integral parts of this approach, make it an inappropriate model for analysing or deriving prescriptions for public pension plans in the world we know, where future conditions are unknown.

5. The Supreme Court of the United States underlined the conditional nature of public pensions when it held that these pensions are not contractual in nature and that Congress has the power to reduce or cut off the benefits at any time (as cited in Ferrara, 1985, p. 193).
6. For example, France is considered to be a State for this purpose. 'France, say, from the Revolution on, and probably from long before, has been near enough to a state with a core constitution for the economic side of things, however variegated its paper constitutions have been' (Weldon, 1976, p. 565n).
7. In contrast, private pension arrangements are largely linked to past savings by the accumulated value of pension contributions. 'Pure government' pension plans have been defined (Asimakopulos and Weldon, 1970, p. 224) as tax-and-transfer schemes, while 'pure private' plans make payments only from funds that have been specifically accumulated by or on behalf of an individual. Some employers, such as governments or firms sheltered from competition, might be in a position to effect transfers. If such transfers are made, e.g. by introducing or improving past service pension benefits, then these employer pension plans can be conceived of as combinations of the pure government (transfer) and pure private (savings) plans.
8. With its inclusion in such a function, and with an expected positive effect on future pension levels, the government may decide to increase public savings. This represents a change from Weldon's (1976, p. 574) position where, although there was recognition of the positive effect of current public saving on future budgetary constraints, it was argued that 'the formal response is to require redistribution over generations to be neutral with respect to accumulation, the national propensity to save has to be maintained'.
9. Another advocate of this approach is Achenbaum (1986), who writes of US Social Security programme that '[A]fter fifty years it is time to acknowledge openly that the true linchpin of social security is that the adequacy of benefits should take strict precedence over the principle of individual accumulated equity' (p. 184).

10. This is Ferrara's latest proposal. For earlier plans the interested reader is referred to Ferrara (1980, 1982).
11. Meyers (1987, p. 138 ff) provides simple arithmetic examples of these windfall gains and losses.
12. This aspect of the benefit formulas can be considered, as noted by Thompson (1983, p. 1438), as a form of life-cycle insurance where all workers are protected against the risk of low lifetime earnings leading to very low pensions.
13. References to these two studies will henceforth indicate only the page number.
14. Public support for the aged was provided from the general funds of state and federal governments in the United States before the maturity of the Social Security system. Thompson (1983, p. 1458) points out that: 'By ignoring the general fund tax payments that earlier cohorts made to support the aged, payroll tax rate-of-return calculations ignore the majority of the burden borne before 1950.'
15. To insulate the system from short-run decreases in taxes due to recessions, they also propose a trust fund equal to at least three years of benefits.
16. For example, suppose an unexpected supply-side shock that lowered productivity by 20 per cent compared to earlier forecasts. Workers might be unwilling to pay for the level of pensions they would have considered reasonable in the absence of this shock. In the case of a brighter future due, say, to innovations that substantially increase productivity, it might be considered reasonable to raise pensions. In either case it is doubtful that political pressures would allow pensions to be determined solely by the supposedly guaranteed real annuities.
17. Changes in income tax provisions could readily alter the real value of pensions paid in accordance with inherited pension legislation.

References

Aaron, Henry (1966) 'The Social Insurance Paradox', *Canadian Journal of Economics and Political Science*, 32 (August) pp. 371–4.

Achenbaum, W. Andrew (1986) *Social Security: Visions and Revisions* (Cambridge: Cambridge University Press).

Asimakopulos, A. (1967) 'The Biological Interest Rate and the Social Utility Function', *American Economic Review*, 57 (March) pp. 185–90.

Asimakopulos, A. (1980a) *The Nature of Public Pension Plans: Intergenerational Equity, Funding, and Saving* (Ottawa: Economic Council of Canada).

Asimakopulos, A. (1980b) 'Public Pensions and Economic Theory', *Journal of Post Keynesian Economics*, 3 (Fall) pp. 49–62.

Asimakopulos, A. and J. C. Weldon (1968) 'On the Theory of Government Pension Plans', *Canadian Journal of Economics* (November) pp. 697–717.

Asimakopulos, A. and J. C. Weldon (1970) 'On Private Plans in the Theory of Pensions', *Canadian Journal of Economics*, 3 (May) pp. 223–37.

Boskin, Michael J. (1986) *Too Many Promises: The Uncertain Future of Social Security*, A Twentieth Century Fund Report (Homewood, Illinois: Dow Jones–Irwin).

Boskin, Michael J., Laurence J. Kotlikoff and John B. Shoven (1985) *Personal Security Accounts: A Proposal for Fundamental Social Security Reform*, Center for Economic Policy Research Publication No. 63, Stanford University.

Bryden, K. (1974) *Old Age Pensions and Policy – Making in Canada* (Montreal and London: McGill-Queen's University Press).

Feldstein, Martin S. (1974) 'The Optimal Financing of Social Security', Discussion Paper 388, Institute of Economic Research, Harvard University, Cambridge, Mass.

Ferrara, Peter J. (1980) *Social Security: The Inherent Contradiction* (San Francisco: Cato Institute).

Ferrara, Peter J. (1982) *Social Security: Averting the Crisis* (Washington: Cato Institute).

Ferrara, Peter J. (ed.) (1985) *Social Security – Prospects for Real Reform* (Washington: Cato Institute).

Kotlikoff, Laurence J. (1987) 'Social Security', in John Eatwell *et al.* (eds), *The New Palgrave – A Dictionary of Economics*, vol. 3 (London: Macmillan Press Ltd) pp. 413–18.

Lerner, Abba P. (1959) 'Consumption-Loan Interest and Money', and 'Rejoinder', *Journal of Political Economy*, 67 (October) pp. 512–18 and 523–5 respectively.

Meyers, Charles M. (1987) *Social Security – A Critique of Radical Reform Proposals* (Lexington, Mass.: Lexington Books).

Munnell, Alicia H. (1987) 'Social Security: book review of Ferrara, Peter J. ed., Social Security: Prospects for Real Reform', *Journal of Policy Analysis and Management*, pp. 456–61.

Pechman, Joseph A. (1978) 'The Social Security System: An Overview', in Michael J. Boskin (ed.), *The Crisis in Social Security* (San Francisco: Institute for Contemporary Studies) pp. 31–40.

Samuelson, Paul A. (1958) 'An Exact Consumption-Loan Model of Interest with or without the Social Contrivances of Money', *Journal of Political Economy*, 66 (December) pp. 467–82.

Samuelson, Paul A. (1959) 'Reply', *Journal of Political Economy*, 67 (October) pp. 518–22.

Thompson, Lawrence H. (1983) 'The Social Security Reform Debate', *Journal of Economic Literature*, 21 (December) pp. 1425–67.

Weldon, J. C. (1976) 'On the Theory of Intergenerational Transfers', *Canadian Journal of Economics*, 9 (November) pp. 559–79.

Weldon, J. C. (1986) 'Economic Processes that Bind Successive Communities', mimeo, Department of Economics, McGill University.

13 Intergenerational Redistribution[1]

Peter Howitt

1 INTRODUCTION

Jack Weldon's theory of intergenerational transfers was a contribution of the first order to economic theory.[2] He took as his starting-point Lerner's (1959) observation that public pensions and other programmes with an impact on intergenerational distribution are not saving plans but rather plans for reallocating the resources currently available between the generations currently alive. Given a realistic amount of uncertainty and ignorance about what will happen over a horizon of thirty years or more, no one can tell what retirement benefits the current young will enjoy. But the programmes now in effect will directly determine how much they must contribute and how much the current old will benefit.

He added to this the important observation that not only is the future uncertain, but the government that will decide those future benefits will be different from the government that decides today's contributions. Future governments will have a different constituency and a different motivation than today's, and therefore will not automatically honour today's promises. There are always the expedients of inflation, deindexation, introduction of new programmes that offset the intergenerational impact of inherited programmes, raising the tax rate on benefits, and reform of programmes, to reduce the net benefit from redistribution below its promised level.[3]

This observation raises the difficult question of the time-consistency of policy.[4] Specifically, even if each and every government wishes its young eventually to enjoy a decent retirement income, what ensures that this outcome will emerge out of a sequence of redistributions in which succeeding governments are not bound by their predecessors' promises?

Weldon was optimistic on this score. He believed that a consistent outcome with adequate retirement income could and would be provided even in the absence of binding promises. The mechanism he envisioned was one in which each government, acting purely in its self-interest (that is, maximising a social-welfare function including the lifetime utilities of only its own constituents) would be motivated to honour the promises of its predecessors, not because it is bound to those promises in any legal or constitutional sense, but simply because of the wish 'to have its own promises accepted and redeemed' (Weldon, 1976, p. 569).

Thus Weldon believed that, Lerner's objections notwithstanding, a kind of intertemporal exchange could be arranged between successive governments. The means for conducting the exchange is 'the introduction of a law that looks to the future, and makes promises of a *contingent* kind, and that is framed so as to induce successor governments to repeat the process and honour those contingent promises' (Weldon, 1976, p. 564).

He also believed that the kind of promise most likely to be honoured by future governments was one that required equal treatment of equals. It would give equal weight to the income of those now retired and to the promised income of those who will retire. He proposed this rule not as a normative benchmark, but as a positive hypothesis of the way governments actually behave. Indeed he criticised Lerner for confusing is with ought on this issue. What Weldon sought was a positive theory of how successive governments act, when driven by a social welfare function that is just as much given to the economist as is the state of technology. He saw this form of intergenerational egalitarianism as the inexorable outcome of strategic interaction, not as an intrinsically desirable rule.[5]

2 THE SOURCES OF CONTINUITY

According to Weldon's theory, what makes a government obey promises is a self-fulfilling belief; the belief that a certain process is sustainable. That process obliges each government to honour the promises of its predecessors, provided that they were made in accordance with the appropriate law, and provided that the predecessor kept the process alive by fulfilling its obligation. The belief on the part of each government is that if it keeps the process alive then so will its successor, but if it does not then its promises will not be honoured by its successor, even if made in accordance with the appropriate law.

Such a belief is implicit in the reference to the wish of each government to have its own promises honoured, as being the ultimate 'source of continuity' in policy. Without it, a self-interested government would have no incentive to honour promises. It is self-fulfilling because if government $t+1$ believes it then it will be induced to honour government t's promises if and only if government t has kept the process alive; that is, it will act in such a way as to fulfill the belief on the part of government t.

Self-fulfilling beliefs like this have also been invoked, for example, by Barro and Gordon (1983) to explain how a central bank not bound by any constitutional or legal rule might nevertheless keep a promise to refrain from exploiting a short-run Phillips curve by using inflationary policies, and by Abreu (1986) to explain why cartel members might all keep their promises to refrain from producing beyond their allocated quotas even in the absence of a binding legal enforcement mechanism. In all cases the self-fulfilling belief is that once an agent breaks a promise, by exploiting some short-run opportunity, then promises can no longer be believed, and every agent will behave opportunistically from then on. In such cases it can be shown, under certain assumptions, that the belief will indeed be self-fulfilling; that the prospect of triggering opportunistic behaviour in the future is enough of a threat to keep agents honest in the present.

There are two major problems with any such scheme. The first is a variant on the well-known chainstore paradox (Selten, 1978). If people are capable of rational strategic reasoning, then the scheme requires people all to believe in the possibility of an infinite future. For suppose that there was no chance of continuing past date T. Then government T would have no incentive to honour the promises of government $T-1$, because there would be no future government to repay it. There would be no threat of future opportunistic behaviour to keep it honest. In anticipation of this, government $T-1$ would realise that its promises are not going to be honoured in any event, so it too would have no incentive to honour the promises of government $T-2$. The reasoning can be extended back to the very first government, which would realise that its promises too will not be honoured. Thus the scheme can never get going. The belief in this case is not self-fulfilling.

The other major problem is that the self-fulfilling belief that underlies the scheme is no different in principle from the kind of belief that would allow Ponzi games and chain letters to go uninterrupted for eternity. As Lerner once observed, the promise to pay people interest forever at the biological rate, by counting on population growth to raise the number of contributors relative to the present number, which Samuelson (1958) proposed as the optimal social security system, is indistinguishable from the sort of hoax the perpetrators of which we routinely put in jail. In all such cases people must somehow be persuaded to believe that the future will always provide enough participants who are willing to keep the process alive, even though those future participants are not signatories to any agreement, and even though they would have a strong incentive to refuse to participate. That incentive arises because they might believe that they could let the process die, and start a new process of their own without having to fulfil their obligations under the previous process.

In other words, the problem is one of multiple equilibria. The optimistic beliefs underlying the scheme might be self-fulfilling; but so would the pessimistic belief that everyone will act opportunistically under all circumstances and pay no attention to promises. Our laws typically assume that optimistic beliefs would not be shared forever in the case of chain letters and other scams. Why should we assume differently when the government proposes such a scheme?

The wisdom of Lerner's observation was not lost on Weldon, to whom Samuelson's infinite-horizon construction was a silly diversion from the intergenerational transfer problem. For this reason he emphasised the contingent nature of promises, which makes his scheme less dependent than Samuelson's upon the assumption of infinity, since it allows for the possibility that the biological rate of interest might not continue unchanged forever. Nevertheless, both Weldon's scheme and Samuelson's are like speculative bubbles. Even if time goes on forever with no change in population growth or in per capita incomes, what ensures that the bubble will not burst? What is supposed to persuade people to believe that the future will always provide participants willing to keep the process alive?

These intellectual puzzles do not, of course, completely discredit the notion of a social security scheme based upon a self-fulfilling belief. After all, fiat money depends ultimately upon the same kind of self-fulfilling belief, and we have seen it sustained for long periods of time. The relevant question is whether Weldon's scheme is more like fiat money or like Ponzi's bank. Is it reasonable to suppose that it exists as a stable arrangement?

Modern theory is of little help in this matter. It can be shown that a Weldon-like scheme is a sub-game perfect equilibrium in a well-formulated repeated game between generations, if and only if time goes to infinity.[6] But the same is true for fiat money, and for speculative bubbles and chain letters.[7] So it would seem from the existing literature that everything hinges on the existence or not of infinity, not on the nature of the scheme. Money and chain letters are equally sustainable or equally unsustainable depending upon the answer to this metaphysical question.[8]

It is somewhat more helpful to observe empirically what distinguishes the socially useful and sustainable institution from the pure con game. One factor seems to be that sustainable institutions tend to grow out of arrangements that are backed by more than trust. The trust grows with experience. That is certainly the case with fiat money, which evolved over the generations from intrinsically valuable precious metals, to more and more indirect claims to those metals based on the promises of increasingly distant and numerous individuals, and finally to purely fiduciary notes. The institutions of private debt have also evolved from initial dependency upon debtors' prison that gave it a real backing.

On this score, one might believe that the institution of the family is now giving way to the less immediate institution of the state as the means of effecting intergenerational transfers.[9] Perhaps the faith we once placed in family ties is being successfully transferred to the welfare state. While this possibility cannot be ruled out entirely, there are grounds for scepticism. Evidence that family ties are loosening is abundant enough, as is evidence of the growth of the welfare state. But we also see evidence that the promises made by the welfare state are routinely violated. Indeed, this is the same evidence that gives force to Weldon's original premise that a present government does not have the ability directly to determine all the intertemporal redistributions that will affect the lifetime welfare of its constituents.

One might argue that this evidence reflects not the violation of promises but rather their inevitably contingent nature. Weldon emphasised that the time periods we must consider in the theory of intergenerational transfers are so long that uncertainty requires promises not to be absolute. Thus we can never rule out the possibility, for example, that *de facto* partial repudiation of nominal debt by means of surprise inflation is just a prearranged response to random occurrences such as wars, made in accordance with the process.[10] But by the same token we cannot rule out the possibility that it reflects the lack of commitment to any promise beyond perhaps that of printing enough money to make good the nominal obligations of government debt.

3 TOO MUCH SOCIAL SECURITY

I have no way of settling these very difficult issues. Instead, my purpose is to explore the possibility that the elements of continuity that Weldon was seeking to explain in policy, the strategic connections that permit exchanges between successive governments, arise from channels that do not involve promises in any real sense beyond that of honouring nominal government debt.

Like Weldon I take as given that the state consists of a sequence of governments, each driven by political forces to maximise a social welfare function taking as arguments the lifetime utilities of the people alive at the time. I shall model the strategic interaction between governments in terms of the modern game-theoretic policy analysis that has grown out of the above-mentioned time-inconsistency literature. However I shall also assume explicitly that there is a known finite horizon to the economy, in order to rule out the kind of self-fulfilling belief that would be needed to make governments honour promises of their predecessors.

I shall first argue that there is an important source of continuity that would exist even in the absence of promises, a source that arises simply from the overlap in the sequence of constituencies. This source exists whenever there is an expectation that succeeding governments will be egalitarian, not in the intergenerational sense of either Lerner or Weldon, but in the sense of imputing to people sharply diminishing marginal utility, and hence being averse to large inequalities in lifetime utility.

Specifically, if today's young contribute more, they will go into the future with a relatively lower initial utility. As a result, the next government, if it is driven by an egalitarian social welfare function, will find itself facing a greater demand to pay pensions. That is, the lower initial utility will tilt its maximisation in the direction of higher pensions. In this way, the next government will act as if compensating its old for past contributions. It will do so even though no promises have been made (or if they have, the government ignores them). It will not fear any retribution on its own young for failure to make compensation. It will just be satisfying current political demands.

This effect clearly gives a government a means of effecting an intertemporal exchange for its young constituents. Raising their social security levy will not force the successor government to pay compensation, but will cajole it into doing so. Thus it will induce a sequence of uncommitted but strategically motivated governments to pay higher pensions than if they did not take these strategic considerations into account.

One might think that this effect is too weak to induce very large pensions in the absence of any commitment or any fear of retribution. In fact I shall argue that the reverse occurs. Over time it will cause the state to redistribute too much in favour of the old.[11]

Specifically, pension benefits each period will be greater than if some almighty and everlasting social planner of an intertemporal federation of governments were to arrange an efficient allocation of social welfare between the governments. This is not to say that pensions will be Pareto-inefficient in the usual sense of leaving room for making one generation better off at the expense of no other generation. But they will be politically inefficient; they will leave room for raising the social welfare of one government without reducing the social welfare of any other. And the way to engineer such a political improvement would be to redistribute less to the old.

Thus if, following Weldon, we regard each government's social welfare function as representing in short form the political demands placed on it by its constituents, my prediction is that in the absence of any mechanism for making promises, the political process in an egalitarian society will not satisfy those demands to the extent technologically possible. As Weldon would have predicted under that assumption, time-inconsistency will arise;[12] the intertemporal allocation of social welfare will not be efficient. But the inconsistency will show up in the form of pension incomes that are too high rather than too low.

4 AN OVERLAPPING GENERATIONS MODEL

There is a finite sequence of periods, $t = 1, \ldots, T$. Each period there is a new generation born, to live for two periods. Population grows steadily at the rate n. Each young person at t has an exogenous endowment y_t of the single non-storable good. Per capita endowments grow at the steady rate g. Lifetime preferences of each member of generation t are separable over consumption when young c_t

and consumption when old x_{t+1}, and are represented by the ordinal utility function:

$$U_t = u(c_t) + \beta u(x_{t+1}) \tag{13.1}$$

where u is smooth, with positive and diminishing marginal utility, $u(0) = 0$, $u'(0) = \infty$, and $\beta = 1/(1 + \delta)$ where $\delta (> 0)$ is the individual rate of time preference. The consumption of generation 0 when young is given historically and the consumption of generation T when old is zero.

Nothing crucial hangs on the separability of preferences, which is assumed for notational convenience. When wanting to characterise steady states I shall add the assumption of homotheticity. Combined with the other assumptions this implies the very special ordinal function:

$$U_t = c_t^{1-\sigma} + \beta x_{t+1}^{1-\sigma};\ 0 < \sigma < 1 \tag{13.2}$$

Weldon would have denounced as silly my assumption that growth rates are constant and the future known. It is, however, very useful, and I shall argue that the main insights of the paper can be generalised to allow for a realistic degree of ignorance and uncertainty.

Each period the government acts so as to maximise the social welfare function:

$$W_t = W(U_{t-1}) + \left[\frac{1+n}{1+\varrho}\right] W(U_t) \tag{13.3}$$

where ϱ is the rate at which the utility of the young is discounted. The function W is an increasing concave function that represents the influence of each individual's preferences in the political process. The greater the degree of curvature of W the more egalitarian the society.

Intergenerational egalitarianism of the Lerner variety would require $\varrho = 0$, but in general ϱ is unrestricted in sign. The factor $(1+n)$ in (13.3) represents the relatively larger numbers of the young in the constituency. When comparing steady states with positive growth I shall consider the special function:

$$W(U) = \left[\frac{1}{1-\theta}\right] U^{1-\theta};\ \theta > 0,\ \theta \neq 1 \tag{13.4}$$

Following Weldon, I attach no normative significance to the maximisation of W_t. Instead, unspecified political forces are assumed to produce that outcome as a matter of fact. For convenience I refer to the government as choosing the allocation each period; but this is just a shorthand characterisation of a collective political process beyond the control of any individual decision-maker.

Accordingly, a more egalitarian society is neither better nor worse, with bureaucrats and politicians that are neither more nor less caring, just one in which the relatively disadvantaged (generally the old when $g > 0$) exert more political influence. In a more explicit formulation that influence might arise from the ability of the disadvantaged to evoke sympathy (although that raises questions of consistency with the assumed non-altruistic utility function of each agent). Alternatively, disadvantaged people might be relatively more disposed to political activism in a more egalitarian society, or the rich more politically inattentive. Another possibility is that the constitution of the more egalitarian society makes populism a more successful political strategy relative to influence-peddling.

The assumption of social-welfare maximisation contrasts with the median voter assumption made by such writers as Browning (1975) and Alesina and Tabellini (1988) in a similar dynamic context, in making the utility of each agent matter in the political process, not just that of one generation or interest group. It contrasts similarly with the assumption by such writers as Loewy (1988) and Kotlikoff, Persson and Svensson (1988) who assume that a preassigned group makes a unilateral decision each period. The fact that people will have an influence both when they are young and when they are old is an important source of intertemporal continuity in the policy process, which is missing from these alternative approaches.

Since the focus is on the net redistribution affected by each government, and its interaction with redistributions of preceding and succeeding governments, rather than on the relationship between the government's instruments and the market equilibrium, assume that there are enough instruments available each period for the government to choose any pair (c_t, x_t) satisfying the current-period budget constraint:

$$c_t + \left[\frac{1}{1+n}\right] x_t = y_t \tag{13.5}$$

The term $(1+n)$ appears in (13.5) in order to convert all items to per-young terms. Although in practice x_t might be the net outcome of various redistributional programmes, no harm is done by referring to it as a pension benefit.

The nature of social-welfare maximisation depends upon the strategic links between successive governments. Before modelling those links, however, it is useful to consider the case in which the political process myopically ignores them. Policy formation in this case follows the procedure recommended on normative grounds by Lerner, without, however, necessarily setting ϱ equal to zero. I refer to it therefore as the Lerner case. Each government chooses (c_t, x_t) so as to maximise W_t subject to (13.5), taking both c_{t-1} and x_{t+1} as given. The solution is given by (13.5) and the marginal condition:

$$\frac{W'(U_t)\,u'(c_t)}{W'(U_{t-1})\,\beta u'(x_t)} = 1 + \varrho \qquad (13.6)$$

The usual Fisherian condition for privately optimal saving in any period before T is:

$$\frac{u'(c_t)}{\beta u'(x_{t+1})} = 1 + r_t \qquad (13.7)$$

where r_t is the rate of interest. According to (13.7) the rate of interest at t is a positive measure of the amount of redistribution at t, holding constant the redistribution at $t + 1$. Also, from (13.6) and (13.7) the rate of interest in the Lerner case r_t^L is given by the equation:

$$1 + r_t^L = (1 + \varrho)\,[u'(x_t)/u'(x_{t+1})]\,[W'(U_{t-1})/W'(U_t)] \qquad (13.8)$$

5 STEADY STATES

If there were no growth in per capita endowments ($g = 0$) and time went to infinity ($T = \infty$), the sequence $\{c_t, x_t\}$ in the Lerner case would converge to a stationary state (c^L, x^L). From (13.8) the rate of interest in that stationary state is the rate of generational time-preference ϱ. Thus under Lerner's intergenerational egalitarianism the rate of interest would be zero, as he originally showed.

Even when T is finite, as long as $g = 0$ the same turnpike reasoning as in Samuelson (1967) shows that $\{c_t, x_t\}$ will spend an arbitrarily large fraction of the time arbitrarily close to (c^L, x^L) as T becomes arbitrarily large. Thus the rate of interest will be approximately ϱ most of the time.

These asymptotic properties of (c^L, x^L) follow from the usual turnpike reasoning even though that reasoning assumes that the sequence $\{c_t, x_t\}$ solves a single time-consistent maximisation problem rather than this sequence of problems. This is because the conditions (13.5) and (13.6) that define the sequence also solve the problem of maximising the dynastic welfare function:

$$\mathscr{W} = \sum_{t=0}^{T} \left[\frac{1+n}{1+\varrho}\right]^t W[u(c_t) + \beta u(x_{t+1})]$$

subject to c_0 given, $x_{T+1} = 0$, and (13.5) for all $t = 1, \ldots, T$.

The fact that such consistent dynastic optimisation produces a stationary rate of interest equal to the rate of generational time-preference rather than the rate of individual time preference δ has been shown in similar contexts by Burbidge (1983) and by Calvo and Obstfeld (1988). It should be emphasised, however, that this dynastic welfare function does not correspond with the utility of any single agent, or with the force motivating any single government. Its maximisation in the Lerner case is merely a chance outcome of a sequence of political decisions in which each government ignores any influence its decision might have on subsequent decisions.

When there is positive per-capita growth ($g > 0$) there is generally no steady state to the sequence $\{c_t, x_t\}$ in the Lerner case. However, under the special assumptions (13.2) and (13.4) there is such a steady state, defined by $(c_t, x_t) = (1 + g)^t (\hat{c}^L, \hat{x}^L)$ for all t, which has the same turnpike property as does (c^L, x^L) in the no-growth case.

It can be seen directly from (13.8) that the corresponding steady-state rate of interest $\hat{r}^L$ is greater than ϱ, for two reasons. First, the growth in x_t makes the marginal utility of x_t fall over time, which makes the rate of interest higher for any given redistribution at t. Second, the growth in utility from the preceding period will cause the government to assign more weight on the margin to the utility of its old constituents, and hence to redistribute more; i.e. to raise r_t holding x_{t+1} constant.

To be exact, $\hat{r}^L$ is given by:

$$1 + \hat{r}^L = (1 + \varrho)\,(1 + g)^{\sigma + \theta(1 - \sigma)} \tag{13.9}$$

Thus even under Lerner's intergenerational egalitarianism ($\varrho = 0$) the steady-state of interest will exceed zero. Indeed if W has sufficient curvature (θ large enough) then $\hat{r}^L$ can exceed Samuelson's golden-rule rate of interest:

$$1 + r^G = (1 + n)\,(1 + g) \tag{13.10}$$

which would yield the constant proportion c_t/x_t preferred by every generation starting with $t = 1$ if time went to infinity.

6 OPTIMAL ALLOCATIONS

Before getting to the strategic interactions between successive governments, consider the question of optimality. First note that under the usual definition all sequences $\{c_t,\ x_t\}_{t=1}^{t=T}$ are Pareto-optimal. No generation's lifetime utility can be raised except at the expense of some other generation.

To see this, note that to engineer a Pareto-improvement x_1 would have to be increased, because that is the only way to make generation 0 better off. Since that would reduce c_1 through the budget constraint, x_2 would also have to be increased, for otherwise generation 1 would be made worse off. Continuation of this argument shows that x_T would have to be increased. But that would make generation T worse off, since it would reduce c_T through the budget constraint and generation T has no future. Thus Pareto-improvements are impossible.

It is possible, however, for a sequence of redistributions to be politically suboptimal. That is, it may be possible to alter the sequence in such a way as to raise the value of social welfare attained by each government. Political suboptimality has no normative significance, since social welfare is a purely positive concept in this analysis. But it does imply a failure of coordination between the choices of successive governments, a failure that could be remedied by a magic central government dictating to this intertemporal federation of overlapping communities, or perhaps by a constitution, or a social contract; the political demands on each and every government could be better satisfied. If the observer had some independent means of estimating each government's social welfare function, political suboptimality would also have positive implications.

A necessary condition for political optimality is:

$$\frac{W'(U_1)\,u'(c_1)}{W'(U_0)\,\beta u'(x_1)} \leqslant 1 + \varrho \tag{13.11}$$

This puts an upper limit on the first government's redistribution, given the inherited c_0 and the next government's redistribution. It also states that the limit is achieved in the Lerner case, where (13.6) holds for all t. Thus any redistribution beyond what Lerner's myopic procedure generates is too much, in the sense that a reduction would make it possible for all governments, starting with the current one, better to satisfy the collective demands of their constituents.

The economic reasoning underlying this result is straightforward. If (13.11) were violated, then c_1 would be too low to satisfy the Lerner condition (13.6) for the first date $t = 1$, given the prospective pension income x_2 of the initial young and the past consumption c_0 of the initial old. But this Lerner condition, as we have seen, must be satisfied if the social welfare at date 1 is to be maximised subject to the budget constraint and to given values of c_0 and x_2. Therefore if (13.11) were violated then social welfare at date 1 could be raised by reducing redistribution at date 1 (raising c_1) and holding all future redistributions constant. This change would also raise social welfare at date 2, when the beneficiaries of the change are alive but not the victims. And it would leave all subsequent social welfares unchanged.

The optimality condition can also be expressed as the condition that the rate of interest at date 1 be no greater than the value r_1^L given by (13.8). Thus the Lerner case generates the highest rate of interest compatible with political optimality. This is noteworthy because in infinite-horizon overlapping-generations models, Pareto-optimality places a *lower* bound on the rate of interest, specifically the Samuelson golden-rule rate r^G.

7 EQUILIBRIUM REDISTRIBUTION

I am now in a position to go beyond Lerner's myopic case and allow each government to look ahead at the effect that its current redistribution will have on future redistributions and, through this channel, on the lifetime utility of the current young. I still assume, however, that each government is unable to make independent promises to its young constituents that will constrain the successor government. Its only instrument is current redistribution.

Even without the ability to grant future entitlements there is a natural intertemporal link arising from the fact that the young have political influence both now and in the future. Specifically, if members of the current polity look ahead they will realise that raising the amount of redistribution this period will harm today's young, who will go into the next period with a reduced level of initial utility, and who will therefore tend to have a greater political influence next period, because of the curvature of the W function.

This means that a government that raises the redistributional levy on the young can thereby 'promise' a repayment. For next period their enhanced political influence will cause an extra redistribution in their favour. Giving now will pay off in the future even though there is no explicit promise; even though the next government will be behaving opportunistically, and hence would not pay attention to any explicit promise even if there were one.

Because of this intertemporal link, the government will tend to redistribute too much, in the sense of violating condition (13.11) for optimality. That is, it will push redistribution beyond the point where the Lerner condition (13.6) is satisfied for $t = 1$. For at that point, as we have seen, the first government's social welfare W_1 would just be maximised under the false assumption that the pension benefit x_2 of its young constituents would be unaffected by period 1 redistribution. Once the first government realises that x_2 can be increased by redistributing a little more in period 1, this extra benefit to its young constituents will induce it to go further, and thus to violate the optimality condition (13.11).

To see more precisely what will happen, I model the sequence of choices as a game between governments, and examine the structure of sub-game perfect Nash equilibria. First consider date T. The pair (c_T, x_T) will be chosen so as to maximise

$$W[u(c_{T-1}) + \beta u(x_T)] + \left[\frac{1+n}{1+\varrho}\right] W[u(c_T)]$$

subject to (13.5) for $t = T$, with c_{T-1} given by the previous government. Since there is no future government to worry about, this is exactly the same procedure as in the Lerner case. It yields a pair of policy functions: $(\hat{c}_T(c_{T-1}), \hat{x}_T(c_{T-1}))$, defined as the solutions to (13.5) and (13.6) for $t = T$. These functions are easily shown to satisfy:

$$\frac{d\hat{x}_T}{dc_{T-1}} = -(1+n)\frac{d\hat{c}_T}{dc_{T-1}} < 0$$

This result shows the intertemporal link that government $T-1$ can exploit. Increased redistribution (lower c_{T-1}) will raise the prospective pension benefit x_T of its young constituents.

At any earlier date t the government takes into account that x_{t+1} will be chosen according to some policy function $\hat{x}_{t+1}(c_t)$. Subject to this constraint, (13.5), and a predetermined c_{T-1}, it chooses (c_t, x_t) so as to maximise:

$$W[u(c_{t-1}) + \beta u(x_t)] + \left[\frac{1+n}{1+\varrho}\right] W[u(c_t) + \beta u(x_{t+1})]$$

Thus government t takes into account the strategic link by which it can affect x_{t+1}, and is in turn influenced by its predecessor's choice of c_{t-1}. But is not constrained by any promises or other obligations. Nor does it make any explicit promises.

This procedure recursively defines the sequence of policy functions $\{\hat{c}_t\ (c_{t-1}),\ \hat{x}_t\ (c_{t-1})\}_1^T$. The implied first-order conditions are (13.5) and:

$$\frac{W'(U_t)u'(c_t)}{W'(U_{t-1})\beta u'(x_t)} = -\frac{W'(U_t)u'(x_{t+1})}{W'(U_{t-1})u'(x_t)} \cdot \frac{d\hat{x}_{t+1}}{dc_t} + (1+\varrho) \qquad (13.12)$$

The necessary second-order conditions for a regular maximum to W_t, combined with the usual comparative-statics techniques, show that $\dfrac{d\hat{x}_t}{dc_{t-1}} < 0$ for all t. Therefore, the first term on the right side of (13.12), which represents the effects of the intertemporal link, is positive for all $t < T$. Therefore (13.11) is violated.

8 CONCLUSION

The above analysis reaches three important conclusions. The first is that even when one government cannot constrain its successors by making promises to its young constituents, it can at least influence its successors by its choice of how much to tax the current young. The second is that when governments take this influence into account and behave strategically, the resulting sequence of redistributions will be politically suboptimal, although not Pareto-inefficient. The third is that the suboptimality will manifest itself in pension benefits that are too large. This final section discusses the robustness of these conclusions to realistic modifications and extensions of the model.

To begin with, it should be noted that the third conclusion depends very much upon the assumption that each government is egalitarian, in the sense of imputing to people sharply diminishing marginal utility. Specifically, it requires the transformation W to be strictly concave. Furthermore, W need not be concave for each government's decision problem to be well formulated, because social welfare at date t can be a concave function of the relevant consumptions c_{t-1}, c_t, x_t, and x_{t+1} even if W is convex.

Two things can be said about this assumption. The first is that conclusion one would still generally be valid as long as W was not linear. Only in the linear case would the next government's redistribution be independent of this government's. Second, it can be argued that concavity of W is at least better than linearity or convexity on empirical grounds. Its importance in the analysis is to make governments favour those who have been previously disadvantaged or have previously made sacrifices. Under convexity society would punish such people. Thus the existence of affirmative action, veterans' benefits, and other such programmes seems to favour concavity.

Next, the demonstration of political suboptimality raises the obvious question of what kinds of institutional reforms might serve to correct the inefficiency. Could an enterprising politician reap a private reward for engineering a political improvement? Addressing this question would take us well beyond the present formal structure in which all interesting politics except for time-inconsistency are buried in the social welfare function.

It is worth emphasising that the mechanism identified above, by which the next government will reward today's young for their sacrifices, does not lead to Pareto-inefficiency. In fact, one can easily imagine circumstances in which the mechanism would bring about Pareto-improvements. Specifically, if today's sacrifices lead to technological improvements or to growth through any channel that involves substantial spillovers, as is emphasised in the modern literature on endogenous growth,[13] then the mechanism may be one way to offset those spillovers. Perhaps at least some of what the private researcher loses on the margin to his imitators and descendants can be made up on the margin by a government that rewards his sacrifices through this mechanism.

The assumption that steady growth and an unchanged political system can be perfectly foreseen is clearly not realistic in this context, as Weldon emphasised. It can be argued, however, that the three conclusions listed above would go through even with a realistic degree of ignorance and uncertainty, subject to at least the reservations of the two previous paragraphs. All that is required for the above mechanism to be at work is the belief that future governments will be egalitarian, in the sense of having a concave *W*. This need not be a rational expectation in the formal sense in order to tilt the political process in the direction of large pensions.

Finally, my reason for assuming that no promises made by the present government will constrain future governments in any way is not the belief that promises don't matter, but the wish to explore other sources of continuity. Promises probably do play an important role, because the commitment to honour nominal government debt, which is clearly high in most developed countries today, is not vacuous. All the expedients for partial repudiation such as inflation come with some direct cost to the government that uses them, in a way that does not require a self-fulfilling belief that future governments will retaliate with similar repudiation. Public opinion polls in periods of high inflation show that inflation is perceived by the electorate to be an important social problem. Whether or not the economist fully understands the sources of that perception, they matter for the political process.

It should be straightforward to extend the above analysis to include government debt, the repudiation of which is costly on the margin. The results of that extension should strengthen the main message of this chapter.[14] Each government will use not only its currect redistributions but also its current promises strategically. Thus pensions will be even higher than without this extra instrument. This is because the extra instrument allows each government to saddle the next with debt that is hard to repudiate on the margin, and which will therefore tilt its decision even more in favour of the old, who will also be the creditors.

Allowing for debt that is costly to repudiate on the margin is also a way of accounting for governments simultaneously promising more social security to the young and finding ways, like inflation, to reduce the commitments made by its predecessors to the current old. It has been observed by many that the baby-boom generation is unique in having been able to exploit both its parents and its children, by inflating away the former's savings and saddling the latter with huge amounts of debt. The preceding argument suggests that this pattern of behaviour is to be expected even when population grows steadily.

Notes

1. I am grateful to my colleagues Joel Fried, David Laidler and Ron Wintrobe for helpful discussions and to Tom Asimakopulos for valuable comments on an earlier draft. This does not however imply their agreement with my analysis.
2. I base this description of Weldon's theory primarily on his Presidential Address to the Canadian Economics Association (1976). The theory evolved out of his earlier work with Asimakopulos (1968, 1970).
3. On examples from Canadian experience, see Asimakopulos (1980).
4. Kydland and Prescott (1977) is the seminal paper in this area. For a survey of recent contributions that focus on distributional issues and their effects on macroeconomic policy through the political process, see Alesina (1988).
5. This at least was Weldon's final published view. He criticised his earlier work with Asimakopulos as much as Lerner's for taking a normative stand and thereby missing the difficult positive issues.
6. See Hammond (1975) and Kotlikoff, Persson and Svensson (1988).
7. Shell (1971) has a fascinating discussion of the paradox raised by infinite time.
8. Rowe (1989) proposes resolving these problems by assuming rule-oriented rather than conventionally rational behaviour.
9. The displacement of the family by the state was also emphasised by Weldon. See, for example, 1976, p. 561.
10. See, for example, Grossman and van Huyck (1987).
11. The argument is similar to that of Browning (1975), who pointed out in terms of a median voter model that if people alive today could vote on the social security tax rate the youngest would vote for a tax that delivered the biological rate of interest, but all others would prefer a higher rate, since they would not have to pay throughout their lives. In this case the model is that of maximising social welfare at each date, instead of a median voter model. Also, each government is unable to choose the tax rate to apply for the future as it does in the Browning model.
12. It is well known that choices made by a sequence of agents, each with rational expectations of how its choices will affect the future, may be Pareto-dominated in terms of the agents' payoff functions. This will be the case if the agents' choices induce people to make irreversible decisions that affect the payoffs, or if the agents have different payoff functions (Strotz, 1956). The latter applies in this case, since the constituencies of successive governments, while overlapping, are not identical.
13. See Romer (1986) and Lucas (1988). Kohn and Marion (1987) have put technology spillovers explicitly into an intergenerational context and explored some of their welfare implications.
14. This also interacts with the above comments on uncertainty and Pareto-efficiency. As Weldon emphasised, promises to the young can be a way of reducing their uncertainty. This will be the case if the costs of repudiation can be counted on more than the egalitarianism of the government. Thus the mechanism of promises might produce a Pareto-improvement, by supplying insurance that private markets do not.

References

Abreu, Dilip (1986) 'Extremal Equilibria of Oligopolistic Supergames', *Journal of Economic Theory*, 39, pp. 191–225.

Alesina, A. (1988) 'Macroeconomics and Politics', *NBER Macroeconomics Annual 1988* (Cambridge, Mass.: MIT Press).

Alesina, A. and G. Tabellini (1988) 'Voting on the Budget Deficit', unpublished, Carnegie Mellon University.

Asimakopulos, A. (1980) *The Nature of Public Pension Plans: Intergenerational Equity, Funding, and Saving: A Study Prepared for the Economic Council of Canada* (Ottawa: Department of Supplies and Services).

Asimakopulos, A. and J. C. Weldon (1968) 'On the Theory of Government Pension Plans', *Canadian Journal of Economics*, 1, pp. 699–717.

Asimakopulos, A. and J. C. Weldon (1970) 'On Private Plans in the Theory of Pensions', *Canadian Journal of Economics*, 3, pp. 223–37.

Barro, Robert J. and David B. Gordon (1983) 'Rules, Discretion and Reputation in a Model of Monetary Policy', *Journal of Monetary Economics*, 12, pp. 101–22.

Browning, E. K. (1975) 'Why the Social Insurance Budget is too Large in a Democracy', *Economic Inquiry*, 13, pp. 373–88.

Burbidge, J. (1983) 'Government Debt in an Overlapping-Generations Model with Bequests and Gifts', *American Economic Review*, 73, pp. 222–7.

Calvo, G. A. and M. Obstfeld (1988) 'Optimal Time-Consistent Fiscal Policy with Finite Lifetimes', *Econometrica*, 56, pp. 411–32.

Grossman, H. I. and J. B. van Huyck (1987) 'Sovereign Debt as a Contingent Claim: Excusable Default, Repudiation, and Reputation', unpublished, Brown University.

Hammond, P. (1975) 'Charity: Altruism or Cooperative Egoism?', in E. S. Phelps (ed.), *Altruism, Morality, and Economic Theory* (New York: Russell Sage Foundation).

Kohn, M. and N. L. Marion (1987) 'The Implications of Knowledge-Based Growth for the Optimality of Open Capital Markets', unpublished, Dartmouth College.

Kotlikoff, L. J., T. Persson and L. E. O. Svensson (1988) 'Social Contracts as Assets: A Possible Solution to the Time-Consistency Problem', *American Economic Review*, 78, pp. 662–77.

Kydland, F. E. and E. C. Prescott (1977) 'Rules Rather than Discretion: The Inconsistency of Optimal Plans', *Journal of Political Economy*, 85, pp. 473–92.

Lerner, A. P. (1959) 'Consumption-Loan Interest and Money', and 'Rejoinder', *Journal of Political Economy*, 67, pp. 512–18 and 523–5.

Loewy, M. B. (1988) 'Equilibrium Policy in an Overlapping Generations Economy', *Journal of Monetary Economics*, 22, pp. 485–99.

Lucas, R. E., Jr. (1988) 'On the Mechanics of Economic Development', *Journal of Monetary Economics*, 22, pp. 3–42.

Romer, P. (1986) 'Increasing Returns and Long-Run Growth', *Journal of Political Economy*, 94, pp. 1002–37.

Rowe, P. N. (1989) *Rules and Institutions* (Oxford: Philip Allan).

Samuelson, P. A. (1958) 'An Exact Consumption-Loan Model of Interest

with or without the Social Contrivance of Money', *Journal of Political Economy*, 66, pp. 467–82.
Samuelson, P. A. (1967) 'A Turnpike Refutation of the Golden Rule in a Welfare-Maximizing Many-Year Plan', in K. Shell (ed.), *Essays on the Theory of Optimal Economic Growth* (Cambridge, Mass.: MIT Press).
Selten, R. (1978) 'The Chain-Store Paradox', *Theory and Decision*, 9, pp. 127–59.
Shell, K. (1971) 'Notes on the Economics of Infinity', *Journal of Political Economy*, 79, pp. 1002–11.
Strotz, R. H. (1956) 'Myopia and Inconsistency in Dynamic Utility Maximization', *Review of Economic Studies*, 23, pp. 165–80.
Weldon, J. C. (1976) 'On the Theory of Intergenerational Transfers', *Canadian Journal of Economics*, 9, pp. 559–79.

14 Pension Reform and Elderly Women: Some Evidence for Ontario Urban Centres[1]

John Burbidge

1 INTRODUCTION

Almost all discussions of pension reform have focused on the plight of elderly women. Several of the recent changes in public and private pensions have been aimed at raising the living standards of this particular group. For example, the Guaranteed Income Supplement (GIS) and Spouses' Allowances have been raised in real terms and the group eligible to receive these benefits has been widened. Ideally, one would like to have a panel data set spanning the reform period to identify what effects the various changes have had on the income, asset-holding and consumption patterns of all concerned. It is well known, however, that there are no Canadian panel data of this kind and, in fact, there is no single Canadian cross-sectional data set that contains information on incomes, assets, debts and expenditures. Have changes in public pensions raised the real incomes of elderly women, and if so, how has the extra income been spent? Do elderly women now save more or dissave less of their incomes? Are consumption levels dependent on the assets held? For example, do the spending patterns of homeowners differ from those of renters? If the elderly do save, can the data tell us something about why they save?

The kind of data one would need to provide answers to these questions does not exist, but the policy importance of the questions demands some sort of response. This chapter attempts to shed more light on the answers to these questions by using simultaneously information from some of the publicly available Family Expenditures (Famex) and Survey of Consumer Finances (SCF) microdata tapes.

The main objective of this chapter is to augment the set of 'facts' about the behaviour of elderly women who live alone. It complements my earlier research with Lonnie Magee and Leslie Robb on Canadian data, and similar research by McFadden, Wise and others on American data. In particular, I provide some evidence to show that real incomes of a certain group of women have increased, that this group has a downward-sloping consumption-age profile, and that these women save a significant fraction of their incomes. My results suggest that elderly saving behaviour may not be induced so much by uncertain length of lifetime or the desire to leave bequests or to provide for medical and nursing home care late in the life-cycle, but rather that the elderly experience near-satiation in consumption. It takes energy to consume – less energy implies lower consumption, and higher saving, if real-income–age profiles are flat or decline slowly with age.

Following is an outline of the rest of the chapter. In the next section, I present a procedure for combining Famex and SCF data sets. Section 3 describes the implementation of this procedure and discusses summary statistics for the main variables. In Section 4, I set out the empirical results on income, consumption and wealth-holding, for a particular cohort of elderly women. The last section summarises the main results and offers some suggestions for further work.

2 COMBINING FAMEX AND SCF DATA SETS

Family Expenditure surveys are usually conducted every two years. In February and March of a survey year, surveyors visit each designated household and assist members of it in completing a lengthy questionnaire on the household's income and expenditures for the previous calendar year.[2] Public Use Microdata Tapes (PUMTs) exist for the calendar years 1978, 1982, 1984 and 1986. The Survey of Consumer Finances collects detailed information on household assets and debts about every seven years. PUMTs now exist for surveys conducted in May 1977 and 1984. These surveys are also administered by a surveyor interviewing members of the household at home; the asset and debt information is taken as of the date of the survey, while information on incomes pertains to the previous calendar year.

Although both the Famex and the SCF surveys are based on the Labour Force Survey sampling frame[3] they differ in several important ways and thus one must be careful in combining information from each to ensure that like is matched with like. For example, Famex focuses on a 'spending unit', which is defined to be 'a group of persons dependent on a common or pooled income for the major items of expense and living in the same dwelling . . . or . . . financially independent persons living alone or as roomers', while SCF focuses on 'economic families', defined to be 'a group of individuals sharing a common dwelling unit and related by blood, marriage or adoption' or unattached individuals (1978 Famex PUMT documentation, p. 130).

For the purposes of this chapter, the two incomes, assets and debts PUMTs constitute the basic data sets and I draw on the 1978 and 1984 Famex PUMTs to infer household expenditures for each record in the SCF. Some Famex surveys are national in scope, while others are smaller and cover only large urban centres (cities with populations of at least 100 000). Since the 1984 Famex was of the latter type, I restrict my attention to urban centres.

This chapter deals exclusively with elderly women living alone. Both SCF and Famex divide households into three categories – single (by which is meant never married), married (with spouse present), and all others. These restrictions – major urban centres and elderly women living alone – resulted in data sets that were too small to obtain meaningful conclusions for regions other than the provinces of Ontario and Quebec; therefore I focus on the larger of these data sets, that for Ontario. Furthermore, there were too few observations on single elderly women, particularly in the 1978 Famex, and thus I was forced to drop the category of 'single' elderly women, leaving only the 'other' category. Unfortunately, the information in these data do not permit one to distinguish, say, between divorced women, who live alone but whose former husbands are alive, and widows, although these two groups could face quite different financial circumstances and one would like to be able to observe them in isolation from each other.

Statistics Canada PUMTs typically report actual age up to 75; all those older than 75 are coded as 76.[4] In the statistical analysis conducted in this chapter, I included all women over the age of 50.

In order to say something about how saving and spending patterns changed across the two SCFs I used the 1978 and 1984 Famex data to infer spending patterns that correspond to the 1976 and 1983 incomes in the two SCFs.[5] Famex and SCF both record information on age, educational level attained, occupation, immigration status, income, market value of home, mortgage and other variables. Using the Famex data, one can estimate a function that describes how each component of household expenditures varies with these characteristics. In particular, I estimated the following equation by ordinary least squares on the 1978 Famex:

$$E_i = X_i\beta + \varepsilon_i \qquad i = 1, \ldots, n,$$

where E_i is an expenditure category such as food for household i, X_i is a 1 by k vector of this household's characteristics, one which is common to both Famex and SCF data sets, β is a k by 1 vector of coefficients, ε_i is an error term, and n is the number of observations. This function can be then employed to predict the spending pattern for each record in the 1977 SCF data set. Similarly, the 1984 Famex can be used to estimate expenditures for each record in the 1984 SCF.

How well will this procedure work? That both Famex and SCF employ the same sampling frame is important because it means that the X-vector really is common to both data sets. One problem is that relative and absolute prices changed, of course, between 1976 and 1978, and again between 1983 and 1984. This is handled here by including after-tax income in the X-vector and by assuming that changes in relative prices over this short interval were sufficiently small that expenditure patterns for these groups of women can be presumed not to have changed significantly.[6] I turn now to a preliminary examination of empirical results.

3 EMPIRICAL RESULTS

The purpose of this section is to use averages of the data to describe the situation faced by these elderly women in 1977 and to compare it to the situation faced by similar women in 1984. I wish to emphasise at the outset that all these data sets are very thin – the number of observations is so low that one must be very careful not to read too much into the results. The exercise is best interpreted as a first step in disentangling a complex story.

A preliminary examination of the data revealed sharp differences between women, depending on whether or not they were homeowners. In all the results of this chapter, therefore, the data sets are split into those who do not own homes and those who do.

The extracts from the 1978 Famex data netted 50 non-homeowners and 39 homeowners. The corresponding numbers for the 1984 Famex were 34 and 21. Implementation of the first stage in the procedure for inferring expenditures required choosing the X-vector discussed above. I employed age, age squared, three variables for education, three for occupation, part-time employment status, immigration status and after-tax income. A complete list of the variables employed, as well as the mnemonic attached to each, appears in the Appendix to this chapter.

The regression equations for total current consumption (TCC) and the components of expenditures confirmed that there is a strong relationship between each of these dependent variables and the independent variables, particularly after-tax income; the R^2s for the TCC equations were between .75 and .90, while those for components of expenditure were in the .40 to .70 range.[7] This suggests that the instruments chosen, particularly after-tax income, should provide fairly accurate predictions of what the households were spending out of their 1976 and 1983 incomes in the SCF data sets. The estimated coefficients from the Famex regressions, the $\hat{\beta}$s, can then be used to predict TCC and the components of expenditures for each observation in the two SCFs; the prediction is simpy $X_j\hat{\beta}$, for the jth record in the SCF.

Table 14.1 lists the means for the variables of interest. As noted above, the data are split into those who own homes and those who do not. In an attempt to make the numbers in the four columns compar-

Table 14.1 Means of key variables in the 1977 and 1984 SCFs, and, in addition, expenditures and saving inferred by splicing the 1978 and 1984 Famexes to these SCFs.

	Non-Homeowners		*Homeowners*	
Variable	*1977*	*1984*	*1977*	*1984*
NOBS	92	128	56	91
Household Characteristics				
AGE	68.32	69.95	68.39	68.36
EDI	0.54	0.44	0.42	0.45
ED2	0.33	0.43	0.43	0.40
ED3	0.12	0.09	0.13	0.13
ED4	0.01	0.04	0.02	0.02
OCC1	0.02	0.04	0.09	0.04
OCC2	0.26	0.19	0.21	0.18
OCC3	0.04	0.03	0.07	0.07
RETIRED	0.68	0.74	0.63	0.71
PARTTIME	0.05	0.05	0.11	0.10
IMSTATUS	0.47	0.40	0.39	0.42

Table 14.1 continued

Variable	*Non-Homeowners* *1977*	*Non-Homeowners* *1984*	*Homeowners* *1977*	*Homeowners* *1984*
Incomes				
EARNINGS	2 564	3 126	3 243	3 129
INVINC	2 411	2 344	2 838	4 690
OASGIS	2 618	3 035	2 377	2 571
CQPP	596	990	661	1 293
UI	45	68	37	23
GOVTR	4 014	4 816	3 412	4 351
PENSIONS	1 075	543	785	1 440
TOTINC	10 409	11 331	10 772	13 888
AFTAXINC	9 839	10 302	9 852	11 903
Expenditures				
FOOD	2 120	1 950	2 130	1 853
SHELTER	3 793	3 083	2 981	3 544
PROPTAX	0	0	859	907
HOUSEINS	0	0	135	186
REPAIRS	0	0	427	490
CLOTHING	603	615	535	621
TRANS	481	613	862	807
TCC	9 249	8 291	8 864	9 119
SAVING	590	2 011	988	2 784
Assets and debts				
DEPOSITS	11 172	12 389	18 444	19 512
BONDS	5 496	4 138	5 217	4 034
CASH	96	78	118	94
STOCKS	914	1 952	510	7 875
RRSPS	133	1 330	1 620	2 686
CARS	436	836	1 049	1 245
HOME	0	0	85 835	68 140
OTHRE	99	1 016	16 454	8 091
BUSASS	0	1 563	0	66
TA	23 780	25 513	131 850	114 326
MORT	0	0	2 195	747
TD	168	583	2 946	4 182
NW	23 612	24 929	128 904	110 144
NWMRE	23 513	23 914	28 810	34 660

(An explanatory list of the variables employed appears in the appendix to this chapter.)

able, I inflated the 'Incomes' and 'Expenditures' rows by unity plus the change in the CPI between mid-1976 and mid-1983; for the 'Assets and Debts' rows I used the May CPIs for 1977 and 1984. Let me try to draw out some of the information in this table.

(a) Household Characteristics

The numbers in the 'Age' row are remarkably constant across the surveys and across the two groups. If it were the case that most elderly women moved from houses to apartments as they aged, then one should observe that, on average, homeowners are younger than non-homeowners. That this is not true suggests that elderly women, who are homeowners, do not divest themselves of their houses to permit a flat or a rising consumption-age profile, as some simple forms of the life-cycle model predict. My results are consistent with those of Venti and Wise (1987) and McFadden and Feinstein (1987), who have studied the asset-holding decisions of elderly Americans.

The education rows point to a strong cohort effect for non-homeowners; even though average age is nearly the same in the 1977 and 1984 SCFs, average educational levels attained are significantly higher in 1984 than in 1977. No significant trends in educational levels are evident for homeowners, and, as one might expect, homeowners tend to have higher educational levels than non-homeowners.

The SCF recorded an occupation for the person only if she had earned any money from employment in the last five years; so to be classified as 'Retired', the person could not have 'worked' at all in the last five years. The occupation rows show that most of these women are retired in this sense. There is some evidence of a trend towards earlier retirement, one which is perhaps a little stronger for home-owners than for non-homeowners, although homeowners appear to retire later than non-homeowners. This tendency is confirmed by the part-time variable in the next row. In addition, the absence of any trend in the part-time variable suggests that there has been no increase in the proportion of these women moving from full-time to part-time to complete retirement. It would be interesting to know to what extent this reflects the wishes of elderly women or the management decisions of firms.

Immigration status has been shown to be an important determinant of net worth, and to a lesser extent household expenditures, for married couple families (see Burbidge and Robb, 1985; Robb and Burbidge, 1989). The most remarkable feature of the 'Imstatus' row in Table 14.1 is its near-constancy; about 40 per cent of homeowners and non-homeowners were not born in Canada in this data.

(b) Incomes

Despite the trend towards earlier retirement, non-homeowners' 1983 average real earnings were more than 20 per cent higher than their 1976 earnings, and real earnings were only slightly lower for homeowners. Pre-tax real investment income, on the other hand, rose by 65 per cent for homeowners and actually declined slightly for non-homeowners. Why? The first five rows of the 'Assets and Debts' items show that the real levels of deposits increased by 11 per cent for non-homeowners and by about 6 per cent for homeowners, that real bond holdings actually declined by a quarter for each, that stock holdings increased particularly for homeowners and that RRSP holdings increased for each group. One important factor, no doubt, was the higher real interest rates of the early 1980s, but why did non-homeowners not benefit to the same extent as homeowners? Investment income, as calculated by Statistics Canada does not include capital gains, and so the difference cannot be accounted for by the capital gains received by homeowners on their much larger stock holdings. Are homeowners better informed about investment opportunities, and therefore invest in assets that yield higher returns? Davies (1979) showed that financial assets were significantly under-reported in the 1969 SCF; differences in under-reporting across these two groups could, of course, account for any of the differences observed. Finally, the small number of observations could mean that these differences are simply noise in the data. In any case, it is clear that much more work is needed to understand what happened over this seven-year interval.

The next four rows of Table 14.1 comprise averages for real government transfers and three of its components, OAS and GIS, Canada and Quebec Pension Plan benefits and Unemployment Insurance benefits.[8] The numbers show that, for non-homeowners, real government transfers rose by 20 per cent, while real total income rose by about 10 per cent, and so, during this period, transfers were growing in importance for this group. The corresponding numbers for homeowners were 28 and 29 per cent. Much of the extra improvement for homeowners came from Canada and Quebec Pension Plan benefits, even though 1983 predates the major increases in survivor benefits made available through the QPP. Between 1976 and 1983 the real value of maximum OAS and GIS rose by about 20 per cent. The 16 per cent increase in average real OAS-GIS benefits for non-homeowners and the corresponding 8 per cent increase for home-owners reflect these increases in maximum benefits and the income conditioning built into GIS payments.

As one might expect, private-pension incomes have a particularly high variance relative to the other income components, and this is especially true of non-homeowners. The 50 per cent decline in real pension income for non-homeowners and the 84 per cent increase for homeowners, therefore, may or may not reflect real changes but what is clear is that the level of private pension income is minor in comparison to the levels of governmental transfers. To the extent these women are widows the survivor benefits from their husbands' pensions are, at least on average, pretty slim.

The last two items in the 'Incomes' list are average pre-tax income and after-tax income. Average real pre-tax income rose by 9 per cent for non-homeowners, but average real after-tax income rose by only 5 per cent; the corresponding numbers for homeowners were 29 and 21 per cent, and thus average tax rates increased for both groups over this seven-year period. Some of what the government was giving with one hand it was taking away with the other.

(c) Expenditures and Saving

It is useful to begin by reminding the reader that these items were generated by splicing Famex and SCF data together, and whatever weaknesses the other numbers in this table possess, the numbers in this section are even less reliable. The averages show that real total current consumption (TCC) declined by 10 per cent for non-homeowners and rose by only 3 per cent for homeowners. Almost all of the decline is attributable to lower expenditures by non-homeowners on food and particularly shelter. More research would be required to determine whether this decline resulted from rent controls or whether these women chose to live in less expensive accommodation or that the difference is due to other factors. Home-owners also spent less on food, but more on shelter, partly because of real increases in property taxes, house insurance and expenditures on repairs and maintenance.

These numbers imply that saving, defined as after-tax income less total current consumption, increased significantly for both groups. Homeowners tend to save a higher fraction of their after-tax incomes. That elderly women saved on average and were saving a higher proportion of their incomes in 1984 than in 1978 is also true in the Famex data. If saving (as defined here) is positive for a single household, it must be the case that net worth, net of capital gains and losses, should be rising over time. Although this identity need not hold for two separate cross-sections, it is instructive to compare and contrast the saving information with the asset and debt information. The last line in Table 14.1 is real net worth minus assets and debts associated with real estate. This variable rose by 20 per cent for homeowners but only by 2 per cent for non-homeowners. It may be that non-homeowners ran down their wealth or dissaved in some of the intervening years, or that total current consumption is underestimated so that saving is overestimated or that non-homeowners under-report their wealth to a greater degree than homeowners, or some other possibility. Whatever the explanation, it is evident that many elderly women, particularly homeowners, save a significant fraction of their incomes.

(d) Assets and Debts

Perhaps the two most striking facts in this section of the table are the dramatic differences in net worth between those who own their homes and those who do not, and the precipitous decline in real home values in these data between the 1977 SCF and the 1984 SCF. I shall take up the latter point first.

My earlier research with Lonnie Magee and Leslie Robb has shown that the presence of a very few wealthy households can distort the means of NW variables in SCF data, and we have developed a set of techniques for handling such 'outliers' (see Burbidge and Robb, 1985; MacKinnon and Magee, 1989; Burbidge, Magee and Robb, 1988). Furthermore, preliminary work with married couples suggests that there are many fewer outliers in the 1984 SCF than in the 1977 SCF. Since the major asset for many types of households is equity in real estate, it is possible that the means for the 'Home' variable in Table 14.1 could be driven by the presence or absence of a few high numbers. The home with the highest market value in my extract from the 1977 SCF was one worth $150 000, measured in May 1977 dollars, which converts to $272 000 in May 1984 dollars. The corresponding number for our extract from the 1984 SCF was 160 000 1984 dollars, so that these numbers support the 'outlier' explanation for the puzzling drop in average real home values between 1977 and 1984.

This can be verified by computing the corresponding averages in the 1978 and 1984 Famexes, which also recorded the market value of the home. It turns out that average real home values were unchanged between December 1978 and December 1984. More work is needed to understand what actually happened to house values during this period; data on market value of home by city would be extremely helpful.

To deal with the first point it is helpful to work with net worth minus net worth in real estate (the last row in Table 14.1). As noted above, these numbers show that this variable, corrected for changes in the CPI between May 1977 and May 1984, were nearly constant for non-homeowners and rose by 20 per cent for homeowners.

To summarise, Table 14.1 provides information on women over the age of 50, who were living alone. It is clear that real increases in government transfers between 1976 and 1983 contributed to the increase in their real after-tax incomes. The income and expenditure numbers suggest that much of this increase in real incomes is being saved, but, at least for non-homeowners, the assets and debts data show no significant change in real net worth. If it is true that real estate wealth was approximately constant in real terms over this period, then the data indicate that homeowners were actually better off.

Table 14.1 tells us little about how incomes, expenditures, saving and net worth vary with age and other household characteristics. In the next section, I attempt to look at some of these issues.

4 COHORT ANALYSIS

In this section, I employ the techniques described in Robb and Burbidge (1989) to simulate the experience of the cohort that was aged 60 in 1977. Briefly, the procedure is as follows. For each of the two groups, non-homeowners and homeowners, I pool the 1977 and 1984 data sets. This requires converting all 1976 income and expenditure variables into 1983 dollars, and all 1977 asset and debt items into 1984 dollars. One can then estimate equations of the following form:

$$Y_i = X_i\beta + \gamma YR84 + \varepsilon_i, \quad i = 1, \ldots, n,$$

where Y_i is a variable of interest, such as net worth measured in 1984 dollars, X_i is a vector of household characteristics, which includes age, and $YR84$ is a dummy variable for those observations from the 1984 SCF. Conditional on the variables in X, γ then measures the real change in Y between 1977 and 1984. By making assumptions about γ, one can use this equation to predict what Y would be for each year, given age and the other characteristics in the X-vector; that is, one can simulate annual observations on a cohort. The particular assumption adopted here is that each variable changed each year by the estimated average annual change between 1977 and 1984 ($\gamma/7$).

Pooling yielded 220 observations for non-homeowners (92 from 1977 and 128 from 1984) and 147 for homeowners (56 from 1977 and 91 from 1984). The X-vector included age (AGE) and its square (AGE2), education variables and a complete set of interactions between these variables and AGE and AGE2, and a variable for immigration status.

As noted above, these data sets are very thin. From Table 14.1 one can see that only about 2 per cent of these women were university graduates. This implies that the simulations conditional on the women who were in the ED4 category are unreliable and they are not reported. Similarly, only 12 per cent are in the ED3 category so that a single 'outlier' could largely determine the predicted values for women in this category, thereby rendering the simulations useless for understanding 'typical' behaviour. Nevertheless, in Tables 14.2 to 14.4, I report predicted values for after-tax incomes, total current consumption, expenditures on food and shelter (all measured in 1983 dollars) and net worth, net worth minus real estate and RRSPs (measured in 1984 dollars), for women in the three educational categories, ED1, ED2, and ED3.[9]

It is transparent from these tables that each variable tends to be higher, given age, at higher levels of education; if one is most concerned to see how poorer elderly women have fared, the concentration of the data in the lower educational categories is actually helpful – this feature of the data enables one to obtain a clearer picture of the most interesting group.

Standard errors are not reported, but it is well known that with ordinary least squares, these would be lowest near the mean age, 68, and greatest at the youngest ages. The negative numbers for RRSPs, which are of course impossible in reality, are insignificantly different from zero; the negative numbers for RRSPs should be interpreted as indicating that the cohort held very low levels of this financial instrument at these ages. The purpose of the rest of this section is to highlight some of the facts in these tables.

Table 14.2 Predicted values of Incomes, Expenditures and Net Worth measured in 1984 dollars, for the cohort aged 60 in 1977, and for those with less than nine years of elementary education

			Non-Homeowners				
Age	AFTAXINC	TCC	FOOD	SHELTER	NW	NWMRE	RRSPs
56	9 968	10 645	2 944	3 586	18 307	18 405	–15
57	9 738	10 371	2 867	3 491	17 678	17 686	4
58	9 522	10 096	2 792	3 393	17 095	17 017	26
59	9 319	9 819	2 719	3 292	16 559	16 397	51
60	9 129	9 541	2 647	3 188	16 070	15 828	80
61	8 954	9 261	2 577	3 080	15 628	15 308	113
62	8 791	8 980	2 509	2 969	15 232	14 838	150
63	8 642	8 698	2 442	2 855	14 884	14 418	190
64	8 506	8 415	2 377	2 738	14 581	14 048	234
65	8 384	8 130	2 313	2 617	14 326	13 727	282
66	8 275	7 844	2 251	2 494	14 118	13 457	333
67	8 180	7 557	2 191	2 367	13 956	13 236	388
68	8 098	7 268	2 133	2 237	13 841	13 065	446
69	8 030	6 978	2 076	2 103	13 773	12 943	509
70	7 975	6 686	2 021	1 967	13 751	12 872	575
71	7 933	6 394	1 967	1 827	13 776	12 850	644
72	7 905	6 100	1 915	1 684	13 848	12 879	717
73	7 891	5 804	1 865	1 537	13 967	12 957	794
74	7 889	5 508	1 817	1 388	14 133	13 084	875
75	7 902	5 210	1 770	1 235	14 345	13 262	959

			Homeowners				
Age	AFTAXINC	TCC	FOOD	SHELTER	NW	NWMRE	RRSPs
56	7 145	9 519	2 244	3 039	80 085	–4 351	–1 339
57	7 472	9 518	2 268	3 055	81 866	–375	–1 019
58	7 790	9 508	2 283	3 070	83 530	3 487	–701
59	8 099	9 490	2 291	3 086	85 076	7 234	–385
60	8 400	9 463	2 290	3 100	86 504	10 867	–71
61	8 693	9 429	2 282	3 115	87 815	14 385	240
62	8 977	9 386	2 266	3 129	89 008	17 789	549
63	9 253	9 334	2 242	3 143	90 083	21 079	855
64	9 520	9 275	2 210	3 156	91 041	24 254	1 160
65	9 779	9 207	2 170	3 169	91 881	27 315	1 462
66	10 030	9 130	2 122	3 182	92 603	30 262	1 761
67	10 272	9 046	2 066	3 195	93 208	33 095	2 059
68	10 506	8 953	2 002	3 207	93 695	35 813	2 354
69	10 731	8 851	1 931	3 218	94 064	38 416	2 647
70	10 948	8 742	1 851	3 230	94 316	40 906	2 937
71	11 157	8 624	1 764	3 241	94 450	43 281	3 225
72	11 357	8 497	1 669	3 252	94 467	45 542	3 511
73	11 549	8 363	1 565	3 262	94 365	47 688	3 795
74	11 732	8 220	1 454	3 272	94 147	49 720	4 076
75	11 907	8 068	1 335	3 282	93 810	51 638	4 355

Table 14.3 Predicted values of Incomes, Expenditures and Net Worth measured in 1984 dollars, for the cohort aged 60 in 1977, and for those with some or completed secondary education

			Non-Homeowners				
Age	AFTAXINC	TCC	FOOD	SHELTER	NW	NWMRE	RRSPs
56	12 566	12 181	2 582	4 369	27 329	27 145	–577
57	12 376	11 857	2 509	4 281	28 247	27 823	–416
58	12 193	11 534	2 437	4 189	29 055	28 409	–263
59	12 017	11 214	2 366	4 093	29 753	28 904	–117
60	11 848	10 897	2 296	3 993	30 342	29 307	21
61	11 685	10 581	2 228	3 888	30 821	29 619	152
62	11 530	10 268	2 161	3 780	31 191	29 839	276
63	11 381	9 957	2 095	3 667	31 451	29 968	392
64	11 239	9 648	2 030	3 550	31 601	30 006	501
65	11 104	9 341	1 966	3 430	31 642	29 951	602
66	10 976	9 037	1 904	3 305	31 573	29 806	696
67	10 855	8 734	1 842	3 176	31 395	29 569	783
68	10 741	8 434	1 782	3 042	31 107	29 240	862
69	10 633	8 137	1 723	2 905	30 709	28 820	933
70	10 532	7 841	1 665	2 764	30 202	28 309	997
71	10 439	7 548	1 609	2 618	29 585	27 705	1 054
72	10 352	7 256	1 553	2 468	28 858	27 011	1 103
73	10 272	6 967	1 499	2 315	28 022	26 225	1 145
74	10 199	6 681	1 446	2 157	27 076	25 347	1 180
75	10 132	6 396	1 394	1 995	26 021	24 378	1 206
			Homeowners				
Age	AFTAXINC	TCC	FOOD	SHELTER	NW	NWMRE	RRSPs
56	14 154	10 404	2 161	3 613	162 180	35 315	5 560
57	13 866	10 367	2 226	3 537	159 567	36 414	5 886
58	13 602	10 324	2 280	3 472	156 875	37 550	6 163
59	13 362	10 275	2 323	3 416	154 103	38 721	6 391
60	13 147	10 219	2 355	3 370	151 253	39 929	6 571
61	12 956	10 157	2 376	3 335	148 323	41 172	6 702
62	12 789	10 088	2 385	3 310	145 315	42 451	6 784
63	12 646	10 013	2 384	3 295	142 227	43 766	6 817
64	12 528	9 932	2 372	3 290	139 060	45 116	6 801
65	12 434	9 844	2 349	3 295	135 815	46 503	6 736
66	12 365	9 750	2 315	3 310	132 490	47 925	6 623
67	12 320	9 649	2 270	3 335	129 086	49 383	6 460
68	12 299	9 542	2 214	3 371	125 603	50 877	6 249
69	12 302	9 428	2 147	3 417	122 041	52 407	5 989
70	12 330	9 308	2 069	3 472	118 400	53 972	5 680
71	12 382	9 182	1 980	3 538	114 680	55 574	5 322
72	12 459	9 049	1 880	3 614	110 881	57 211	4 916
73	12 559	8 910	1 769	3 700	107 003	58 884	4 460
74	12 684	8 765	1 647	3 797	103 046	60 593	3 956
75	12 834	8 612	1 514	3 903	99 010	62 338	3 402

Table 14.4 Predicted values of Incomes, Expenditures and Net Worth measured in 1984 dollars, for the cohort aged 60 in 1977, and for those with some post-secondary education

			Non-Homeowners				
Age	AFTAXINC	TCC	FOOD	SHELTER	NW	NWMRE	RRSPs
56	16 433	15 597	2 669	5 315	27 644	27 437	–71
57	16 053	15 070	2 575	5 081	26 117	25 875	208
58	15 707	14 568	2 486	4 857	24 900	24 624	470
59	15 394	14 091	2 404	4 643	23 993	23 686	715
60	15 114	13 640	2 328	4 440	23 397	23 058	943
61	14 867	13 213	2 258	4 246	23 111	22 743	1 154
62	14 653	12 812	2 194	4 063	23 135	22 739	1 349
63	14 472	12 436	2 136	3 890	23 469	23 047	1 526
64	14 324	12 086	2 085	3 728	24 113	23 666	1 686
65	14 210	11 760	2 039	3 576	25 068	24 597	1 830
66	14 128	11 459	2 000	3 434	26 333	25 840	1 956
67	14 080	11 184	1 967	3 302	27 908	27 395	2 066
68	14 065	10 934	1 941	3 180	29 793	29 261	2 159
69	14 083	10 709	1 920	3 069	31 989	31 439	2 234
70	14 134	10 509	1 905	2 968	34 495	33 929	2 293
71	14 218	10 335	1 897	2 877	37 311	36 730	2 335
72	14 335	10 186	1 895	2 796	40 437	39 843	2 360
73	14 485	10 061	1 899	2 726	43 874	43 268	2 368
74	14 669	9 962	1 909	2 666	47 620	47 004	2 359
75	14 885	9 889	1 925	2 616	51 677	51 052	2 333
			Homeowners				
Age	AFTAXINC	TCC	FOOD	SHELTER	NW	NWMRE	RRSPs
56	31 876	22 068	5 049	1 410	386 769	254 565	8 119
57	29 290	21 184	4 821	1 751	356 532	225 657	7 058
58	26 874	20 340	4 601	2 066	327 806	198 679	6 087
59	24 629	19 537	4 389	2 354	300 591	173 630	5 205
60	22 554	18 775	4 185	2 617	274 888	150 512	4 412
61	20 649	18 053	3 990	2 853	250 695	129 323	3 709
62	18 914	17 372	3 802	3 064	228 014	110 064	3 095
63	17 350	16 732	3 623	3 248	206 844	92 734	2 570
64	15 955	16 133	3 451	3 406	187 185	77 335	2 135
65	14 731	15 574	3 287	3 537	169 038	63 865	1 788
66	13 677	15 056	3 132	3 643	152 401	52 324	1 532
67	12 793	14 578	2 985	3 722	137 276	42 714	1 364
68	12 080	14 142	2 845	3 776	123 662	35 033	1 286
69	11 536	13 746	2 714	3 803	111 559	29 282	1 298
70	11 163	13 390	2 591	3 804	100 967	25 461	1 398
71	10 960	13 076	2 475	3 779	91 887	23 570	1 588
72	10 927	12 802	2 368	3 727	84 317	23 608	1 867
73	11 064	12 569	2 269	3 650	78 259	25 576	2 236
74	11 372	12 376	2 178	3 546	73 712	29 474	2 694
75	11 849	12 224	2 095	3 417	70 676	35 301	3 241

Expenditures on food always decline with age and this decrease is not forced; that is, even for the lowest educational level, the person has the resources to eat more if she so desires. For non-homeowners, expenditures on shelter also decline with age, falling by a factor between 2 and 3 between 56 and 75. The decrease in expenditures on food and shelter contribute to significant declines in total expenditures (TCC). Since real after-tax income also falls with age but at a much slower rate, non-homeowners in all three tables are saving at older ages. Net worth tends to decline and then to rise in Tables 14.2 and 14.4, which supports the numbers for saving. The numbers in Table 14.3 lack this consistency – here despite substantial saving, as implied by the income and expenditure numbers, particularly those for older ages, net worth has an inverted U-shape. While the data are not necessarily contradictory – capital losses, which are not included in Statistics Canada's estimates of income but which are reflected in estimates of net worth, could 'explain' the differences – I think the assumption of steady change, upon which these numbers are based, is certainly open to doubt. It would be very helpful to have more information on what happened in the intervening years between 1977 and 1984. Finally, I note that holdings of RRSPs tend to rise with age and educational level for non-homeowners.

The picture for homeowners differs somewhat. Like non-homeowners, their expenditures on food decline with age but their expenditures on shelter rise with age. Even though total expenditures decline the rate of decrease is less than it is for non-homeowners. After-tax real income declines with age for ED2 and ED3 (Tables 14.3 and 14.4), but it actually increases for ED1 (see Table 14.1), where it starts \$2800 below the level for non-homeowners at age 56 and rises to \$4000 above the level for non-homeowners at age 75. Because of the problems noted above – low numbers of observations and the presence of outliers – the net worth data in all three tables are suspect. The presence of a few wealthy households at younger ages in the ED3 category distorts both the NW and NWMRE columns of Table 14.4. The NWMRE and RRSPs columns of Tables 14.2 and 14.3 support the view that homeowners are saving substantial sums late in the life-cycle and that they have significant holdings of RRSPs.

These tables help to provide a clearer picture of the financial situation faced by a certain specific group of elderly women. While one hopes that predicted values from regression equations provide a picture of 'typical' behaviour, one does miss the extremes in this kind of exercise. For example, one woman, a non-homeowner, reported her annual income to be $955 (measured in 1983 dollars), and another, a homeowner, reported her annual food expenditures to be $107 (again measured in 1983 dollars).

5 SUMMARY AND CONCLUSIONS

This chapter is another component of an ongoing research programme to compile a set of facts upon which more realistic life-cycle models can be constructed for the purpose of improving our understanding of important policy issues. Let me draw attention to the following facts in particular.

First, between 1976 and 1983, real government transfers increased and this led to a significant increase in real after-tax incomes for the group of elderly women studied here. Second, while some of this increase in incomes went to higher real expenditures on shelter, especially for those who were homeowners, much of it went into increased saving. Third, like other groups of the population, elderly women's total expenditures decrease with age – even though they have the financial resources (real incomes and wealth) to consume more, they choose not to do so. Some versions of the life-cycle model predict that consumption expenditures increase with age. The American literature has enquired why reverse annuity mortgages do not exist – these would permit the elderly with housing wealth to enjoy a higher (or unchanged) level of consumption after retirement than that enjoyed before retirement. My results, which are consistent with those of Venti and Wise (1987) and others, suggest that these financial instruments are rare because the typical person does not want them. Fourth, some have argued that a significant fraction of those between the ages of 55 and 64 are liquidity constrained in the sense that they would like to be able to consume some of their public pension benefits earlier (see Kahn, 1988). The data presented in this chapter indicate that most elderly women are not liquidity constrained in this sense. The one group that might be liquidity constrained are women with low levels of education who are homeowners. My data, and again this is consistent with the findings of other researchers, suggest that elderly women wish to live in their own homes as long as possible. The bottom half of Table 14.2 shows that homeowners with low levels of education experienced an increase in real incomes with age and that their wealth levels in their 50s were low.

Following the lead of the QPP, recent changes in the CPP permit contributors to start collecting retirement benefits at age 60. In addition, the Workmen's Compensation Board in Quebec has permitted those entitled to receive what amounts to an indexed real annuity to trade higher benefits before age 65 for lower benefits after age 65. Would the government consider introducing this kind of flexibility into OAS/GIS? If the last fact mentioned above can stand up to more careful scrutiny, the Federal government might wish to do so.

Having said this, let me remind the reader of the weaknesses in the data used here and draw attention to some of the many possible directions for improvement. First, as noted several times above, data limitations forced me to work with very few observations, and thus the 'noise-to-reliable-information' ratio may be very high. Second, I have used a very simple technique for splicing the Famex and SCF data sets and these results should be checked against those obtained with more sophisticated techniques (see Meghir, 1988, for example). This extension might help to remove some of the inconsistencies noted above between the saving numbers and those for changes in net worth. Third, while I have avoided the mistake of using endogenous variables (such as those for occupation and part-time status) as explanatory variables in the section 4 regressions, the statistical model does not properly account for the transition between work and retirement, as it should do. Fourth, one could also argue that I should use a more flexible functional form for estimating, say, income–age profiles, because one might expect that OAS/GIS induce discontinuous jumps at ages 60 or 65. Finally, there is strong evidence of an outlier problem in this data and future research should also take this into account.

Since so much of the modern research programme has been aimed at understanding why the elderly save, it may be useful to speculate on what these data may imply for this research programme. As I observed in the introduction, one hypothesis worth exploring in future research is that the elderly, who typically have poorer health and less energy, experience near-satiation in consumption.

APPENDIX List of the Variables Employed

Note: Variables marked by an asterisk are not dummies.

(1) Household Characteristics

AGE – age (*)
AGE2 – age squared (*)

Education

ED1 – less than nine years of elementary education
ED2 – some or completed secondary education
ED3 – some post-secondary education or post-secondary certificate or diploma
ED4 – university degree

Occupation

OCC1 – managerial, administrative and related occupations or occupations in natural sciences, engineering, mathematics, social sciences, religion, medicine and health or teaching, or artistic, literary or recreational occupations
OCC2 – clerical, sales or service occupations
OCC3 – mining, processing and machining, product fabricating, assembling and repairing, construction and other occupations not stated above
RETIRED – never worked or last worked more than five years ago
PARTTIME – worked mostly part-time last year

Immigration Status

IMSTATUS – not born in Canada
Omitted category – born in Canada

(2) Incomes (*)

EARNINGS – total earnings
INVINC – total net income from investment
OASGIS – Old Age Security and Guaranteed Income Supplement
CQPP – Canada/Quebec Pension Plan benefits
UI – Unemployment Insurance benefits
GOVTR – total government transfer payments
PENSIONS – retirement pensions, superannuation and annuities
TOTINC – total income
AFTAXINC – after-tax income

(3) Expenditures (*)

FOOD – total expenditures on food
SHELTER – total expenditures on shelter

PROPTAX – property taxes
HOUSEINS – homeowners' insurance premiums
REPAIRS – maintenance, repairs and replacements
CLOTHING – total expenditures on clothing
TRANS – total expenditures on transportation
TCC – total currrent consumption
SAVING – saving (≡ AFTAXINC – TCC)

(4) Assets and Debts (*)

DEPOSITS – total deposits, including savings certificates
BONDS – Canada savings bonds and other bonds
CASH – cash on hand
STOCKS – total stock holdings
RRSPS – Registered Retirement Savings Plans
CARS – market value of cars, trucks or vans, primarily for personal use
HOME – market value of owner occupied home
OTHRE – equity in real estate other than owner-occupied home
BUSASS – equity in business, farm or profession
TA – total assets
MORT – mortgage outstanding on owner-occupied home
TD – total debt
NW – net worth
NWMRE – net worth apart from real estate (≡ NW – HOME – OTHRE + MORT)

Notes

1. This has been a difficult chapter to write. Every time, *every time*, I have sat down to work on it, I have been unable to escape the meaning of 'a contribution to a *memorial* volume for Jack Weldon'.

   Jack taught the 4th-year honours theory course at McGill. Lee Panetta, Ron Simkover and I used to pester him mercilessly with questions – but he got all of this back and more in helping to supervise my Ph.D. thesis. I still have his comments on the first draft; literally every page was covered with blue ink – the comments and questions seemed endless (and these were the nightmarish kind, the ones that have you convinced the thesis is washed up), but somehow he made writing a thesis fun. In dealing with my doctoral students since 1974, I can't count the times I'd have been grateful for a small fraction of his patience, wisdom and humour.

   Tom Asimakopulos and Jack Weldon were working on public and private pensions long before it was fashionable to do so. Their work, unlike most of the more recent literature, provides a rationale for pensions and they both played an important role in shaping the changes in pension policy that have occurred in Canada. The effects of some of these changes on the financial status of elderly women are documented in the present chapter.

I thank the editors for helpful comments and the Social Sciences and Humanities Research Council of Canada for financial support. Data manipulations were performed with GAUSS, version 1.49B, written by L. E. Edlefsen and S. D. Jones.

2. Information on food expenditures is collected using diary techniques, and this information is then combined with the recall information for all other expenditures.
3. This is a multi-stage, stratified, clustered, probability sample; see Statistics Canada (1973) for details on the methodology of these surveys.
4. The 1984 SCF PUMT reported age up to 80. It would, of course, be helpful to have actual age reported for all observations.
5. There is a Famex survey for the calendar year 1976, but it is not publicly available.
6. Robb and Burbidge (1989) and others have found that expenditures move very closely with after-tax incomes in Family Expenditures data.
7. Copies of the printouts from these regressions are available upon request.
8. The PUMT for the 1977 SCF did not separate the Province of Ontario's transfers, such as the Guaranteed Annual Income Supplement, from other governmental transfers.
9. These tables were generated with the dummy variable for immigration status switched off, and thus the numbers apply to women born in Canada.

References

Burbidge, J. B., L. Magee and A. L. Robb (1988) 'Alternative Transformations to Handle Extreme Values of the Dependent Variable', *Journal of the American Statistical Association*, 83, pp. 123–7.

Burbidge, J. B. and A. L. Robb (1985) 'Evidence on Wealth–Age Profiles in Canadian Cross-Section Data', *Canadian Journal of Economics*, 18, pp. 854–75.

Davies, J. B. (1979) 'On the Size Distribution of Wealth in Canada', *Review of Income and Wealth*, 25, pp. 237–59.

Kahn, J. A. (1988) 'Social Security, Liquidity and Early Retirement', *Journal of Public Economics*, 35, pp. 97–117.

MacKinnon, J. G. and L. Magee (1989) 'Transforming the Dependent Variable in Regression Models', *International Economic Review*, forthcoming.

McFadden, D. and J. Feinstein (1987) 'The Dynamics of Housing Demand by the Elderly: I. Wealth, Cash Flow and Demographic Efects', National Bureau of Economic Research Conference on 'The Economics of Aging', New Orleans, March.

Meghir, C. (1988) 'Complementary Data Sources', University College London.

Robb, A. L. and J. B. Burbidge (1989) 'Consumption, Income and Retirement', *Canadian Journal of Economics*, 22, pp. 522–42.

Statistics Canada (1973) *Family Expenditure in Canada*, vol. 2, cat. no. 62–536.

Venti, S. F. and D. Wise (1987) 'Aging, Moving and Housing Wealth', National Bureau of Economic Research Conference on 'The Economics of Aging', New Orleans, March.

Author Index

Subject Index

SPRINGER NATURE

GPSR Compliance

The European Union's (EU) General Product Safety Regulation (GPSR) is a set of rules that requires consumer products to be safe and our obligations to ensure this.

If you have any concerns about our products, you can contact us on ProductSafety@springernature.com

In case Publisher is established outside the EU, the EU authorized representative is:

Springer Nature Customer Service Center GmbH
Europaplatz 3
69115 Heidelberg, Germany

The manufacturer's authorised representative in the EU is Springer Nature Customer Service Centre GmbH, Europaplatz 3, 69115 Heidelberg, Germany. If you have any concerns regarding our products, please contact ProductSafety@springernature.com

Printed and bound by CPI Group (UK) Ltd, Croydon, CR0 4YY
13/10/2026
02232373-0012